ROOSEVELT'S
REVOLUTION

ROOSEVELT'S

REVOLUTION

The First Year—
A Personal Perspective

REXFORD G. TUGWELL

Macmillan Publishing Co., Inc.

NEW YORK

Macmillan Publishing Co., Inc.
866 Third Avenue, New York, N.Y. 10022
Collier Macmillan Canada, Ltd.

Library of Congress Cataloging in Publication Data
Tugwell, Rexford Guy, 1891-
Roosevelt's revolution.
1.   United States—Politics and government—1933-
1945.   2.   United States—Economic policy—1933-
1945.   3.   Roosevelt, Franklin Delano, Pres. U.S.,
1882-1945.   I.   Title.
E806.T83   353.03'13   76-22741
ISBN   0-02-620370-7

FIRST PRINTING 1977

Printed in the United States of America

*This book is
gratefully dedicated
to my wife,
who not only thought
it should be written
but helped in its preparation.*

Contents

I

AFTER THE ELECTION

Contents

II

THE TURN TO ADMINISTRATION

III

BATTLES—MOSTLY LOST

Contents
IV
1933 ENDS; 1934 BEGINS

Prefatory Note

INTERPRETATIONS OF PAST events are subject to questions about accuracy, about disinterest, and about the importance of the events being recorded. Nevertheless, those who have taken part in passages of history they regard as worth attention continue to write what they recall. I am no exception. What I say can be taken with any preferred amount of skepticism; nevertheless, it is here put down as I understand it.

What I do not admit is that the first Roosevelt year was unimportant. Also, it must be granted that I was at least present and had something to do with what went on. I may not have been disinterested; but I was there in the middle of events, and the considerable time since they occurred may have given me a certain detachment.

It was an exciting year, and at a distance of several decades, it seems even more important than it did at the time. We were too busy then to make accurate assessments. There was so much to do and so few hours in the days or days in the months that we hurried from one stint to another without much intermission. If we had not already thought about what had to be done, there was little possibility that we could catch up; but, of course, plans had been roughed out. The depression had provided the insistent motive.

Historians seem inclined to the view that a page in the American ledger was turned in 1933 and new entries began to be made; but actually only a few of the undertakings were really novel. They had been proposed again and again, most of them, and if they had not been started, they had been argued for. When it was all over I once made a list of New Deal ventures begun during Hoover's years as secretary of commerce and then as president. I had to conclude that his policies were substantially correct. The New Deal owed much to what he had begun. Unfortunately, his enterprises had been overtaken by a flood of disasters. There was no precedent for such a massive debacle.

Nevertheless, some things ought to have been done that Hoover would not do, and about others he was constricted by what he liked to think of as principles. He identified these as American ways of life (he actually used that locution) and regarded himself as standing in the way of those who would destroy them. They had to do mostly with a rugged individualism he was unwilling to see diminished.

Roosevelt was more willing to compromise. He believed as much as Hoover in the virtues of independence, but he was open to the sights and sounds around him, and when people were starving and homeless, he realized that it had become impossible for them to look out for themselves and their families. What had happened to them had come from outside; it was something they could not even understand. If it required unbalancing governmental budgets to furnish relief, and public intervention to restore their courage, he was willing to lay aside, if only temporarily, his conviction that characters might be undermined.

Roosevelt had been forced to conclude while governor of New York that only federal intervention could overcome the crisis of those years. He had at first used the resources of the state for relief but had very soon run into the indisputable fact that these resources were not nearly enough and never would be enough. He intended, when he became president, to muster the latent national wealth. This would require departure from courses he would have preferred. Setting things right called for reforms and new devices, and not all were within the value system he had in common with Hoover. Still, he hoped that his departures would contribute to a renewed individualism. The judgment of certain annoyed contemporaries that he was a radical was quite wrong. He was a conservative, but not a dogmatic one.

On inauguration day the nation was in the deepest trouble it had known since the Civil War. It has ever since been called the Great Depression, and the capitals used by commentators seem justified.

Industrialization was well under way by then; but it is necessary to note that in 1933 the economic importance of agriculture and industry, of rural and urban interests, was still about equal. This accounts for our preoccupation with the conditions farmers found themselves in; their depression had begun in 1921 when their expanded wartime markets overseas had suddenly disappeared. It accounts also for the intolerable unemployment problem of factory workers. This had reached something like thirteen or fourteen millions—depending on who was doing the counting. If farmers could not sell their crops they could not buy what the urban workers produced. Later generations have hardly been able to imagine what deprivation, insecurity and actual suffering followed from these conditions. Some years later, two-dollar wheat and an unemployment rate of 6 percent caused politicians to fear for their reputations; in 1933, wheat was below 50 cents and the unemployment rate was some 30 percent.

The magnitude of the problem put it beyond the limits of any traditional solution; and subsidiary to the economic debacle there were numerous other disjointures demanding correction. Hoover, who was a man of compassion, had nevertheless lost control of the situation. He had conceived that the business cycle could be turned upward. Ways to do this had been outlined in studies he had commissioned when he had been secretary of commerce. The difficulty was that whatever was done was meant to meet small crises and now there was a big one. Relying on the independent initiative of Americans was to ask of them something beyond their capabilities; but marshaling all the resources of government to help them, and forgetting the consequent dangers to character, seemed to him a departure from what was allowable. The measures he took were never enough. Private charities and limited loans to the states disappeared like water sinking in desert sands.

Hoover gave way to Roosevelt with the deepest misgivings. He considered his successor to be irresponsible, unprepared, and lacking in respect for traditional values. Strange and dangerous measures were likely to be undertaken. He himself believed so firmly in free enterprise that he could only contemplate with horror the socialistic devices he was convinced Roosevelt had in mind. What Hoover thought, however, was no longer of any importance after the election of 1932. He had been repudiated.

Roosevelt had a new chance; but unless his efforts proved remedial he would be in trouble too. His performance—the inspiring inaugural, the sequestering of gold, the messages asking the Congress to grant him emergency powers and then large funds for relief, the brief but reassuring fireside chats—all these were dazzlingly optimistic, and if things did not greatly improve immediately, at least something was being done and more was coming. Besides, his program seemed to be intended to match the dimensions of the disaster. He said frankly that he hoped it would be right and would be enough, but that if it proved to be wrong or insufficient, he would be the first to say so and to recommend trying something else.

This did not please the reactionaries but it did establish a new level of presidential responsibility. Hope was a good deal more visible than accomplishment for a while, and the anticipated mistakes were made; but much was done that eventually made matters better. The mistakes were presently overridden and the successes were enough to relieve the worst distresses.

The administration began with hurried legislation during what was afterward called the Hundred Days; then there were months of hurried organization. Even this short time brought some ventures into disrepute; others, though, were succeeding. There was relief; there were public works; there was protection for homeowners; and farmers began to get payments for compliance with a nationwide plan for diminishing the surpluses. The National Recovery Act had originally been a scheme for industrial reorganization; but added to it when it passed were labor reforms and relief provisions. These would preempt attention; and the hoped-for reform would die before it came to life.

I was involved in some of this, and even when I was not involved, I was in a position to know what was going on. I was both admiring and critical. Both these emotions are, I am sure, reflected in my account.

If I had to do again what I did in the year I write of, I would do much differently. What is said here has to be read with the gloss of my inexperience. My convictions about public policy were mature, but I was an innocent in Washington. I saw my real self only as a helper, but I found it impossible to accept many of the politicians' mores and so I set myself in opposition, mostly futile and puzzling to sophisticates. This opposition seems now to an older, and perhaps more cynical, individual to have been undertaken from a position and with an armament that ensured failure. One thing I can say without reservation: I learned much. If I have made some of what I learned available to my readers that is all I have intended for this account.

Prefatory Note

At the end of this book is a brief chronology of the first Roosevelt year. The reader, trying to follow the rapidly unfolding events, may turn to it as a guide.

RGT

LIST OF FIRST-YEAR AGENCIES

RFC   The Reconstruction Finance Corporation. Set up by Hoover, and enlarged by Roosevelt, to assist embarrassed financial institutions.

AAA   The Agricultural Adjustment Administration, the organization set up to control farm production and increase farmers' incomes.

NRA   The National Recovery Administration, authorized by the National Recovery Act of June 16. The intention was to reduce destructive competition by establishing codes of fairness for each industry.

FERA   The Federal Emergency Relief Administration; Hopkins' first organization.

CWA   The Civil Works Administration; Hopkins' second organization.

WPA   The Works Progress Administration, later the Works Projects Administration; Hopkins' third organization.

TVA   The Tennessee Valley Authority.

PWA   Ickes' Public Works Administration.

CCC   The Civilian Conservation Corps. Organized to take youths off the streets and employ them in work camps at conservation projects.

HOLC   The Home Owners Loan Corporation. To take over mortgages of those who were threatened with the foreclosure of their homes.

FCA   The Farm Credit Administration. A consolidation of several agencies set up in the past to furnish credit to farmers.

FSRC   The Federal Surplus Relief Corporation. An agency established to distribute to the needy surpluses of agricultural products.

I

After
the Election

CHAPTER 1

Expectations

AFTER THE ELECTION in November 1932, messages of goodwill began to pour in upon Roosevelt. There was unmistakably an expectation of immediate action that would set things right. This was something of a surprise to those of us who had been involved in the campaign. We explained it to ourselves as a demand for reassurance, for a credible promise of change.

Roosevelt suddenly became a savior found in the electoral processes Americans believed in. What made this seem strange was that obviously Hoover had been voted out of office and Roosevelt only incidentally voted in. Moreover, the campaign had revealed almost nothing the president-elect actually meant to do. The Democratic party was committed to no more than picking up certain elements of orthodox progressivism shelved by Woodrow Wilson when the First World War had disrupted all plans for reform. Roosevelt had not gone much beyond this in any of his pronouncements. Nevertheless, although these policies were irrelevant to the crisis of 1933, he was looked to for the cure of the country's sickness. It would be several months before he could even begin (inaugurations then were on March 4); meanwhile things could get much worse; but this was somehow overlooked in the euphoria of prospective change.

Those of us who were his helpers had been aware that during the campaign there had been a growing personal rapprochement between him and those who were disenchanted with Hoover. His confident voice had been heard from their radios, and he had been seen standing on the back platforms of trains or waving from the back seat of his open car. Then too he had been spotlighted at enormous party rallies.

People had begun to feel possessive about him, a feeling that was deepened when, in February, a deranged man shot at him several times as he sat in an open car in the midst of a crowd in Miami. By what would seem almost a miracle, the assailant missed him completely, although Mayor Cermak of Chicago, seated beside him, was wounded. Nothing but some such precipitating incident was lacking for a great outpouring of public concern. To us the change in attitude since the election seemed more striking than it appeared to be to him. He took it as a matter of course. His tranquil and competent private secretary, Marguerite LeHand (known to all of us as Missy), looked at me strangely the first time we met after the shooting incident and said, very simply and quietly, "There *is* a star, you know." She can have had no reason to doubt it afterward.

He fascinated the public; and he used his charm now in a lavish way. Those of us who worked with him during the months before election often wondered why he bothered to use it on us. We concluded that it was not conscious, but rather something become habitual. There was, besides, his confidence. He never doubted, it could be seen, that he would succeed in what had to be done. Besides, he had faith in a tendency to betterment that would not be denied. He would be its agent—and its beneficiary. Since he relied on this, he had no need to hesitate. He would try the devices he knew of, and would try others if he must. It was fortunate that he had a detailed firsthand knowledge of the country and of the variety among its people.

The members of what had been called his "Brains Trust" had been, and continued to be, uneasy about an inconsistency he was holding to in spite of such warnings as some of us put forward. Late in the campaign he had made what now seemed a most unfortunate speech in Pittsburgh promising a 25 percent reduction in government expenditures; but in other speeches he had committed himself to what would certainly be very costly unemployment relief. This was about as contradictory as it was possible to be. The promise of economy pleased businessmen who wanted less spending, and the prospect of help relieved the fears of the unemployed. He rather weakly argued that government economies would pay for relief and public works. There were, however, twelve or thirteen million unemployed and the simplest arithmetic showed how far the savings would go: they could be no more than 2 percent. Furthermore, the savings were to be made by discharging government employees, and these would then be unemployed and their reduced spending would diminish the market for goods and services. But what was needed was more employment and more demand, not less of either.

He was ignoring these contradictions, and, it must be said, so was almost everyone else. His position as president-elect seemed to give him immunity to criticism. It was not until after his first "fireside chat" that his radio personality began to be talked of and written about as technically remarkable. It is hard to explain how this reputation grew and expanded. His campaigning for the vice-presidency back in 1920 had not made him an oratorical reputation. It was true that when he had nominated Al Smith as the "Happy Warrior" in 1924, the speech had been well received. It had even been suggested by *The New York Times* that he might make a better candidate than the one he was nominating. But his radio talks as governor had made no notable impression. I had listened as he made several of these. He was obviously reading texts he had not given careful directions for, and seemed to have little interest in. Before he made the "common man" speech in April there had been little attention to what he said. Now he was listened to and watched even more intently. These changes were in his auditors, not in him.

When he escaped the assassin's bullets in Miami and a great tide of congratulations poured in upon him, it was clear that at least for some months, and perhaps longer, he could count on public support for whatever he proposed. This might well give him more than the traditional presidential honeymoon. It was no doubt because of this that he determined well before inauguration to demand certain reforms in addition to measures made necessary by the disasters of the depression. But neither those who wanted these changes nor those who opposed them anticipated all that was to come during the Hundred Days. It would be revealed bit by bit in successive messages to the Congress. Only those of us who helped to prepare these messages in the interval before inauguration had any notion of what was coming; and even we were occasionally surprised.

I have since concluded that some of his proposals were impromptu; but not the more important ones. For instance, the central idea of NRA—allowing industries a large measure of self-government—had been discussed many times in our Albany talks. His assumption that he could propose it without preparing the public must have been based on a conviction that under the stresses of those months acceptance

5

would be easy. This was true as well of his determination to demand delegation to himself of emergency powers. I had had intimations of this months earlier, if I had been sharp enough to appreciate what I was listening to. I was present in February, when he instructed Lewis Douglas, who was to be his budget director, to prepare a draft of what was later called the Economy Act. He prefaced his remarks with allusions to the old Trading with the Enemy Act of 1917. This had given President Wilson the powers he needed in wartime. Roosevelt said that only the president could really make economies. The Congress would never reduce the government's spending. Douglas—who was then a congressman—agreed. This exchange took place during a drive from Hyde Park to Albany; I sat between them, unhappy because I thought such an act unwise and because neither was interested in any objections. He was right about the reception of this economy move, however. It was approved by everyone except those who were to lose their jobs. Why it was supposed that a reduction of government expenditures would help to cure a depression was beyond me; it must be, I concluded, because there had to be an attribution of blame and bureaucrats were convenient.

As for his proposed reforms, the climate was favorable. If the bureaucrats were unpopular, bankers at the moment were more so. Wall Street was again the wicked place it had been during the progressive era. The financial establishment was being blamed for what had happened. The program of relief for businesses through the Reconstruction Finance Corporation had not succeeded. Loans to large institutions had failed to trickle downward to the smaller ones. It had inspired little confidence even in the recipients. The banking system was disintegrating and depositors were losing their money.

Yet those who were worst off were adapting. For instance, a species of community new to the American scene had been developing on vacant lots, at railroad junctions, and in fields on the fringes of towns and cities. One had spread itself on the flats by the Hudson where we could see it from Morningside Heights. It was like many others: it had patched-up huts made of flattened cans, fruit boxes, and cut-up automobile tires; there were muddy passages for streets; and a strange kind of informal government had appeared. Many, though not all, of the inhabitants were derelicts; some were younger people who had left home because food had run out and with it parental care. Others were whole families evicted from their homes. These gatherings were called Hoovervilles, a cruel comment on presidential failure.

What could be done to arrest the degeneration of the whole economic complex? What could be done for those who had been employed and who were now simply unable to find jobs? I recall one typical discussion of the nation's sorry state in a Washington hotel room on a December evening. Henry Morgenthau and I were meeting with Senators Wagner, Costigan, and La Follette in one of those Mayflower suites that became so familiar in succeeding years. We had just talked with Roosevelt in Albany, reporting our success in what we had come to Washington to do—get the farm leaders together for a discussion looking toward agreement on agricultural legislation. He seemed cheerful and confident when I talked with him. He asked me to discuss with Senator Wagner the work camps for youths we were planning. It had been one of my assignments to look into the possibilities of such a scheme. We thought thousands could be taken off the streets and given useful work in forest improvement. The Forest Service had the necessary expansible organization, and there was plenty of development work to be done. This scheme had the double attraction of giving young men an income and useful work while at the same time improving the public domain. My conversations about it with the Service officials had become quite detailed, and it was time to enlist sponsors.

This, we agreed, was only one of the projects necessary if the national paralysis was to be overcome. The progressives in the Congress had long been advocating stronger action. During the campaign Senator Wagner had urged Roosevelt to be bolder. Like so many others, however, he had not been given much satisfaction. He appreciated the problems of being president-elect, but was afraid that Roosevelt had not evaluated properly the dimensions of the economic debacle and the small effect of all the remedies Hoover had tried. The Reconstruction Finance Corporation, so much relied on, had degenerated, Wagner thought, into a relief organization for big business, and it ought to be supplemented by other measures. The progressives thought we might get things started even before inauguration if Roosevelt would lend his support.

La Follette had, for a long time, been pushing for more public works. We agreed that by distributing the excess incomes of the well-to-do among the deficit group and so supplying purchasing power, the economy might be kept in reasonable motion. This was certainly the most practical starting place. Neither of us thought that large deficits would be necessary. The existing pools of sterile savings seemed sufficient. The transfer offered no technical difficulties. The problem was to persuade the conservatives in the Congress that it must be done, and this would be impossible unless Roosevelt should insist.

Following this meeting, preparations for what became the Civilian Conservation Corps did get under way. Roosevelt asked me to consult further with Major Stewart, then the head of the Forest Service, and a group of foresters began work at once. I found, as I already suspected, that they had made similar proposals themselves, and had been turned down by Hoover. As to the larger measures of unemployment relief, I had to report back to my progressive friends that Roosevelt was still considering what it would be politic to do: in other words, what the party elders—Hull, Pittman, Robinson, Byrnes, Harrison, and others—could be got to accept. Also that he was wary of Baruch who had so much influence with these elders and hoped to have a prominent place in the new administration.

Nothing more came of these efforts before inauguration. The subsequent success of the Civilian Conservation Corps, however, is well enough known. The foresters would be disconcerted by the kind of organization finally set up, including not only the Park Service, but state conservation agencies as well; and they would be reluctant to have recruitment and administration entrusted to the Labor Department and the Army; but they could only consent. Much confusion would result, but in the end a quite notable success.

Concerning other plans, Lewis Douglas and I quarreled very early. I protested to Roosevelt too, about the serious inconsistency that was rapidly developing. Douglas was busy persuading congressmen to give permission (in the current appropriations bill) to reduce personnel, abolish functions, transfer bureaus, and the like—the idea being to save that 25 percent Roosevelt had committed himself to in his now-famous Pittsburgh speech.

It seemed to me that reducing expenditures would turn out to be impossible. The demand for relief and public works would be irresistible, and would require vast appropriations. I argued with Douglas that his efforts would get Roosevelt into trouble. His soft brown eyes turned hard. Economy was the great need of the day, he said, not relief. I have to say that it was difficult to dislike Douglas; I thought he would probably be an effective director of the budget, although I later changed my mind concerning the qualifications for that position.

More statesmanlike planning and less determined cutting of expenses would soon be qualities prayed for, but never achieved during my time in Washington.

On coming back to my office at Columbia on December 28, I made a note. With a colleague I had taken a long walk after dinner on Christmas day. It had taken us along 110th Street and back by 125th Street. We had seen unemployed men, wrapped in rags and patches against the winter cold, standing by hundreds in long lines waiting for food to be made available by some charity; others were drifting along the streets, fugitives from a hostile economy.

There was nothing new about this, but still it reinforced a feeling of urgency. The time was approaching when what we had been discussing would be put to the test. I summarized the conclusions we thought Roosevelt had reached. If he carried out what we believed to be his intentions, we thought it would be a good start. Political skills of the highest order would be required, but those he most certainly possessed.

This note reminds me again that the measures adopted by Roosevelt were not, as many critics have since suggested, improvisations. Anyone who will study the conclusions reached in Berle and Means, *The Modern Corporation and Private Property*, and those in my own *Industrial Discipline and the Governmental Arts*, completed but not yet published, must conclude that this is so. Although when it should come time to legislate, extraneous matters would interfere, and although some laws, especially NRA, would be badly administered, Roosevelt was prepared for what was to come.

It was agreed that the war debts had to be reduced; but we were certain that the government's expenditures would need to expand, even if only temporarily. We had urged that only an increase in purchasing power would be an effective stimulus for the economy; but we realized that Roosevelt was not quite convinced. He was still open to the arguments of Douglas and the business leaders, who insisted that economizing would restore confidence and that confidence would lead to the restarting of enterprises. If his first moves were not consistent and if some of them proved to be mistaken, it was not because he had neglected his homework, it was because he had not yet made some choices among alternatives that eventually he would have to make. It was partly, also, because he had to convince others. He could not act alone.

9

CHAPTER 2

Leaving Columbia

CONCERNING MY OWN preparation for what was to come, I was a
professor of economics at Columbia and by now a member of the
University Council. This did not mean that I had much of a reputation. My several books and articles were not regarded by the senior
professors of the graduate faculty as significant contributions. I had
not been made a member of the Faculty of Political Science, the
Sanhedrin of Columbia's sages. My teaching was in the undergraduate
college, something my detractors quickly discovered. What they did
not mention was that I had helped to develop a genuine educational
innovation. This was the beginning comprehensive course we called
Contemporary Civilization, originated by two remarkable men. One
was John J. Coss, of the philosophy department; and the other was
Dean Herbert E. Hawkes. Between them, as the university had gone
back to normal activities after the war, they had conceived and were
putting into effect the novel scheme that was just starting when I
joined the group in the fall of 1920.

They had begun by objecting to the prevalent custom of allowing
students to choose from among a department store of offerings, thus
fractionalizing their studies. Graduates were emerging with a mis-
cellany of superficial knowledge that had no more than a coincidental
relevance in their later lives. It was conceived that a body of knowledge
concerning man and his problems ought to be made available. If all
students had such an introduction, and if it was carefully thought out

and skillfully presented, the life of reason in an increasingly complex world would be measurably advanced.

Our course was a reach for both relevancy and comprehensiveness. The difficulties were formidable. The expanding academic community had organized itself into departments, and each of these had jealous hierarchs. The Hawkes-Coss proposal would break into this system, taking something from each and molding a new whole. Opposition, or, at the least, indifference, could be expected. Still, Columbia College was a good place to try. The graduate professors in Fayerweather Hall regarded Hamilton Hall, our domain, as a kind of farm for trying out young teachers, anyway. They themselves were busy with research, consultations, and the oversight of dissertations. Undergraduate activities were as remote as if they took place on another campus. What we did was too unimportant to be seriously noticed.

For the younger faculty who were asked to join this enterprise, there was obviously a risk. Effort given to it would get no attention from those who controlled recommendations for advancement. Each of us would have come from graduate work in an existing department and eventually would have to develop a specialized subject. Contemporary Civilization would detract from the main purpose of our careers. Those who were attracted to the enterprise could only rely on Coss and Hawkes to get for them the recognition they would need for advancement. If it was difficult for us as teachers, we were convinced that it was enormously beneficial for the students; but success depended on certain arrangements. We had to make a syllabus; we had to have small classes; each of us had to teach all the subjects touched on; and we had to meet the same students five days a week. It was a rigorous discipline.

Still I have always felt that this was my happiest experience as a teacher. I had to expand my own education, often studying subjects I had neglected, especially philosophy and intellectual history. I could contribute what I had learned in economics, law and the other social sciences. Colleagues could help me in their disciplines. It was exciting for all of us. We became friends as well as fellow workers.

I must say that a beginning skepticism about the classical economics I had studied so long was intensified when my studies brought to bear on it the contributions of philosophers and historians. It had become a set of rules for free competition. The model was not then, if it ever had been, recognizably real. In the economists' texts, the discipline had become abstract and refined. An absolute free play for competitive forces was assumed. I had already concluded that this was so far from reality that policy based on it would never be successful. This view was not allowable among most academics; but there was another school of American economists who called themselves, rather awkwardly, institutionalists. They insisted that by exploration and description, genuine forces, rather than mythical ones, could be discovered and that policy should have as its purpose their realistic control. I was attracted to this theory, but I had worked with Simon Nelson Patten at the University of Pennsylvania and he had opened other possibilities. Patten led me to believe that there was a discoverable order in affairs that we must try to understand. This order would be found by experiment and exploration.

I contributed this economic experimentalism to the work, year by year, of improving the course in Contemporary Civilization. Presently I wrote, with the help of two colleagues, one of its texts. It was called *American Economic Life and the Means of Its Improvement*. The title, I think, indicates the intention. It departed from accepted maxims and brought into economics the pragmatic influence of John Dewey, who was then teaching at Columbia, as well as the experimentalism of Patten.

There were many institutions where our syllabus, or some variety of it, was in use by 1932, and most of them adopted *American Economic Life* as well. There was, indeed, such a notable change taking place in higher education that in 1931 I was asked by the Laura Spellman Rockefeller Foundation to explore this development, write a report, and indicate how the movement could be furthered. I was engaged in this as our work with Roosevelt began in the spring of 1932.

I made the study, wrote the report, and offered some recommendations. The supporting studies commissioned among my associates were issued in two volumes by the Columbia University Press under the title *Reconstructing Education*. Work with Roosevelt during the spring and summer had given me some confidence that the ideas and devices I had been advocating would prove practical if adopted as public policies. Roosevelt at least had taken them seriously even if the campaign had been more calculated to reassure uneasy voters than to suggest actual means for recovery.

Whatever else it was, my work with Roosevelt proved to be an academic mistake, something I ought to have anticipated. Ray Moley, as the organizer of the Brains Trust (whose experiences I have described in a book of that name), had recruited other faculty members;

but besides myself only Adolf Berle had survived. Working with Roosevelt had to be done against a good deal of liberal distrust, voiced most aciduously by Walter Lippmann. The complaint was that Roosevelt had not been forthright about international issues; that he had compromised with Tammany; and that he had avoided saying precisely what measures he would take for recovery—probably because he did not know what needed to be done.

Such critics granted him nothing on his record and allowed nothing for his problem as the candidate of a party very loosely held together. There were, among its members, a few Populists, left over from Bryan's days, and some Progressives who were by now disillusioned with recent Republican policies; but it was controlled by its conservative elite who, somewhat earlier, would have been called Cleveland Democrats. Roosevelt's aim was a gathering-in without alienating any of these. This might be thought an impossible undertaking; but the depression was an effective solvent of differences.

Hoover, in 1932, was well on the way to losing all support except that of the most loyal Republicans. If he was determined to defeat himself the professionals among the Democrats were all for letting him do it. In their view it followed that Roosevelt's strategy should be the simple one of not offending anyone. So he must stick to lively but innocuous statements. Nothing drastic, nothing unexpected—this was the advice; and Roosevelt followed it. This had annoyed those who had hoped for a forthright attack on big business in the accepted progressive style; and most academics shared the displeasure. And I, of course, was disappointed by his generality.

Those who suspected him of unorthodox intentions about finance centered in such places as our School of Business, where J. Parker Willis was the most opinionated of the seniors. Willis had a high reputation among financiers; he had been the drafter, for Senator Glass, of the Federal Reserve Act passed in Wilson's administration. Willis at once assumed that Berle and I were encouraging Roosevelt in fantasies about easy money. I was soon made aware of this and arranged for him to visit Roosevelt. I was present and was amused to hear Roosevelt ask pointedly why the reserve system had not prevented the financial crisis we were now in. Willis' inability to explain did not make him happier about Roosevelt—or about Berle and myself.

I must say that my former closest associates granted me more tolerance. Even those, like Hawkes and Coss, who had never voted anything but the Republican ticket gave me a different kind of rating.

They knew I had questioned many notions and institutions they regarded as unshakable, but they took pains to find out rather more about the situation as it developed and allowed me the tolerance I needed.

I did not think my separation from Columbia was likely to last long; indeed, I did not regard it as a separation at all. This was the assumption when Nicholas Murray Butler invited me to his office in Low Library, whose windows overlooked the plaza where academic activity centered. He had been president since 1901 and had presided over the university's development into an institution of great reputation—one of the country's few really notable centers of learning. I had not quite accepted the adverse judgments of my liberal colleagues about Butler. He was actually an appropriately majestic figure among academic statesmen. It was true that his posture in later years had invited parody. His corpulent dignity, his remoteness from day-to-day administration, his much-publicized consortings with prominent persons at home and abroad, his position in the upper levels of Republicanism—all lent themselves to the humorous depreciation of juniors.

I had never talked with him alone and had no idea what might come from the unexpected meeting. He offered me a comfortable chair and ignored his desk. He said he had heard that I might go to Washington and asked if it was true. I said it was: as he was aware, I had assisted to some extent in Roosevelt's preparatory studies and it was evidently considered that I could be of some use in the new administration. He said of course I must go if I wanted to; but the university was important too, and I would be missed. I thanked him and said that my first loyalty was to Columbia, that I should have only a temporary assignment, and, as much as anything else, would value the experience I should get.

He said he was not certain that any advice he could give would be of any use; but reminded me that he had been similarly tempted on several occasions. It seemed that at least two presidents had wanted to make him secretary of state, that he had been offered ambassadorial posts, including that at the Court of St. James's; also that he had been urged to become a candidate for the presidency by influential supporters. After consideration he had rejected every such opportunity because of his conviction that his place was at the university. He felt justified now since Columbia's position had grown to be so unassailably excellent in all that gave such an institution its reputation. It had even survived so far the difficult years of the depression with hardly any scars. It was true that physical expansion had been interrupted; but the faculty was being protected. The university now comprised the most illustrious scholars on this side of the Atlantic. To be one of such a company was distinction enough for anyone. These were considerations I must have in mind as I planned my future course.

I was so impressed, not only with his pride in the university's refulgence, but with the unusual thoughtfulness of his indirect advice, that I went back to Hamilton Hall and called Moley to tell him that official life was not for me. What changed my mind was a talk with Roosevelt.

I was not as familiar with the house on East 65th Street, where he now was, as I had become with the mansion in Albany and the home at Hyde Park. It was the house bought for the newly married Roosevelt by his mother, next to hers, one of a row, when it was thought he would become a New York lawyer. The stony exterior enclosed the same furniture for living as the brownstones all over this part of New York. Roosevelt was using the second floor. Here he had been interviewing numerous people who had something to say about what ought to be done. Most of the visits were urgent, and in these days of bank closures and spreading economic paralysis, there was a strange unreality about everyone's behavior. What could not possibly happen was nevertheless happening.

I noticed, as I sat with him, that others were doing most of the talking. This was a change. Roosevelt's habit had been to say something at once when visitors approached and go on until he got around to the subject he was interested in; but now he seemed to be listening more. If he had made up his mind what he must do, as I felt certain he had, at least in economic matters, it had not been publicized. I knew that he meant to see that such banks as seemed solvent were to be reopened; he intended also to sequester gold entirely; but what part I had had in discussing these plans was now in the past. He told me I was to be positioned in the Department of Agriculture—with other possible assignments—but I understood, without his saying so, that one of them was not to be finance. I had argued for a rejected policy and disqualified myself for participation in what was to be done.

I had passed the point of arguing further; anyway, visitors in other rooms were discussing the situation in low but excited voices. Some were waiting to see him; some had come from seeing him. I had not yet learned to distinguish the Secret Service men from the others; but I recognized some upper-echelon financial people among those present.

This was quite different from most former conversations. Anyway, it was not a time for discussion. I still had more than half a mind to tell him I was not suited to the kind of life I could see ahead, and that he must leave me out.

He was not exactly short with me when we were left alone; but he was unequivocal. I was simply instructed. I was to take my assignment as an assistant secretary. The farmers had to be got back in business. I could not get out of it now. I left, making no objection. I was apparently committed. He was right. There was tension in the air. We had talked a good deal. Now the time to act was coming.

CHAPTER 3

The Developing Crisis

THE UNEMPLOYED, all through this third winter of depression, had voiced no protest and in that sense were not a problem. Those among them who had once had good jobs were still struggling and dreading the time when their credit could no longer be extended. Since they could not buy many goods, stores were no longer crowded and manufacturing plants were idle. By now it was evident that debts were still an intractable problem. Banks had made loans to manufacturers and held collateral but its value had evaporated. Consequently, they could not meet their depositors' demands, and, when their cash was exhausted, were forced to suspend payments. It was becoming plain that all the banks would soon be closed. It was this rather than unemployment that got public attention.

One of the Democratic suspicions at this time was that the Republicans were trying to manage events so that the complete breakdown, now inevitable, would be delayed until after the inauguration and so would not be chargeable to them. They had opened this line of argument immediately after the election. The worsening of conditions, they said, was the result of Roosevelt's refusal to cooperate with Hoover in checking the downward slide. The confidence of businessmen had been returning in 1932; but fear of radical measures when Roosevelt took over in Washington had checked it. The rising panic was in anticipation of a new regime, not a failure of the old one. Enterprises would not be started if they had to contend with policies sure to make profitable business impossible.

Roosevelt was not much disturbed by this ploy, but he watched closely as the tension increased. There was more and more evidence that the climax would come in early March. Hoover did make attempts to persuade his successor that he ought to join in reassurances. One had to do with foreign debt moratoriums; but another had to do with support for sound money—a promise not to devalue the dollar. But Roosevelt rejected or ignored these advances.

All during the depression, businessmen had been ill-served by their sources of information, and it was still so. The newspapers no longer reported facts. They were resorting to optimistic fiction. Nevertheless, realistic merchants had recognized what was happening. They were cutting prices to reduce inventories. Insurance companies had begun to refuse policies; they did not know how to invest new funds any more than they knew how they could meet their coming obligations. By now most of them were virtually bankrupt. Bankers and businessmen knew their enterprises were insolvent; but they hoped government loans might give them a few more weeks or months of life. Perhaps they might somehow survive. They had frightened Hoover with forecasts of business and bank failures, and they were now attempting the same tactics with Roosevelt. Hoover's RFC had responded bravely to their appeals, and loans to corporations had been made in what then seemed immense amounts; but the assistance was never enough.

The situation was made worse by the wholesale hoarding of currency. During January this became a certain indication that a crisis was widely felt to be impending. Those who had cash were hoping to reserve at least something for the coming shortage. By the middle of February the entire banking system was in immediate jeopardy; moreover, this danger was well known. The final phase began on February 14, when the banks of Michigan's whole southern peninsula were closed for eight days by governor's proclamation. This included Detroit and involved institutions supposed to have assets of a billion and a half dollars. Since it was obvious that a suspension of such size must involve other areas, fears mounted everywhere. Security prices fell precipitously in succeeding days, and hoarding increased. Nearly every open bank had a queue of depositors clamoring to withdraw their funds.

On February 18, Missy LeHand had called and said Roosevelt wanted to see me. Hoover had written another letter asking him to join in a statement that would "restore confidence." Since I had been involved in earlier answers to Hoover's advances, he wanted my help in replying to this latest one. He was afraid that anything he might say would limit his future options. I no longer urged the measures I knew he would not take. The letter was quickly composed. Then he spoke of ways to locate the "sound" banks and get them back in business. Even if the trouble was systemic, as I thought, he was not ready to do anything further at once. He told me he understood that Arthur Ballantine and Francis Awalt, Treasury officials, had some helpful ideas and would stay on as long as they were wanted. He would accept their offer, he said, and the emergency measures could be drafted at once. I understood that I would not be involved in this. I would have other things to do. But it was a quiet evening's conversation, and, although I thought what was proposed could do no more than put things back where they had been when all the trouble started, I said no more about it. It was the last time I talked with him about the financial situation until after the banking crisis had been eased.

When, on the morning of March 2, I went down to join the others traveling to Washington on the special train, the cave-in of the whole country's financial institutions was almost complete. The Michigan precedent was being followed and the closing of banks was on everyone's mind. It was hard to think or talk of anything else. The Democrats were taking over with the economy crashing and general paralysis about to set in. It was hard to sustain much elation over the ending of the long Republican era.

March 3 is likely to bring wind and chill to New York, and this March 3 was no exception. But at least there was neither snow nor rain. As so many times in past years, I took the bus that crossed over from Riverside Drive to Fifth Avenue at 110th Street. It was one of the old doubledeckers. When it stopped and passengers were taken on, it seemed unlikely that it could ever heave itself back into motion, and when it did it made a horrific commotion.

Henry Wallace would meet me at 65th Street. He had been in New York during the past few days, seeing various people, but hiding from reporters. We had visited in my apartment or office when it seemed safe, and had once gone to a theater. His characteristic stiffness was wearing off; but it was something he could not overcome altogether. He was naturally a solitary and a mystic, not a mixer in the political fashion. Yet he should have been better prepared than I. His father had been secretary of agriculture when he had been growing up; but his diffidence was apparent. He had approached in a hesitant way what for him was a considerable difficulty—the matter of clothes. How did a member of the cabinet, a presidential intimate, a statesman—

and we both smiled—dress? I had already prepared. Would he like me to go shopping with him? He certainly would, he said with relief.

With only a few days left, there was no alternative to a quick, ready-made outfit. So I went with him to a Fifth Avenue store with an air of confidence that might have been less if I had had to confess that it was my first visit too. It was a good choice. There was an amazing collection of cutaways, striped trousers, tailcoats, English shoes, silk hats and all the rest, down to shirts and ties. I told the salesman that he was outfitting a future cabinet member. Looking at what Wallace was wearing, he hardly believed me at first; but he soon came around and was helpful. I have an idea that Wallace never really forgave me for the striped trousers that went with the cutaway. He would later josh me about appearing at meetings of farm leaders in flannel slacks and a tweed jacket—eastern campus style. I would only have to point out that at that very moment he was wearing striped pants and that they were no more Iowan than flannels and tweeds. He was keeping them under the desk, he said.

The assembled friends and political associates, new and old, of the Roosevelts were spilling over onto the outer, chilly steps when we got to 65th Street. Roosevelt always traveled on the Baltimore and Ohio from Jersey City to Washington. I never knew the reason for this. Perhaps he just preferred the scenery; but I suspected an old dislike of the rival Pennsylvania railroad. The choice made necessary a procession of limousines to carry us across the river. The excitement natural to such an occasion was inevitably intensified by the nationwide economic paralysis, but the amenities had to be observed. It was not altogether a company of strangers but Wallace confessed that he knew none of the others and had to be introduced all around. This journey was the first of the new administration's social occasions.

I found some acquaintances, but it was the first time, for instance, that I had met Josephus Daniels, who was by then a legendary ancestral figure. Daniels, of course, had been Roosevelt's sponsor in 1913, when Wilson had agreed to his appointment as assistant secretary of the Navy, and had been his superior during the following years of war. The young Roosevelt had not always behaved loyally to either the secretary or the president. He had been hawkish about the impending conflict with Germany when official policy had called for neutrality, and on occasion Wilson had been impatient with him. Daniels had always smoothed things over and in the end had gained his junior's respect. He was now to have his reward. He was to be ambassador to Mexico.

Daniels, being a shrewd but kindly man, spoke at some length with me about the campaign, and when I confessed my disappointment about its many evasions, he counseled patience. Young men like myself might not understand the necessity of loyalty, he said. "Franklin did not understand it in 1913," he continued, "but he learned—and you will learn. Politics is a complicated business. You will not always understand his maneuvers; but you must not question them."

Roosevelt's special car was the last on the train. He sat toward the rear so that he could see the countryside as we passed through and called one after another of us for a talk. He discussed with Will Woodin, who was now, by a last-minute choice, to be secretary of the treasury, the plans for getting the banks open again. When he got to Washington, he would send at once for the holdover treasury officials, and Woodin, looking frail and retiring, was given instructions.

He remarked to me what I had often noticed as I had gone back and forth to Washington during the past few months, that chimneys were smokeless—and it was industrial country we were passing through. As we came to Philadelphia he recalled that this was familiar territory to me, and I told him a little of my experiences as a student among the buildings and streets as we drew slowly past. Nothing more was said about what we had to do in agriculture. We had talked this matter out. He said nothing about it to Wallace either in a serious way. In fact, when Wallace returned from his conversation, his conscience was bothering him. He said, "It's incredible. The country is in ruins; and we seem to be on a kind of Sunday picnic."

There were not half a dozen people on the special train who knew much about what might be done before the week was out or how far plans had been developed. Roosevelt's apparent cheerfulness, Wallace obviously felt, was so preposterous as to approach irresponsibility; but I knew that some of the proclamations to be issued during the next three weeks were already roughed out. I explained this to Wallace and it seemed to modify his uneasiness about the frivolity of a political celebration on a train rolling slowly through the winter-scarred countryside.

One of these proclamations had to do with the convening of a special session of the Congress on March 9. Another proclaimed a nationwide bank holiday. In Roosevelt's *Public Papers* there is a note to the effect that he had consulted with Senator Thomas J. Walsh, his choice for attorney general, about these proclamations. This is a mistake. We were never able to get in touch with Senator Walsh before his sudden death on a train coming to Washington from Miami. Homer Cummings, who took Walsh's intended place, was not appointed until the last minute and he cannot have been consulted until after the inauguration. It must have been the holdover officials who had done the drafting.

The moves to be made were actually tentative. No one could know whether any or all of them would have the effect intended. The use of the Trading with the Enemy Act to declare the bank holiday and to suspend the buying and selling of gold, as we had discovered, had been rejected by Hoover and Secretary Mills. Its use now might be thought an act of desperation. But Roosevelt had made up his mind that what was most needed now was to act and to keep on acting as though what was being done was obvious and legitimate. Awkward questions were out of order.

Concerning the Trading with the Enemy Act I had a story for Woodin, who still doubted the legality of sequestering gold. I recalled the situation in February and the persistent dollar speculation in such foreign markets as Amsterdam and Vienna. Gold was moving abroad in vast quantities and was being hoarded at home. It was urgently necessary to get control of the situation. We might go off gold entirely, of course, and set up a different monetary base. Some of us had thought the time had come to do this. Since, however, this would precipitate a long debate and acrimonious controversy, Roosevelt had looked for another solution. Something clearly must be done at once. Consulting widely among New York acquaintances he regarded as public-minded—Russell Leffingwell of the house of Morgan was perhaps the most trusted—he had concluded that gold must be sequestered entirely, hoarding forbidden, and shipment abroad prohibited. Otherwise prices would keep dropping, the liquidity crisis would grow worse, and assets could not be unfrozen.

It was Rene Leon, a retired Wall Streeter, who called attention to the Trading with the Enemy Act, passed in 1917 as a war measure. It was, he thought, still available. It had been repealed in part after the armistice; but as Leon read the repealer, it stopped short of removing the president's authority to forbid trading in gold. This may have been legislative carelessness—it probably was—but if it was fact, a president could act by executive order as Wilson had done. Although Roosevelt could not be sure, this seemed the only possibility short of asking the Congress for legislation and risking the consequences of frantic speculation during an indefinite delay.

He had asked me to find out. I had gone to Washington, got in touch with Daniel Bell at the Treasury, and asked him to tell me confidentially whether he interpreted the act as Leon suggested. Bell had smiled, reached into the top drawer of his desk, and brought out a marked copy of the act. The passages we were interested in were underlined in red. "So," I said, "others have considered segregation by executive order." He answered that the passage had been studied intensively. It had been concluded, however, that repeal could hardly have been meant to end at a semicolon, as the Leon interpretation suggested.

I needed no other evidence that Hoover and Mills had seen the possibility but had been afraid to proceed. I asked Bell not to mention my inquiry; then I called Roosevelt and told him that such a move had been canvassed but had been rejected. "Well," he said, "Hoover couldn't get a quick confirmation from the Congress. After March 4th, *I* can. So you go and talk with Key Pittman, Jim Byrnes, and Cordell Hull. Ask them first where they think the repealer ends and whether I would be justified in basing an executive order on the assumption that it ends at that semicolon."

This I did. Everyone agreed that although there had been careless drafting, and Leon was probably correct, quick action would be advisable. The thing to do was to prepare a congressional prohibition about trading in gold, exporting it and even possessing it. It should be presented immediately after the executive stop order. Its passage would legalize the order. Woodin had not known about this, but he was not too much surprised. The question, he said, was whether the sequestering of gold and even the reopening of the banks would be enough to reestablish confidence.

What finally determined Roosevelt's decision to support the present banking structure, and to allow the present system to be regenerated, was, of course, the rising level of fear about all our institutions. He had been unable to put together in his mind an alternative to private banking that seemed workable. During the spring he had asked himself, and us, who would contrive and run a nationalized system. He felt that the alternative was impractical. Berle, after our discussions, was certain this was what led to his decision, and I was inclined to agree.

Many of those on the train, and many others who were to join in the inaugural celebration, would not have enough pocket money to pay their hotel bills or to meet the other expenses of the journey. This caused a kind of apprehension they had never before experienced. The same strange emptiness must have been felt by people everywhere in the country. There were millions who had already faced worse possibilities than not being able to pay a hotel bill. As their jobs had disappeared and their funds had melted away, even food and shelter had become uncertain. In this company, however, fear of such an elemental kind seemed intolerable.

There had been some discussion about abandoning the elaborate ceremonies. Roosevelt's answer to that had been short and quick: of course not, even if they should seem somewhat incongruous. It was better to risk some criticisms than the added anxiety cancellation would cause. And so, when we reached Washington, Roosevelt's newcomers were put into automobiles and I, at least, had my first experience of a presidential cavalcade with motorcycle outriders. None of the spectators along Pennsylvania Avenue paid any attention to the rest of us after the Roosevelts had gone by. Presidents were expected to display a certain splendor, even if somewhat muted for democratic sensibilities. Others were no more than an extension of the presidential presence.

CHAPTER 4

The Capital

DURING THAT NIGHT and the next day, conferences about the financial situation went on feverishly in Roosevelt's suite at the Mayflower. The professionals Roosevelt had not called on before were now available, and I had no part in the discussions. But on March 4, Wallace and I went to our future offices to call on our predecessors. I had a comical moment when the incumbent assistant secretary, R. W. Dunlap, informed me that no one had told him he had to leave. Since my appointment had not been made official, I had no immediate reply to make. It was ridiculous but I retreated. Within a few days, however, an announcement did appear, and on my next visit Dunlap was more reconciled to retiring. I asked him to instruct me in what my duties would be. He said that he signed the road contracts (agreements between the states and the Bureau of Public Roads) and presided at the hearings prescribed in some of the regulatory acts. Otherwise his time was his own. He had no authority over any of the bureaus.

I naturally assumed that he meant to be facetious; a troubled expression lost itself somewhere in the bald spaces above his eyes. "You'll find," he said, "that an assistant secretary isn't much around here." He did remark, however, that he spent some time out at Beltsville. After inquiry I discovered that Beltsville was an experimental complex a few miles east of Washington in a state of arrested development. Dunlap, being a farmer, undoubtedly felt more at home in the fields and stables than in the office he was so reluctant to give up.

He was right about assistant secretaries. Like American vice-presidents, they were nonpersons who were expected not to remind anyone of their existence. They had no responsibility for policy. Their only real duty was to become acting secretary when their principal was away.

Before long I yielded that corner office to Mordecai Ezekiel, the economist we were to depend on so much, and moved into another nearer the center of activity. I found that members of the department did not regard me as so much of an outsider as I had feared. The scientists and administrators had always endured politicians of the Dunlap kind, and they seemed to be relieved that for once they had superiors they could communicate with. I soon found that I did have departmental duties in spite of my involvement in such matters as getting a farm relief bill framed and doing numerous jobs for Roosevelt.

I soon began to regret my undertaking to make the reduction he had in mind. He was holding to a conviction that much of the department's work was unnecessary. It could be reduced by half, he thought; and although I knew that this was exaggerated, I was well enough aware that some projects had been extended beyond all reason. Some cutting would certainly be possible, and the scientific work would be better for it. Still, it was presumptuous for an outsider to insist on a rearrangement likely to inconvenience many capable people. I was somewhat less embarrassed because I meant to make my stay brief, as I had promised President Butler I would. At least I could try to do no damage.

A university such as Columbia engaged such affection and loyalty that most of its teachers lost any desire to change. If they achieved professorship, they expected to serve out their active days quietly and busily. I soon found it was much the same with most of the people who were working in the department. But workers in government are, above all, realistic. They had made accommodation to other changes. They would absorb this one. It was an advantage for us that both Wallace and I had credentials of a sort, mine academic and his scientific. Although he had been known mostly as editor of *Wallace's Farmer* in Des Moines, he had been an experimenter. Indeed, he had had considerable success in the hybridization of corn and the commercial distribution of the improved seed.

March 4 began with Roosevelt's swearing-in and his inaugural. The speech was intended to begin the restoring of confidence. There was, he said, "no failure of substance." Nature still offered her bounty, but generous use languished in the very sight of abundance. He then tramped hard on those he considered responsible. Primarily it was "the rulers of the exchange of mankind's goods" who had failed through their own stubbornness and incompetence.

It would be difficult to reconcile this speech with the policy of the first months, when Roosevelt's best efforts were directed singlemindedly to the reestablishment of the very institutions he had denounced. But, of course, he did have faith in the institutions; it was their managers he castigated. Obviously he believed the country to be of the same mind. That was implied when he said that "the money changers" had "fled from their high seats in the temple of our civilization." Only one who was completely aware of his singular responsibility would pour into the ears of a listening nation such a scriptural comparison as followed about restoring "the temple to its ancient truths."

Actually, I asked myself, what "ancient truths" were there to be restored to the high seats in the business temple? It was hardly made clear by the two passages recalling Americans to ethical standards they had neglected but had never ceased to profess. He went on to say that these dark days would be worth all they had cost if they taught us that our true destiny was not to be ministered unto but to minister: "There must be an end to a conduct in banking and in business which too often has given to a sacred trust the likeness of selfish wrongdoing . . ."

Were banking and business *sacred trusts*? They had not been thought to be. They were rather occupations intended to make profits—and the more the better—by any means within overly permissive rules. The wide separation of ownership from management in the modern corporation had not helped to "humanize" business or to make it more ethical. *Caveat emptor* had replaced *caveat vendor*.

His hearers were obviously expected to recall the other sentence of the parable. And that he had the whole of the tenth and eleventh chapters of Mark in mind was equally plain.[1] In the tenth chapter it is said: ". . . and whosoever would be first among you, shall be the servant of all. For the Son of Man also came not to be ministered unto, but to minister, and to give his life as a ransom for many"; and in the eleventh chapter it is related that Jesus came to Jerusalem after his triumphant progress and "entered into the temple, and began to cast out them that bought in the temple, and overthrew the tables of the money changers, and the seats of them that sold the doves; and

---

[1] I say Mark rather than one of the other gospels even though the same story is told—with some variations—in all of them, because of Roosevelt's reference to *ministering*—a word that occurs only in Mark.

he would not suffer that any man should carry a vessel through the temple. And he taught and said unto them, 'Is it not written, my House shall be called a House of Prayer for all the Nations? But ye have made it a den of robbers.' "

Then there was the next sentence of that story: "And the chief priests and scribes heard it, and sought how they might destroy him; for they feared him . . ." For some reason I had not seen the draft of this speech and could only suppose that he had written most of it himself; but Moley has given an account of its writing (in *The First New Deal*, 113*ff.*) at Hyde Park, late in February; and evidently it had been put together in the usual way.

Like many others I watched the parade from temporary stands across from those occupied by Roosevelt and the new cabinet. It came billowing down Pennsylvania Avenue from the Capitol. There were squads and squadrons of marching clubs, fraternal drill teams, silk-hatted and frock-coated Tammany braves, military detachments, and uniformed bands. Gifford Pinchot stood in his open governor's car, and waved to the junior bullmooser who was now president. For four hours the gaudy color of politics, its brassy tunes, its bosses and helpers passed by as Roosevelt sat on a shooting stick or stood on his braces with the help of son James, erect, smiling, waving to each passing unit of the parade.

The mood contrasted with the morning's solemnity. His "So help me God" as Mr. Chief Justice Hughes had held out the Bible had rung bell-like from the amplifiers in his high tenor. Work would begin tomorrow. Today the Democrats were ending their long exile, and they meant to enjoy it.

As he liked to tell the story later, the new president woke next morning with an urge to get started. When he had been wheeled from the living quarters across to the executive offices and was seated, for the first time, behind the presidential desk, he found himself alone. It was Sunday. There were several buttons; but no one answered the bells. For some time he sat there, a little unnerved, unable even to dictate notes. The whole capitalistic system was smashing up. He had offered himself as its savior; and here he was, helpless! He shouted and finally someone came. Then he called his first cabinet meeting and started the Treasury holdovers on the task of rescuing the financial system.

CHAPTER 5

The Department

I T IS NOT EASY for outsiders to understand the loyalty of those who serve in government agencies. There are devoted attachments—to a department, to an agency, to a bureau or division. No one speaks about it in high-flown language. Nevertheless, the sentiment can be very strong and can call out efforts no pay could produce.

The armed services have this kind of hold on those whose soldiering is professional, and what is true in the military is only less true of workers in laboratories and experiment stations, in services of inspection, and even in agencies that gather and organize information. It would surprise no one to have it said of foresters that their dedication is complete; but it would surprise a good many to be told that the same thing is true of a bureau having to do with plants, animals, insects, or, say, managerial techniques or statistics. Yet, as I got to know my fellow workers, I soon realized that it was this that kept government going. It gave the department a really remarkable morale.

It sometimes seemed to me that everything possible was done to discourage it. The press spoke slightingly of "bureaucrats," and they were favorite subjects for congressional sarcasm. They were told every day that they were time and money wasters who got useless jobs by patronage and held them through influence. It was true that our department, as a whole, like others, seemed to have been assembled by chance with only coincidental relation to farming. It included the Weather Bureau, the Bureau of Public Roads, and the Food and Drug Administration, for instance, as well as more credible bureaus devoted to

29

agricultural activities; but this was no stranger than that the Department of Commerce should have the Lighthouse Service, the Treasury the Coast Guard, or the Department of the Interior the Division of Territories. It was obviously long past time for rearrangement; but meanwhile, if there was some lack of departmental identity, there did remain those inner affiliations of the bureaus, services, and administrations; and in our case those were what counted—or would until we undertook the immense and baffling effort involved in the renewal of agriculture.

I was aware before I began that the reduction Roosevelt expected was distasteful; but he was insistent. He said the department was a lodging place for Republicans who were more interested in serving their patrons on the hill than in doing anything useful for farmers. There was some truth in this; but I was appalled by his determination to end all research. I reminded him that breeding experiments were essential, and that the control of diseases and pests had to be carried on; but he was not convinced.

I could not deny the multitude of political appointees in minor positions. Everywhere I looked there seemed to be a Mormon. That perennially demanding senator from Utah—Reed Smoot—had been influential. I tried to explain that these were not essential to the organization and that they would soon be replaced by equally deserving Democrats. What would be damaging would be to eliminate the scientists and their technical helpers.

I recognized the source of his prejudice and the illustrations used to support it. It came, of course, from Cornell. The agricultural college there was a stubbornly reactionary center, a principal conserver of faith in states' rights and the family farm. It was the center also of an economic theory. This was the belief that a shortage of money had caused the decline in prices and brought on the depression. According to this theory, farmers, if left alone, would set everything right provided only that money was properly managed. Individualism, free competition—a return to the old ways and old virtues—was the right policy. Cornellians were also opposed to experimental work being done by the department. They would have had it all done at the state experiment stations and Roosevelt agreed.

In spite of my quickly documented descriptions of departmental accomplishments, he accused me of being won over by specious appeals. One of my recitations recounted the conquest of hog cholera. Another was the saving of citrus crops by the introduction of new insects. I also cited the danger to forests from blister rust and other diseases and recalled the devastation caused by the cotton boll weevil. He was most susceptible, I could see, to the effort just being organized to combat Dutch elm disease. I told him that unless it could be checked, every elm in the East would go the way of the chestnuts, whose skeletons were standing everywhere in woods and fields.

I pointed out how necessary it was to find alternate crops for the old corn and cotton country from the Atlantic to the Appalachians: I thought he ought to have a special interest in this, because a farm he was trying to bring back from ruin near Warm Springs in southwestern Georgia was defeating his best efforts. In his convalescent years he had driven about the southern countryside and talked with many farmers. From this he knew what the agricultural depression had done; but he also knew that economic recovery would not defeat the boll weevil or restore fertility to worn-out land. For such problems the department had the only answers there were. I pressed my case.

Cornell was devoted to saving New York State's hill farms in the late stages of decline. The West had much more efficient operations. The land was flat and could tolerate machinery much better than eastern hillsides. New York farmers raised some wheat and corn; but mostly they had to buy grain for feeding. They had pastures for only about half the year; their stock had to be in barns during the winter; and this was a severe disadvantage in competing with areas farther south. Besides, much of New York, like New England and Pennsylvania, was badly eroded.

This last had given rise to an act of imagination at Cornell that had interested Roosevelt: the buying up of exhausted farms and moving their owners to better situations in valleys, if they wanted to start over, or persuading them to retire to some village if they were old and discouraged. This Tompkins County experiment had been supported with state funds and was a success even if only on a small scale. The land retired from farming could be returned to forest or used for parks. This could be considered a pilot project for more extensive use.

On the inoffensive scale of the Cornell project, resettlement had no enemies. Later, when we tried it on a national scale, it would develop so many that its beginning with emergency funds would never be further authorized by the Congress. Even the Cornellians opposed it. There was no consistency about this; they were willing to support such cautious experiments as the rescue of local hill farmers, but from the first they were hostile to any and all federal programs. They did want their local dairying protected by the federal government from outside competition; but this was an unusual concession. Otherwise they felt that if farmers were treated fairly by tax laws, had good roads, and could get credit at low interest, nothing else need be done except to raise prices. This, they insisted, could be done by manipulating the price of gold.

Such attitudes are visceral. Roosevelt's sentiment was Cornellian; he liked to see prosperous family farms; he thought they were good places for people to be. He would even have liked to entice the unemployed out of the cities and establish them on such places. He had done some of this—or Harry Hopkins, as deputy relief administrator, had done it for him—in New York; and he was encouraging the planning for a federal homesteading scheme. On the other hand, he saw that the immense surplus of staple crops—cotton and wheat, especially, but also warehouses stuffed with lard, butter, eggs, and other semi-perishables—had to be reduced. Certainly no more farmers were needed. The immense surpluses were a problem neither he nor others could ignore. So, in spite of his reluctance, he listened to the arguments of those of us who felt that heroic—and perhaps costly—measures must be undertaken. It was the first necessity, we insisted, for general recovery. If farm people—they made up nearly half the population then, counting owners, tenants, sharecroppers, laborers and small villagers—could not sell, they could not buy; and if they could not buy, no one need supply the goods and services they would like. Thus, closed factories, unemployment, general paralysis!

This was the agricultural problem in 1933. It was much more pressing than departmental affairs; and Wallace and I owed it our first attention. We had to devise legislation to replace what we had tried but failed to get in the lame-duck session before inauguration; and then its administration had to be organized, and this would have to be done while Roosevelt—and everyone else—was immersed in the complex banking crisis.

It may be difficult for later generations to understand why agriculture was so important to recovery. It must be recalled that prodigies of production during the war had left the country's granaries and warehouses filled to overflowing with immense surpluses when the war was over; and these were being added to by each new crop. Prices had fallen so far because of this that farmers could not pay their debts or buy new machinery and the other supplies they needed. Until their purchasing power was restored, half the population was simply out of the market for manufactured goods. It was a first necessity to relieve this paralysis. The banks could be reopened by huge infusions of government credit; the unemployed could be given income by devising public projects; but farmers must have some relief as well.

Our adjustment scheme was meant to accomplish this by reducing farm production to what could be sold in domestic markets at profitable prices. The Cornellians thought this was outrageous interference. Farmers, they said, always prospered in times of rising prices. They knew how to make them rise. They had a deceptively simple formula: simply acquire increasing amounts of gold; each ounce would be worth less in other commodities. The supply of dollars in relation to commodities could be manipulated. Whether Roosevelt would really adopt this scheme we did not know; but the signs were ominous.

☆ | CHAPTER 6 | ☆

At Some Distance

IN THE DRAMA of those days, the new president was playing his part like an experienced actor. His ambivalence during the campaign had caused some skepticism; but there had been instant public response to his inaugural, and his first decisive moves were watched with fascination. Anything done to banks in the way of discipline was sure to be approved; and retrenchments—cutting salaries and firing employees— were rebukes to a generally disliked bureaucracy. That these moves would only make the problem worse ought to have been anticipated; but everything said or done somehow seemed right at the moment. The traditional honeymoon for new presidents, exaggerated in Roosevelt's case, made the Congress compliant to his demands. Nothing he proposed was critically examined or, if it was, very few listened to the critics.

Those who were putting the financial organization together again after its collapse knew well enough what they were doing. They were, in fact, the ones who had presided over it as it had gone to pieces. They stayed on for some time until the solvent banks were reopened and something like normal operations were restored. Even Secretary Mills delayed his departure. He, like Hoover, viewed the Roosevelt accession as a disaster for the nation but was relieved to discover that rumors about nationalizing the banks were false.

The succeeding phases of emergency from the crisis were, after the closures, the appointment of conservators, and then the bringing to bear of massive federal assistance. With some increase in business activity and a rise in the price level, the banks would gradually be able to liquidate their assets and begin to make new loans. Roosevelt had judged that however much reform was needed, the first thing to be done was to resume. After that, something could be done to make it less likely that such a disaster would occur again.

Conservators were to distinguish the institutions whose assets were only temporarily unsalable from those with ones that were worthless. For the first, an enlarged RFC took over their loans; with this assistance they could go back into business. For others, liquidation had to be arranged with gradual payment to depositors of whatever funds could be realized.

There was such interest in these rescuing operations that the suspension of gold shipments abroad by executive order and then the validating by the Congress of the sequestration order affecting all gold was taken as part of the resumption plan. There was suspicion, latent for some time in the financial community, that there was more to come. Since the gold standard affected bank reserves and its price affected the value of dollars, creditors realized that they would be repaid in cheapened currency. That, however, was not happening at the moment. Anyway, their fears were of no interest to the public.

When, after some weeks, at least some banks were open again, there was time to think of other matters. At one of the early cabinet meetings Wallace raised the question of farm relief, and it was discussed briefly. The only real violence in the country was out in the corn and wheat country, and it was already sharing headlines with the banking crisis. Farmers were loudly protesting low prices and were using force to prevent foreclosure proceedings.

When he came back to the department from this meeting, Wallace was so worried about the possibilities that he suggested a private talk with the president, and presently it was arranged. It was not yet warm in Washington but the grass was green on the lawns outside the windows and the trees were budding. I noticed that it had not taken long to cover the walls of the oval office with the naval prints Roosevelt regarded as essential wherever he went. His desk was already accumulating a clutter of statuettes and gadgets; and there were piles of papers he had to get through every day. He was pushing one away when we came in, and talking at the same time.

It was an easy and pleasant conversation. It was remarkable how cool he was in all the confusion; but of course his small staff had gone to work without much fuss. Marvin McIntyre arranged appointments; Stephen Early handled the newsmen; Missy LeHand was next door in a small office with the cabinet room just beyond; and Louis Howe was acting as general factotum. In his jealous way, Louis had established himself as the principal presidential assistant. He meant to see that Roosevelt made no mistakes, that he paid proper attention to the political elders who counted, and that he should not be upset by the office-seekers and interest-peddlers who were gathering in Washington. He watched over Roosevelt now much as he had when Roosevelt had been a young assistant secretary of the navy.

The confusion in the outer rooms, where all the privilege-seekers, together with newsmen, milled about, did not reach the inner office. Between the two was McIntyre's domain, guarded by Secret Service men who let through only those who had made appointments. In the chairs around the waiting room there were usually several people eyeing one another or carrying on low-voiced conversations. Roosevelt was always behind schedule.

Wallace, being our secretary, was supposed to put our case, but he was hesitant and slow to get started. Eventually he began in a burst of words accompanied by awkward gestures. Roosevelt at once interrupted to ask whether the farm leaders had agreed on any plan for relief. Wallace had to admit that they were as far apart as ever. They had done much declaiming ever since there had been a prospect that the new administration would support some legislation; it was still going on; but each of the farm organization leaders was still maneuvering to get his own scheme approved.

Wallace described John Simpson of the Farmers Union, raucously demanding price fixing in tones reminiscent of Populist oratory; also the processors' lobbyists who were insisting that if everything was left to them they would see that farmers got higher prices—of course at consumers' expense. Also he admitted that those who insisted against reason that surpluses could be sold in foreign markets had not given up. Our own plan for crop control was taking shape and, we thought, gaining adherents, but there would be opposition from several sources: the processors, of course, who were powerful persuaders of congressmen; but also the heads of several farm organizations with other schemes in mind. We had the support of the largest of these, the Farm Bureau, but the western Populists would settle for nothing less than outright price fixing. There was also the Grange—the oldest of the farmers' organizations and, as well, the most hostile to governmental interference. Wallace, having admitted this, came to an abrupt stop.

By this time McIntyre had suggested several times that we were overstaying our time and there was, in fact, no more to be said. Roosevelt was cheerful enough. He was getting almost unanimous praise for the brave words of the inaugural and for the vigor of his first moves; but as to the farm problem, he plainly regarded it as our job to get agreement among the farm leaders. We had hoped that somehow he would intervene and take the lead; but evidently he would not. We left in bad order. When we got back to the department we glumly agreed that a new effort must be made to get something like a consensus. That conviction was all very well; but we had nothing more to offer than we had had all along. Perhaps the situation had to get even worse before we could overcome the jealousies and differences keeping the factions apart.

☆ | CHAPTER 7 | ☆

Exile

THE WHITE HOUSE in those first weeks was under siege from many
sources. For one thing, not all the politicians had heard, or if
they had heard, did not believe, what Farley was telling them about
patronage: there would be a moratorium on jobs for deserving Democrats until the emergency legislation had been passed. The excuse
was the crisis. Most of the claimants became more tractable when
promised later satisfaction but there were those who regarded themselves as exceptions. When they failed to persuade McIntyre over the
phone that they ought to have an appointment with the president
they undertook intimidation by face-to-face confrontation. So the lobbies
swarmed with angry and frustrated politicians who considered that
their elementary rights had been denied.

It was easy enough in those relaxed times for anyone who looked
respectable to walk into the White House. He would be eyed by the
guard at the gate but not asked if he had an appointment. He could
get as far as McIntyre's door if he announced confidently that he was
a congressman, but there he was stopped. Louis Howe had heard from
Farley about the most insistent petitioners. Roosevelt himself had his
own preferences among them. He even sent for some. Usually, however,
those who were admitted by McIntyre were not the petitioners in the
lobby. These watched the privileged callers go on into the oval office
with offended glares.

For Roosevelt to get through such days might seem an exhausting
ordeal: twenty or thirty people to see, most of whom wanted some-

38

thing; perhaps several hundred papers to look at and sign; then lunch at his desk. So it would go until late afternoon. Only occasionally was there an outing of any kind. Dinner, if not formal, was at least black tie in the family dining room with a company chosen not by himself, mostly, but by Eleanor and her secretary.

There were times when he could relax enough in the evening to see a movie, the apparatus for which had been set up in the upper hall; but very often he had more conferences or more papers to get through, and he seldom got to bed with a detective story before midnight. He did sleep well; he always had. He counted on it. Since he was used to official life, even if not so strenuous as that in the White House, he could be said to take his duties easily; and certainly he was always cheerful.

When he was really concerned about something he could usually, as he said, give things a push. He was not surprised when bureaucrats found ways to soften or evade their orders. This he was shrewd about. It was always possible to be pleasantly threatening and, if he took the trouble, to devise a way of following through. The worst troubles of this sort involved the older bureaus; but the newer agencies developed methods almost as effective. He was experienced enough to locate resistance, and if it seemed important, break it down. He lectured me on this general subject reminding me of his eight years as assistant secretary of the navy. "They'll fool you," he said. "They're used to confusing people in the front office; they'll always exaggerate their usefulness; and the only way to make orders stick is to take away their money." I protested that I was used to people in laboratories and offices and thought I could reason with them. "No," he said, "people in laboratories and offices are the worst kind. You'll never really know what they are talking about and they'll make it seem disastrous to interfere with their projects."

At the end of this first March visit we were getting up to leave when Wallace said to Roosevelt that he supposed there could be no objection to his discussing with me not only agricultural problems but the various other problems discussed in cabinet meetings.

"Oh no," Roosevelt said, "you mustn't do that. Cabinet meetings are confidential. Josephus Daniels never told me anything when I was an assistant secretary . . ."

We went out. When we had got through the crowd in the outer office and had climbed into his big black car, Wallace looked at me and asked, "Now how do you account for that?"

"For one thing," I said, "you shouldn't have asked him."

"I thought I had to," he said. "You know him better than I do, and I knew you were more in his confidence. I didn't propose to worry about that or let it come between us."

"He didn't by any chance wink at you, did he?" I asked.

"No," he said, "I never saw him look more solemn."

"I'll tell you one thing," I said, "if that's the way it's going to be, I'm going home now instead of a few months from now. I didn't come down here to be an assistant secretary. He told both Moley and me he wanted us to do jobs for him that he couldn't trust others to do."

"You heard the same thing I did," he said. "I can't tell you what it meant."

When I asked Moley what to think, he laughed it off. If I wanted to see a really awkward situation, he said, look at him. He was an assistant secretary, too. His superior, Hull, was an opinionated ex-senator with one fixed idea—free trade. Even if he, Moley, was only nominally in the department, how could he always keep out of Hull's way? He couldn't imagine that Roosevelt had changed his mind about our confidential duties. He said we would not be in departments at all if Louis Howe hadn't been so jealous that he would not have anyone in the White House but McIntyre and Early, who were old subordinates from Navy days. If I had trials, his were worse.

Ray's offices were in a corner suite of the old State, War and Navy building across a narrow street from the side entrance to the West Wing of the White House. He could go in and out without being noticed; but since he was the only speechwriter he might make the journey several times a day. How Hull felt about this could be imagined.

The prohibition against being privy to cabinet discussions soon came to a comic end. Wallace went away on a speaking trip in April and on cabinet day I inquired of McIntyre what I should do. He said, "You're the acting secretary; and secretaries are supposed to come to cabinet meetings."

On this assurance I went, taking Wallace's place at the table next to Secretary Swanson of the Navy, who genially shook hands. Roosevelt rolled himself in and swung into the chair at the head of the long table. He was talking before he got settled and went on talking. If he thought I ought not to be there, he gave no sign. When he went around the table later for reports, beginning with State and Treasury, and got to Agriculture, I spoke briefly about the troubles in Iowa and Nebraska and said Wallace was out there now. He might come back with something more than was reported in the press; but the situation was bad. We ought to get on to some legislation as soon as possible.

That was that. I heard nothing more about not sharing cabinet confidences. Besides, as we soon discovered, there *were* no cabinet secrets. Such of its members as had come from the legislative branch regarded publicity as one of their perquisites. Most of them were already supported by well-developed groupings who were still relied on to further their ambitions. None of them seemed to recall how unusual it was for a cabinet member to become president. These characteristics of the national government were only gradually discovered by those of us who were new to Washington; but it was quite clear within months, even when Roosevelt was securely ensconced in popular regard, that at least three of his cabinet were gathering support of this kind, rather quietly, but with obvious determination. I disliked to acknowledge that Wallace was one of these; but there soon could be no doubt. Of all that first group, he would come closest to succeeding. That, however, was not evident at the moment.

☆ | CHAPTER 8 | ☆

Confusion

THE CRISES WE HAD to work our way through may seem, to a later generation, as remote as the nation's early wars. Problems of precisely the same sort will never appear again. Yet they had significance as an instance of the necessity for governmental interference when a free enterprise system finds itself in trouble beyond its self-repairing capabilities.

It is a discouraging admission that our rescue of agriculture by heroic efforts would in the end be futile. During the years to come, farmers would eventually be so much reduced in numbers as to very nearly disappear, their place being taken by agribusinesses using much more capital and much less labor. Our excuse for saving the then-existing farmers is that it was something we had to do just then if the country was to be got moving again; and it did get moving, slowly at first, but moving. Farmers' renewed purchasing power had a good deal to do with this; in fact it was indispensable.

As to my assignment in Agriculture—to reorganize, to reduce unnecessary projects, and generally to tighten up—the results were minimal. Anyway after a while this seemed, even to Roosevelt, so unimportant that it faded out of our discussions. While it was going on during the spring in our department as in others, there was resentment and confusion. This seemed to me ironic, because these same departmental people would soon be asked to invent projects to employ far larger numbers than would be dispensed with in the reductions.

Reorganization would then seem to be something we might have been allowed to defer until a more tranquil moment.

How retrenchment came to be so firmly fixed in Roosevelt's mind is still something of a mystery; but of course this was not the first —or last—instance of the nearly complete disappearance of consistency. It will seem incredible—it is still incredible to me—that the conflicting policies of those early months not only existed in the government and operated side by side, often colliding, sometimes canceling each other, but that they also existed somehow side by side in Roosevelt's mind. If I am asked how this could be I should have to answer in unsatisfactory—because too general—terms. They have to do with the timing of decisive actions, and with political demands so often incompatible with sensible decision. It may be that a president has to proceed in this way, putting behind him at well-matured times one commitment after another, allowing those not yet having generated the necessary pressure to continue unsettled.

This ambivalence was not new. It had characterized the campaign when Roosevelt, pledging himself to economy, had also promised assistance for the unemployed. He was obviously moved by other than economic reasons. He felt strongly that something had to be done for unfortunate fellow citizens and that only government—the federal government—could give relief. But he did not like it any more than Hoover had.

Strangely enough, my arguments that the bolstering of purchasing power was necessary to recovery were what had first attracted him to me; and for some time I had thought him convinced. I had argued that once the economy was again operating at its customary level, governmental income would be enough to reduce the deficits incurred for such purposes. The way to recovery was through this temporary acceptance of unbalanced budgets. This might not work out so smoothly as in theory it should; but certainly the restoration of purchasing power was the first necessity.

We had gone over this ground so thoroughly before the campaign that I was at a loss to understand why the Economy Act had been insisted on. It had stopped the public works then in progress and reduced the incomes—and so the purchasing power—of the workers involved. These might not be many, but when others were being asked to enlarge employment, to have the government reduce it was inconsistent. Economy, of course, had been promised in the unfortunate Pittsburgh speech castigating Hoover's extravagance. It had been intended to bolster the "confidence" of businessmen who were expected to take risks and expand employment; but that this simply would not happen I had thought he now understood. Real and instant purchasing power, not promises for the future, was what was needed.

Vigorous subordinates will always try to commit their superiors to policies they believe in; but it cannot be denied that just then there was an excess of such attempts. Perhaps they were allowed because Roosevelt himself was of two minds about so many matters. He even seemed to persuade himself that opposites were identical—that, indeed, some unlikely synthesis had come about. On the other hand, it may be that he deliberately tolerated inconsistencies, waiting for the issues to become clear. If these uncertainties and postponements were calculated they still were exasperating and the cause of many embarrassments.

Roosevelt did not have to explain himself to anyone. He seldom argued with those around him now as he had in the Albany evenings I have described in *The Brains Trust*. What he did—and this I recall an indignant Frances Perkins holding forth about—was to tell us, quite as though he expected to be believed, what he expected to come of actions and arrangements we knew were contradictory. Our willingness to be faithful subordinates was severely tested.

Wallace and I, discussing this, had to conclude that sooner or later there would have to be an embarrassing retreat from one or the other of the positions about the means for recovery. Were we going to bolster incomes, fully recognizing the emergency nature of such a course and the dangers of inflation, or were we going to pare down expenditures to restore businessmen's confidence? It seemed to us absurd to suppose they would be persuaded to resume activity because of renewed faith in Roosevelt's devotion to sound money and free enterprise. Yet he seemed to expect it.

We had a similar situation in agriculture. We must do a lot of spending before returns could be expected from a rejuvenated farm economy. Would he accept this? He would not. He insisted that we must impose a tax to pay for our program; but if this was done it would raise prices and reduce the consumption of farm products. We could not get him to acknowledge the contradiction. So in the bill we were drafting we included a processing tax, knowing that it would reduce still further the purchasing power of those who must buy the farmers' products.

There was still another annoying issue. He accepted—or seemed to—the trade-union fallacy that reducing the hours of work stretched out the jobs to be done and allowed more men to participate. There was only so much work, according to this theory, and it should be widely shared. This notion was pushed very hard by the union lobbyists; and Senator Hugo Black had introduced a bill making mandatory the thirty-hour week, precisely on the theory that reducing hours would result in employment for more workers. There was difficulty in heading off its passage, and it would have been adopted if a diversionary title (7A) had not been added to the National Recovery Act. This provision legitimized collective bargaining and abolished child labor, reforms trade unionists had long wanted. It did not end the argument about the stretch-out, however; nothing would convince labor leaders that reducing hours of work did not make more jobs, and it continued to stick in Roosevelt's mind.

I had confirmation of this one day when public works were well under way—if I may digress to speak of it. Roosevelt and Fiorello La Guardia, who in 1933 had become mayor of New York, were talking about funds for the New York airport afterward named for the mayor. They were happily agreeing that bulldozers and other powered machines should be banned. There should be only hand tools so that more men would be employed. I listened with some exasperation. Finally I suggested that if their only purpose was to provide employment, trowels might be used instead of shovels. That way, I said, *many* more men would be employed. It was an inspiration. I have seldom seen two people, plowing along an agreed course, so dramatically interrupted. The illustration needed no elaboration, but the pause allowed me to say that many airports were needed, not just a single hand-crafted one in New York. I finished by asking how the cost could ever be justified. That, I think, was decisive. La Guardia, who was a frequent visitor, admitted to me afterward that the first cost of shovels as against bulldozers was less, no doubt, but that the accomplishment would be so much less that he might never finish one airport, to say nothing of building others.

While the rescue of the banks was going on in the weeks after inauguration, Moley occasionally filled me in on what was being done. I had known what way we were going when he told me on the Tuesday after inauguration that the immediate restoration of confidence was to govern policy. I was disappointed to see that he was satisfied with this. It confirmed my fear that we were going to make matters worse by continuing contradiction. That this was wanted by the bankers I could believe; but I thought, and had argued, that the immediate enlargement of employment would have been more sensible. For the Economy Act I would have substituted a public works measure of La Follette's providing for expanded employment and thus increased public buying power. He was still urging its adoption. Since I was meeting frequently with the progressive senators, I could at least encourage like-minded friends. I hoped something might come of it when late in March Senators Norris and Costigan agreed to go with La Follette to Roosevelt with a protest and an alternative plan. This included expanding public works and an appropriation for direct relief; but for that moment the president was going another way.

I am writing still of the earliest days. I had for a long time been close to the progressives—particularly, of course, La Follette, Costigan, Cutting, and Wheeler; also some midwesterners in the House, though the progressives there were disorganized by the loss of La Guardia, who had been their leader for fourteen years past. Then too I found effective helpers in the department and these were detached from routine duties to assist in reorganization.[1]

As was inevitable, my association with Adolf Berle was no longer a frequent one. He had been made a consultant at the RFC but was not regularly in Washington. Still he was respected by Roosevelt and we sometimes met for consultations. I was compensated for losing him by gaining, before the end of spring, Jerome Frank and Harry Hopkins. My old relationship with Moley had become less intimate because of our different duties. We had gone through much together; but now the loyalty involved in our relationship was less to each other and more to our common principal. In practice this nowadays involved differences.

I told myself that we were not playing at something; a nation's policies were being shaped and petulance was not something I could allow myself. I did not like the turn taken in the banking crisis; I was disturbed that nothing was done at once to increase purchasing power; I knew that the economy bill would diminish the effect of relief measures; I objected to cutting down a staff I knew would be needed later on. On the other hand, I had hope in the prospect for farm

[1] These included Lee Strong and Knowles Ryerson, heads of bureaus, and William Jump, finance officer. There were also Mordecai Ezekiel and Louis Bean, economists and statisticians, and John R. Fleming and Russell Lord of the Division of Information. These last were ceded to us by Milton Eisenhower, chief of that division.

legislation. It might even be improved by having been fought over and lost in the winter of 1932-33.

There was confusion, conflict, and some mistaken policies, but everything was fluid and nothing could be considered settled finally. Things might come right before it was too late.

CHAPTER 9

Issues

THE IDEA OF A "voluntary domestic allotment" which Wallace and I had been advocating as a way of curbing overproduction was beginning to substitute itself in the minds of the important congressional Democrats for the older idea of dumping surpluses in foreign markets. It was finally being accepted that European countries had farmers of their own who were not disposed to see American products sold in competition with theirs at sacrifice prices. The problem would have to be solved right here at home, not at the expense of foreigners. This was a reluctant concession. For more than a decade successive so-called McNary-Haugen acts had been pushed by an aggressive farm bloc. Coolidge and Hoover had rejected these, and finally a Farm Board had been created to find ways of diminishing the ever-growing surpluses. It had ended up with elevators and warehouses bulging with unsalable products. Thus the Hoover agricultural policies had the same futile outcome as his other plans for the economy. The legislative farm bloc was by now at least discouraged, if not ready for the extreme remedy of crop reduction.

There were enough staple products in storage to last through two seasons if nothing should be added in the coming year, and, of course, the spoilage was immense. The problem was still the disposal of surpluses and the preventing of further additions. Meanwhile farmers would have to have some kind of income. Our scheme would compensate them for using fewer of their acres. It could be called adjustment—adjustment to the market—but actually it was a way of raising their prices while they reduced production and the stored products were being used up. We knew that most legislators disliked this; they preferred not to discommode farmers, who, like others, expected government to make it possible for them to go on in customary ways. They wanted simply to raise·crops as usual and be paid a good price. We hoped, nevertheless, to see our scheme accepted. It was not so easy as shipping unwanted products abroad; but it was realistic.

There would be even more vicissitudes than we foresaw. We thought that the impossibility of exporting surpluses was by now recognized; but George Peek, as well as others, was unconvinced. As will be seen, he was to be important in the first phase of operations; and anyone who reads his subsequent account[1] or General Johnson's tribute to Peek[2] will understand something of what was coming to us. Peek had been a farm-implement manufacturer, and he had charged his troubles to the inability of farmers to buy his machinery. He had long ago set out to get them more income. He claimed—or Johnson claimed for him—to have invented the "equalization fee" embodied in the successive McNary-Haugen bills. This involved shipping products to foreign markets for whatever they would bring and distributing the yield to the growers.

Having left the Republicans in 1928, convinced that he could get no help from them, Peek felt that he had some claim to Democratic attention in 1932; and he was active in getting it. Since his old association with Baruch during the war was well known, Roosevelt had never encouraged him. We had heard, from time to time, of his efforts to further legislation; but his continued insistence on the invasion of foreign markets seemed to Wallace and Wilson, as well as to me, downright nonsense. But supplementing the sale of farm products abroad, Peek had another scheme. This was the making of agreements with the processors—meat packers and millers of grain—to pay farmers more for their products. About these agreements, as a form of farm relief, both Wallace and Wilson were thoroughly skeptical. Wilson

[1] *Why Quit Our Own?* by George N. Peek with Samuel Crowther (Princeton, N.J.: Van Nostrand, 1936).

[2] In *The Blue Eagle from Egg to Earth* (Garden City, N.Y.: Doubleday & Co., 1935).

had invented the voluntary allotment scheme and had the natural pride of authorship. He was also apprehensive about benefiting the processors at consumers' expense. Wallace knew that such an arrangement would result in higher prices and so in reduced consumption. They had assisted me in convincing Roosevelt that crop reduction, however unpopular, was necessary.

It had been as early as the winter of 1931-32 that Wilson had tried to interest Hoover's Farm Board in his proposal. They had gone so far as to invite him to Washington, and had assigned Mordecai Ezekiel, then their economist, to do some research on the scheme. Ezekiel had urged the board to accept Wilson's advice.

About this time, Henry I. Harriman, then president of the United States Chamber of Commerce, became interested in Wilson's early version of the plan. During the spring of 1932, discussion had gone on among Wilson, Ezekiel, Wallace, Harriman, and that extraordinarily inventive character, Beardsley Ruml.[3] My own interest was aroused by Ruml, who described the plan as it was then outlined and invited me to a meeting of this group. It was this that had ultimately taken me to Chicago just before the Democratic Convention, where I had picked up enough from Wallace to write a passage for Roosevelt's acceptance speech.

Meanwhile, Senator Norbek of South Dakota had been persuaded to sponsor a Wilson appearance before the Senate Committee on Agriculture and Forestry[4] about the time I was making my first trip to Albany and discussing the national situation with Roosevelt. A little later the House Committee on Agriculture had had a subcommittee looking into the matter and a bill had actually been introduced providing for "adjustment charges" (really a processing tax) and authorizing the payment of benefits for reducing production.[5] In addition to this, Congressman Clifford Hope of Kansas had introduced bills[6]

[3] Then dean of the Social Science Division at the University of Chicago and later a vice-president of Macy's in New York, as well as general adviser to many public bodies.

[4] Then considering proposed changes in the Farm Board Act and the Farm Loan Act. Wilson's statement appears on pp. 55-61 of the *Hearings*, 72 Congress, 2nd Sess., April 1932.

[5] Chairman Jones of the committee, on June 4, introduced the Voluntary Domestic Allotment Act (H.R. 12461). It lacked some features of the plan considered essential by Wilson, however, and he doubted its usefulness.

[6] H.R. 12918 and 19219, the Voluntary Domestic Relief Act, July 7, 1932.

containing the proposal. Wilson had so far succeeded in his benevolent machinations. There had followed Roosevelt's campaign speech in Topeka on farm problems; and after that he had been regarded as committed to the plan. This was a success indeed for a professor in an agricultural college in Montana.

In view of all these occurrences it is interesting that Hoover's Farm Board—by then thoroughly discredited—made a kind of belated attempt to recover respectability. When Roosevelt expressed his preference, and it seemed certain that he would be elected, they reversed their long opposition to crop reduction. When their annual report was issued late in 1932 they added a special message to the Congress recommending legislation to carry out the Wilson plan.[7] About this time we had held our meeting in Washington to work up a measure for the lame-duck session. We had hoped to get this passed and out of the way before Roosevelt's inauguration.[8] Our bill had passed the House as the Agricultural Adjustment Act on January 12, 1933, but had failed to pass the Senate. Because of this failure a new draft would now have to be introduced.

Something more must be said about the way the embarrassing surpluses had come about. Westward migration during the nineteenth century had resulted in the opening of new lands in the high plains, and this movement had accelerated during the war. The breaking-up of the short-grass lands had had a tragic result. But in spite of recurrent droughts and many crop failures there had been expanded plantings to meet worldwide demands. A succession of favorable years had produced unusually large crops. When the war ended there was an abrupt failure of the foreign market. Wilson himself had been a home-

---

[7] "Recommendations for Legislation, Special Report to Congress," December 7, 1932.

[8] Ezekiel has commented on this meeting, ". . . the basic elements . . . were hammered into fairly definite shape and first steps were taken in drafting into bill form, with F. P. Lee acting as lawyer in the proceedings. There were many hot arguments, especially with Earl Smith of Illinois, over the exact nature of the proposals, and it was only at the last minute that it was decided to include hogs as one of the commodities. There was considerable discussion as to whether dairy products were to be covered. The New York people were very unenthusiastic about dairy products coming in the bill. George Peek was present toward the end of these discussions but had little or no effect on the idea then being developed. Shortly after that a meeting was held at Albany to which you invited me at which the first draft of the farm plan was briefly discussed with Governor Roosevelt . . ." *Private Memorandum.*

steader in a Montana river bend, and this experience had led to his invention of the "voluntary" reduction scheme. He thought government must simply arrange for farmers to join in a general reduction movement.

Wilson's plan originated in western experience with wheat. It was necessary, however, to be aware of the South; and there was some question whether it would do for cotton what he promised it would do for wheat. Moreover, Earl Smith of Illinois, president of the powerful Illinois Farmers Association, expressed the belief that it would not do at all for the corn and hog economy of the Midwest. It was always difficult to understand motives among the farm politicians; and we never knew whether Smith's active Republicanism, the fact that the scheme was one he could claim no credit for, a weakness for the interests of processors as well as of farmers, or perhaps other motives determined his attitude, but he was influential. Then there were the dairy interests. Their representative, Charles Holman of New York, was always the slipperiest and most effective of Wilson's opponents—but from motives it was not difficult to understand. He was infected with the general hostility emanating from Cornell.

Another consideration was this: Although it was called a "domestic" plan, and was intended to reduce dependence on foreign markets, American staple crops traditionally had a worldwide market, and farmers had an interest in attempts to keep it. The planning of resources for the world's people was a long way off; but we all knew that it must come when the temporary situation had been stabilized. Then American products would again be demanded by European consumers.

What had to be done now, in 1933, was therefore temporary, but it was critically necessary. This was why many congressmen had come around to the acceptance of reduction. The powerful farm leaders who were either indifferent or actually opposed, had lost their old persuasiveness. Earl Smith of Illinois was uncertain; John Simpson of the Farmers Union—who thought farmers' riots were the proper tactics—would never agree to any compromise. But the Farm Bureau Federation, largest and most powerful of all the organizations, was with us. This was for reasons of its own; but we knew we could not succeed without its support.[9]

---

[9] The Farm Bureau Federation was a curious—and indefensible—mixture of private association (with all the stigmata of a pressure group) and agricultural college repre-

This was the situation of Wallace, Wilson, Ezekiel, myself, and our helpers as we began our work in March. But the ills of the farmers formed, at this early moment, only a rumbling in the Washington background; the monetary crisis was more dramatic and was monopolizing attention. It is curious, and yet understandable too, that our first few weeks in office should have been the most relaxed we, in our sector, would have in all our time there. The old agencies could be temporarily left to themselves, and we were able to do a good deal of conferring. We needed to if legislation was to be written and plans made for the administrative organization we would have to create.

Wallace did not yet feel or act like a cabinet member. He took shyly to his large office and sat uneasily sideways at the big desk in its center. He looked at first as though he had just strayed in from somewhere and wanted nothing so much as to find a way out. It took him some time to appear as though he was no longer just a farm-paper editor on temporary leave to do some catching-up in Washington.

I had little enough sophistication about proper official behavior; but Wallace was quite hopeless. The personal assistants of the outgoing secretary stayed on for a time. They were tactful, and smoothed over for both of us embarrassments about protocol that can torment a new official even if such things mean little to him; or perhaps especially if they mean little to him, for then he is sure to be slow in catching on. To show up in white tie and tails when black tie is called for; to realize suddenly and too late that he does not know how to address an ambassador; to arrive unequipped with cards when custom calls for their use—such matters plague the most high-minded officials if their positions require conformity.

These were mostly Wallace's problems. Since few individuals were lower in protocol lists than assistant secretaries I was let off a good deal, especially at first. It was some months before Wallace's family

---

sentatives in the field, since all county agents were graduates, and since the experiment stations and the extension departments were closely tied. But also about one-third of the funds were furnished by the federal government and one-third by the states. Here was a case of government furnishing the funds for the support of a powerful lobby to influence itself. Philippine independence, Cuban tariffs, and sanitary regulations which kept out Argentine beef were much influenced by this organization. This was all changed in later years; but it was what we had to deal with as we began in 1933.

moved from Des Moines to Washington; and he characteristically solved the living problem by taking the same furnished apartment in the Wardman Park Hotel that his parents had occupied in the Harding administration; he felt quite safe in following their precedent. He appeared slightly incongruous in those elegant surroundings, but he gradually came to seem more at home. Presently he could be certain that, however he might feel, his outward appearance was orthodox. This was largely because Edward had taken him for his own. Edward was rated as a messenger at the department; but he had become a sort of factotum, and he adopted this secretary as he had others. He was glad for Wallace's awkwardness and ignorance, since that allowed him to take charge. He extended his services from the office to the apartment as well.

I was quite happy at the shabby old Cosmos Club; but Wallace suggested that I come out to live with him for a few months. Since he was alone there and seemed to mean it, I did. We lived there together through the "Hundred Days." I must confess to have been happier at the old club. It then occupied two connected houses on a corner of Lafayette Square just across from the White House. This was historic territory in Washington. Henry Adams had lived on the square where the Hay-Adams Hotel now was; and St. John's Church occupied another corner. The park itself was a pleasant place. Its centerpiece was the statue of Jackson on a rearing horse; but its character was placid enough. Its benches were sparsely occupied by visitors who fed the pigeons and rested. At lunchtime, government workers opened their parcels and enjoyed an hour sitting there on the benches. The club itself was old and its leather chairs worn. Its dining facilities extended into gardens in the rear. The servants had apparently been there forever. They moved slowly, but that too was in keeping with all else.

Of the likenesses and differences Henry and I had to get used to in each other, the most puzzling, perhaps, was that he had more of the characteristics I was supposed to have than I did. This may seem a little involved, but it was true. He carried pictures of statistical tables in his mind; he thought in exact quantities; and his mind moved outward to the enlarged consequences of small facts and occurrences with ease and rapidity. This was to be an invaluable trait in the formulation or reformulation of policy made necessary by the events of the next few years. I used to think admiringly that his equipment for the secretaryship must be the most appropriate and complete of any person's who had held that office. And I saw no reason to modify that judgment as his leadership in scientific work, as well as economics, began to make itself felt throughout a difficult period.

I was to learn, as time went on, what his failings were. Indeed he spoke about some of them himself, and deplored the insufficiencies they revealed. His ambition for higher office soon became somewhat more than latent. This led him to avoid controversy and to compromise more than he should. He was too intelligent not to recognize this. He, more than I, was caught up in an ongoing process whose momentum was nearly irresistible. For decades farm politicians had been rooting themselves in Washington. They extracted from federal revenues the funds they needed; the state colleges trained the sons and daughters of farmers not only in the methods but also in the ideas and prejudices of their group and class; and these in turn supported and backed up the lobbyists. It was a tested and effective establishment.

It had long been recognized that there were sinister covert relations with the processors of farmers' products. This had spread into the department's bureaucracy so that there was the suspicion, sometimes voiced by acute critics, that the department represented the farmers' enemies rather more than farmers themselves.

Besides this, there was a technological change going on, one strenuously resisted. It might have been expected that the prolonged depression would have caused some searching of heart and mind, that some question might have arisen as to whether the family farm was to last, and whether agricultural improvement ought to center in making farmers prosperous without some change in their methods of production. But questioning was discouraged. This I was repeatedly told, was because farming was "a way of life," not just a method of production. Wallace, whether his intelligence approved or not, was cast in the role of leader. He was the farmers' man in Washington. He had to accept the common beliefs. He put it this way at a somewhat later time:

Undoubtedly there will be more mechanized farming, but increased mechanization may eventually mean more family-sized farms rather than fewer. For a time it seemed as though new inventions were helping the big farmer more than the small one. But increasingly there is an interest in inventions designed to make it possible for the small farmer to compete on a more even basis with the large one . . . The steam engine, and the factory based on steam, collected people from the farms and put them in cities. It is conceivable that rural electrification, the automobiles and hard roads will eventually to some extent reverse the process. At any rate around the cities there will be a great increase in the number of "part-time" farmers.[10]

This is a properly qualified statement. It was not made in 1933 but several years afterward, when the signs, I would have thought, were even plainer. Wallace, however, was still conforming even then. In that same article he would go on to say that in wheat, corn, and cotton areas, some large-scale operations must be regarded as inevitable; but the family farm could be saved in poultry, dairy, fruit, and vegetable country. "All that is needed is genuine awakening," was his conclusion. His illustrations were drawn from those regions where even he would have had to admit, if challenged, that mechanization was inevitable.

In AAA legislation Congress has repeatedly shown a desire to use federal power on behalf of the small farmer at the expense of the larger one. Small farmers are paid a higher rate per acre or bushel for complying with AAA regulations than large farmers. In referenda the vote of the small farmer counts for exactly as much as the vote of the large farmer. Very small farmers are given special exemptions in the case of marketing quotas.

What did not appear in this, of course, was the recognition that a powerful lobby was using its pressures to favor the obsolete, the anachronistic, as against disturbing change. Being basically honest, he did, however, go on to expose the reason for all this:

More and more thoughtful people in the United States appreciate what was long ago made a part of continuing policy in France—that an enduring nation can be built only on the foundation of a prosperous farming class operating farms which in the main are family-sized.

Both the Roosevelts had this same reluctance to distinguish between realistic and sentimental objectives. It seemed to me important that the least expenditure of labor and capital needed to produce food and fiber should govern the use of the land. There were by now new sources of power, new breeding methods, new controls of disease and new ways of utilizing products. Each of these was certain to influence

[10] Henry Wallace, "The Future of the American Farmer," *The New Republic*, November 8, 1939.

agriculture; and to say that each must be made to fit the family-farm pattern was absurd. They had revolutionized industry, and they would certainly revolutionize agriculture.

This was doubtless too rational for political purposes, and my refusal to share in the emotionalism on this subject was held against me by all those who preferred not to recognize the consequences of technology. Wallace, having been washed up to the top of the agricultural hierarchy, might have become the shaper of the force behind the coming revolution. He chose not to do that.

It was ironic that, in spite of what he said, the small farmers who were so much praised had miserably few government benefits from the operation of AAA. These would go to the larger operators, not to the smaller ones. Millions of those "sturdy peasants" would be stranded. They would either sink into poverty where they were or move to city slums in search of other employment. The problems of another generation were created by the policies of 1933, and absolutely nothing was done to avert what was plainly to be a disaster. A city worker displaced by improved processes was at least near to retraining opportunities, not to mention sources of assistance in time of trouble; an agricultural worker, or sharecropper (and their number was roughly equal to the total number of "farmers"), had far fewer such resources and far greater initial handicaps in any change of occupation. The trouble was most serious all across the South, where wages were supplanting the share-crop arrangements in force since the abolition of slavery and where laborers were being replaced by machines. Evictions, lynchings, and race troubles were especially frequent on the border between dominantly black and dominantly white communities. The few well-meaning outsiders who were working for very decent objectives so often confused personal publicity for themselves with improvement in the situation of the victims that they were seldom effective. There had also been some unfocused talk about land for displaced tenants. This was quite naturally not supported by those whose ownership status was beyond question. There were fewer secure farm-owners now, of course, with the full pressure of depression bearing down; and any assistance for croppers and black workers would have to be provided by Hopkins' social workers who previously had had no rural responsibilities.

The greatest difficulty in doing anything for these rural people, however, was that so few of those in more fortunate circumstances acknowledged the extremity the poorer families had already reached and the hopelessness of their situation. There was a tendency to say that they at least had a roof over their heads and enough to eat.[11]

What nonsense that was is easily enough seen in the perspective of later years; but it was not questioned when it was said.

[11] Roosevelt continued to share that view. In 1931 he had made a radio speech "Advocating Distribution of Population toward the Source of Food Supply" in which he had not only made a kind of back-to-the-land appeal but had also implied rather clearly that country unemployed were at least better off than those in the cities. "What does unemployment in the city mean? It means that the whole family is not only put out of work and out of cash, but is also out of food and is threatened with losing a roof over its head. . . . There are unemployed people in the agricultural sections of the country, though they total only a small minority of the whole of the unemployed and I think it is fair to say that with certain exceptions most of these people in the country are not faced with actual starvation or actual eviction. . . . While agriculture is in a thoroughly bad way, actual distress and starvation and lack of clothing exist primarily in the cities of the nation.

"Is it worthwhile for us to make a definite effort to get these people in large numbers to move out of cities where there are thousands and hundreds of thousands of unemployed and bring these people closer to the actual sources of food supply? It seems to me that to that question we must answer an emphatic *Yes.* . . . We must try to work out a definite plan by which industry itself will seek to move certain forms of industry out of the congested centers where unemployment is greatest into the smaller communities closer to the primary food supply." *Public Papers*, I, 516-18.

CHAPTER 10

The Economy

Historians can hardly be blamed for being puzzled by Roosevelt's beginning an economy drive and then almost immediately asking for several billions of dollars to be used for relief and work projects. It could not be denied that reductions in government personnel and the stopping of such construction as Hoover had started added to the numbers of the unemployed and reduced purchasing power.[1] At the same time it had become clear that the attack on our economic paralysis had to begin by giving consumers the means to buy. It simply has to be admitted that Roosevelt was not yet certain what direction he ought to take and was, in fact, going both ways at once.

A ready shelf of public works had been recommended to Hoover, who had then been secretary of commerce, as long ago as 1921 by a committee whose chairman had been Wesley C. Mitchell. Following the report, an emergency office had been put to work producing plans; and as a result a number of projects had been ready to start in 1929

---

[1] The Economy Act was signed on March 20. It had been requested in a message enlarging on the theme that "for three long years the federal government has been on the road to bankruptcy." This, Roosevelt said, had caused the collapse of the economy. Almost at once after inauguration stop orders had shut down what public works Hoover had started, and it was well known that everyone's pay was to be cut and that all agencies would be required to reduce personnel by 25 percent. Authority was even asked for to eliminate such agencies as seemed unnecessary. On the other hand an act was signed on May 12 that would authorize the CCC and a relief and public works program.

when unemployment had become serious. It was a small office and the projects were limited; but it was something.

The difficulty had been that Hoover could not bring himself to approve of spending beyond visible income. Also he would not approve *giving* to the states rather than *lending* to them, and since they soon exhausted their own borrowing power they were unable to continue giving relief.

Hoover had defended himself by repeated statements of principle against the progressives who were badgering him for more public works and even relief. Independence was the foundation of American life, he said; people must not be *given* the means of living. He described "rugged individualism" as a principal American virtue. There might be such public employment as could be afforded; but outright relief was tolerable only for those who could not work.

It can hardly be imagined how often the word "confidence" had been repeated during his last months in office. It was being said that the economy had faltered because Roosevelt would give no assurance that he would follow a conservative course. The demand had first been heard in Roosevelt's circle from Baruch, and it had been repeated by General Johnson when he was loaned to our Albany group by Baruch whose employee he was. It had been Johnson who had drafted the Pittsburgh speech implying that Roosevelt, after all, was not the radical he had been supposed to be. He would balance budgets by reducing expenditures and would be a friend to business. Those were the intended conclusions; but he made no similar statements after election and during the months before inauguration; the idea had spread that he was indeed having radical thoughts. Any confidence the Pittsburgh speech may have conveyed soon evaporated.

How much Roosevelt believed in the efficacy of restored confidence it was impossible to say. His inaugural had proclaimed a war on the depression. He had called people back to the belief in their institutions and chided them for wholly fanciful fears. If the economic system was to be restarted it was certainly necessary to restore confidence in it; but who, I wondered, would believe in a system so thoroughly discredited? It was evident that Roosevelt meant to persuade them that only a few miscreants were responsible. They would be expelled from "the temple."

It was in pursuit of renewed confidence that the Economy Act was presented and easily passed. Its logic involved certain conditions. One was simple reassurance about the soundness of money; creditors wanted their debts repaid in dollars of stable value. Another was the reduction of expenditures with the lowering of taxes this would make possible. It followed that government would be less likely to harass business. Troublesome bureaucrats would promulgate fewer regulations and demand fewer reports.

It might have been thought impossible to explain, when so much had been said about national bankruptcy and Republican extravagance, why the enormous sum (for those days) of $3.3 billion was presently requested for unemployment assistance when obviously the government had no such funds to appropriate. This difficulty was passed over very lightly in the accompanying message; but it was hinted that the deficit would be reduced as government expenses were cut and the taxes paid by restored businesses came in.

This promise seemed reassuring but Roosevelt had something else in mind. He meant to raise the price level so that the vast burden of debt could be liquidated. Professors Warren of Cornell and Rogers of Yale were lurking in the background. They had no doubt that they knew how to work the miracle of recovery. They were going to "reflate" by manipulating the price of gold in a market monopolized by the government.

Still, the struggle in Roosevelt's mind was not over. If there was to be inflation by one means or another, confidence among businessmen might be shattered. But it appeared that Roosevelt himself was still not happy about the prospect. He hoped that reflation would restore prices to their former balance; but he was apprehensive about acceptance by the business community. It was, after all, a departure from "soundness." Perhaps when prices had been restored to their former levels the process could be stopped. He believed that the Warren-Rogers scheme would give him adequate control. But could he convince his public that this was his intention and that it could be accomplished?

Among the people around Roosevelt, the dispute about inflation, held over from the campaign months, was indeed still alive. There were those who believed in creating purchasing power—effective demand, in economists' language—and those who protested that if businessmen only had some reassurance they would bring about recovery without government interference. Then there were those who argued that unemployment had become a national disaster and they seemed to have the best of it. But Roosevelt continued to hear from businessmen that what was needed was to stop governmental extravagance and to give assurance that money would continue to be sound. This last was important to the financial community because its members were the nation's creditors and they were hearing raucous and unsettling sounds from the Midwest. Farmers wanted "easy money," and they did not care how they got it.

There still existed, it must be recalled, a powerful farm bloc in the Congress, and its members understood what their constituents wanted. The Republicans—and some more conservative Democrats—had withstood demands of this kind since Cleveland's day. Wilson had not given in to their pleadings but had succeeded in establishing the Federal Reserve system. This had gone a long way toward taking power away from "Wall Street," the farmers' *bête noir*; but bankers in the St. Louis, Little Rock, and Atlanta Federal Reserve centers had been as hard on debtors as those in New York. Roosevelt was aware that there was a massive demand for at last "doing something about money." He was caught between the country's creditors and those who had borrowed more than they could repay.

The Cornellians, with Morgenthau as their agent, assured Roosevelt that reflation was essential; and they found themselves in a strategic position when Woodin fell ill and Morgenthau became secretary of the treasury. Their panacea was slightly different from that of the numerous easy money proponents in the Midwest. They were contending that the gold standard could be made flexible. The fixed legal relationship between gold held in reserves and currency issued by the banks was their point of attack. If the price of gold could be raised by government, the worth of the dollars based on it would decline. It was only necessary for the Treasury to fix the price it would pay for all gold brought to it; and if all gold *had* to be brought to it, and could no longer be held privately, dollars could be made to buy much or little. If they could be made to buy much right now, farmers could repossess their mortgages with more easily acquired funds. They would be more easily acquired because their products could be sold for inflated prices.

The Cornell scheme had been discussed with Roosevelt along with many other monetary proposals. The catch in the plan had seemed plain enough. It was that currency, in fact, was no longer so closely related to gold that the value of dollars would be greatly affected by what happened to its price. But Roosevelt, in spite of his confident air, was fearful about recovery. Frances Perkins was telling him that unemployment was still increasing. Things were getting worse. He was convinced that the whole country had simply lost faith in itself and had to be assured that the depression could indeed be conquered. What was universally wanted was a return to conditions as they had been before 1929 when everyone had been prosperous. Dissent from that as a proposition was confined to those who knew well enough that the conditions of 1928 had produced the debacle of 1929 and, if they were restored, would sooner or later produce them again; but these doubters were few.

Roosevelt concluded that he could not ignore the demands for raised prices. He could not—when debtors were still deeply apprehensive— tell them they were asking the impossible. At the same time there were all those unemployed, and something would have to be done about them. He agreed that the best thing would be to get them back the jobs they had had before. They would have them back if businessmen could hire them. Businessmen would rehire them if any future could be seen in starting their enterprises again—and if the banks could loan them the necessary funds.

He felt compelled to do something. Presently he could mollify those who continued to disagree; but he could not do it until some activity had begun and the paralysis had been overcome. If he was pulled two ways at once, it was because he dreaded making a choice between two powerful interests. He also thought, as politicians do, that the inconsistency in following both courses would soon be forgotten. This dilemma tormented him all during the months before inauguration; and even afterward he had not come to a firm conclusion. Still he must act.

Getting business to resume operations did come first. The banks had to be reopened; the railroads, insurance companies, and other large industries had to be helped; and sources of credit had to be reestablished. The conservators would attend to the banks and a vastly expanded RFC would make loans or buy the assets of the others. So much could be done even before the needs of the unemployed were met and before the manipulation of the gold market was undertaken.

The special session of the Congress, called for March 9, was supposed only to validate the bank holiday and the prohibition of trading in gold, actions taken by executive order on his first days in office, but once this was done and seemed to be immediately acceptable, the problems of the unemployed demanded attention. The situation was becoming more and more critical. The country was indeed paralyzed. It had to be got going—even if heroic measures had to be used. Care must be taken, however, not to deepen anxieties or seem to depart too far from accustomed practices. It was a president's duty to reassure, not to frighten.

Reassurance was therefore the theme of the radio address on March 11—the first of the "fireside chats." It began by explaining that the banks were being rescued, that they would resume honoring depositors' demands. The cash for this was being provided by loans from the RFC on perfectly good, but temporarily frozen, assets. He asked those who were still fearful to have confidence in what was being done: if everyone would now go on as he had before the crisis, take his money out of hiding places and entrust it again to the banks certified to be sound, stability would be assured. "I do not promise you," he said, "that every bank will be reopened; but most will be, and they will be trustworthy." A bad situation had had to be overcome; but that phase was over now.

"It has been wonderful," he said, "to catch the note of confidence from all over the country . . . even when all that was being done was not clear . . . " He was right about that. There was a new spirit abroad. But things were not clear.

It was Moley, of course, who had drafted the fireside chat, as he had the campaign speeches and the inaugural. As in most of the speeches, however, Roosevelt's own touches are identifiable. They gave warmth and reassurance. Then too, it was known that the address was made directly from the White House. He spoke very clearly in his high tenor. It was not a typically regional voice from anywhere in America. The Groton-Harvard accents were very special, and they might have been taken as superior or precious but they were not. On the contrary they conveyed a sense of mastery. Something was being done about the debilitating sickness of the country.

Reservations and dissents would begin later; but Burt Snell, the Republican leader in the House of Representatives, voiced the general feeling. The house was burning down, he said; let the president put out the fire. The effect of the speech was magical; but no one knew better than Roosevelt that he had to produce more than reassurance. The magic was temporary. Nothing the government could do would take the place of genuine recovery. Would that start soon? He was still considering what further actions must be taken. If it seemed afterward that a whirlwind of confident activity took place during April and May, there were actually many uncertainties, many days and nights of discussion and questioning while Roosevelt came to his conclusions.

AAA

ONE OF THE WHISKERED former secretaries who looked down on me from a portrait in my big square office was James Wilson. His face was a reminder of the department's many servants who had believed in its mission and defended it shrewdly from interfering politicians. These predecessors had been skilled in mobilizing the persuasions needed to advance the department's causes. It had been hard in Wilson's time for a squeamish man to get along at all, considering the deals he had to make. I wondered, in spite of the strength so obvious in his jaw, how he had survived three presidents and nine Congresses, from 1897 to 1913. It was he who had really created the department; at least he had provided the beginning of its physical plant and encouraged the expansion of its researches and experiments.

A story illustrating his ingenuity was still told among survivors from his regime. He persuaded the appropriate committees of the Congress, during years of easy income, to authorize a home for the department. Until then it had been a tenant of the Patent Office. He had succeeded in getting twin buildings placed between the Smithsonian Institution and the Bureau of Engraving, a situation with little to recommend it except the one characteristic he wanted. It left a space between two wings obviously waiting for a center, something not noticed by the Congress until too late for change. The designing had been done secretly, and the customary fences had hidden the separated foundations from prying eyes. There was a considerable row when his duplicity was discovered; but the central building did finally get built.

It stood there now, gray stone, undistinguished, with curious decorative excrescences, chosen, it was said, by Wilson himself as appropriate agricultural symbols. It housed the secretary and most of the supporting administrators, whose numbers would have amazed Wilson. In his day there had been less than a dozen; now there were hundreds.

The two wings were still devoted on the one side to Plant Industry and on the other to Animal Husbandry. Together they had represented, and in some sense still did represent, the department's main activities. Housed in one was the effort to grow two blades of grass where one had grown before, and in the other the increasing production of milk, meat, eggs, and lard. Each had developed independent administrative routines and was largely autonomous. They were, however, vulnerable to an earnest effort at economy. They had started many projects but evidently had given up few. I soon found that out; and even William Jump, our remarkable budget officer, admitted this when pressed.

I inquired further what was to go on in the unfinished offices on the other side of C Street, only to be seen from our own back doors. They were, I was told, more office and laboratory buildings. The conglomeration looked no more substantial than the temporary war-time buildings still scattered around Washington. The defense for them was that they allowed almost all the department's activities to be gathered in one complex; but they were an architectural outrage.

Jump explained, out of his long experience, how often central control of the vast department had been tried and why it had always failed. One difficulty was that so immense and so diverse an organization could even be *known* about only with the greatest difficulty; and he was sure that no one understood what went on in all its parts. No secretary or assistant secretary within his memory had even tried to become familiar with its diverse undertakings; and none had been able to influence very much its scientific work. The first thing to be done, he suggested, was to improve the central services. Of course, he warned, the activities were bafflingly unrelated to each other. What the Forest Service, the Food and Drug Administration, and the Weather Bureau had in common was indiscernible; and what they had to do with agriculture was remote.

As I sat under James Wilson's portrait, meeting visitors and studying papers from the never finished piles on my desk, I could look across the mall at the unfinished columns of what would some day be the Department of Labor. There had recently been a controversy about the mall. Park planners had had its trees cut down because they did not stand in orderly rows. The big expanse was now a plowed field with new trees planted more to the designers' liking.

Before we were settled in our offices, the national bank holiday had been proclaimed. At the same time, gold exports and payments had been prohibited. We had no responsibilities about all this, and so we had time to begin discussing the administering of the domestic allotment scheme if it should be approved. The trouble was that we could not guess what amendments might complicate things or how long passage might be delayed. There was reason for thinking it might be many months. The present special session of the Congress had, after all, been called to meet the financial crisis. Presumably after legislating about this, it would adjourn until the next January.

Until the concern about the banking troubles was relieved, we could not expect attention for our bill. We did think that emergency credits might be classified as urgent, since they were needed to still the agitation over dispossessions in the Midwest. But we were well aware that our domestic-allotment scheme was unpopular with many congressmen, including Marvin Jones, chairman of the House Agricultural Committee, who would presumably have to sponsor it. We thought we might have a hard time ahead, and it would be made harder by the machinations of George Peek and others who thought domestic allotment a theorists' vagary. It might be nearly a year before agitation and dispute could settle into a legislative agreement.

As we dealt with our domestic problems, we were aware that an election was taking place in Germany. We read that the Nazis had won 288 seats in the Reichstag and the Nationalists 53 more, making 52 percent of the total. Hitler's star was well over the horizon. The president, when I next saw him, wanted to talk only about Hitler, speaking of him as though his menace was immediate. There was general underestimation of the shrewdness accompanying Hitler's paranoia. Even Roosevelt wondered if the Germans would be deluded for long by so obvious a demagogue.

He spoke also of Mussolini, whom he regarded in a different way. He went on to say that both Hitler and Mussolini were dangerous enemies of democracy and all its processes; but what was going on in Italy did seem to be a rational effort to modernize. There was some harking back to the glories of Rome; but there was definitely more tongue-in-cheek about it than about the solemn German conjuring of demigods from the mists of a doubtful mythology. Still the Germans were more efficient than the continually disorganized Italians. They were the ones to be watched.

There was a good deal more than the reopening of the banks to be worried about, but certainly the principal worry was whether the regulations issued by the Treasury would ease the crisis. All New York banks remained closed. The clearing house declared itself ready to go ahead with the issuance of certificates " . . . if national action is deferred," but there was some hope that reopenings would come quickly.

When, about the middle of March, I stopped by Missy LeHand's new office just off the president's, she spoke softly of Cermak's death. The strange troubles of the world would run their courses; others would die; but Roosevelt would be spared. He would because he must. Her awe was not less because of familiarity. At another time she had said, "He laughs, and often seems unreliable. Sometimes he is stubborn. Can he really answer people's prayers?"

When Roosevelt spoke of this same news about Cermak, he voiced the appropriate sentiments, but there was none of the "But for the grace of God . . . " piousness about it. An accident had occurred, and it had turned out to be a fatal one. He had, in fact, to concern himself with something else in the news. At foreclosure sales in Iowa, farmers were agreeing that one of them would bid one dollar for anything offered. None would bid higher. This, he remarked, was as near to rebellion as the depression had brought Americans. He had spoken before of the strange passivity under pressures of the times. It was, he thought, because no individual could be blamed. Now, however, minds were being made up. The debtors had centered on the foreclosures.

Despite this new urgency that seemed to be rising in the country, we in the Department of Agriculture could not respond. We had more planning than acting to do just then. Wallace had not yet settled down. He was still worried about being surrounded by strangers. His office was a large one with windows toward the north and west. He could look out across the plowed-up mall to the unfinished row of buildings on Constitution Avenue; but by turning his head he could gratify his Iowan eyes with a stretch of grass between himself and Washington's monument. We occasionally walked together across the lawns, talking. It was on one of these walks, after we had led up to it rationally enough by deploring the so-called Economy Act, that we conceived between us a formula for opening the way to immediate action on farm relief. It might succeed in satisfying Roosevelt's demand for agreement among farm leaders.

It occurred to us that the protracted wrangling we were dreading might be evaded by an omnibus emergency bill authorizing the use of all the proposals being pushed by competing lobbyists. Decisions could thus be deferred and perhaps altogether removed from legislative bickering. Successful action, we thought, might smother arguments; and, best of all, we might get to work at once.

This was the real beginning of our spring campaign, and, as we thought, our contribution to recovery. We went at once to Roosevelt. We pointed out that it met the conditions he had been making all along. The lobbyists might support a bill that authorized everyone's scheme. If they did the Congress would pass it. We could then proceed experimentally. If domestic allotment proved unworkable, we might turn to subsidized exports or to the use of agreements with the processors for raising prices. Possibly we should want to use all the proposals serially or in combination, although we had every intention of concentrating first on the one we preferred.

Roosevelt agreed at once. The impending fight over policy would be put off; and this appealed to him as a relief from at least one harassment. There was also the consideration that such a bill could be prepared very quickly. It would, he said, give the Congress work to do while some other proposals he had in mind were being got ready. There had been quicker action on his emergency bills than he had counted on. Who ever heard of laws being passed in one or two days? He warned us, however, that we were asking for trouble. The lobbyists would leave the hill and descend on the department. "But," he said, "you can send them over here if they give you too much trouble." It turned into a light-hearted conversation. We all wondered why we had not thought of such a solution before.

When the Congress validated the first fiscal proclamation overnight, Roosevelt had been undecided at first whether to limit the emergency session to that—or to try for further legislation under the pressures generated by the crisis and with the strategic hold he had on a new and disorganized majority. If he did this, as he was beginning to think he might, our bill might make a recess unnecessary.

He agreed that we should call the farm leaders in and have a discussion preliminary to drafting. He asked how soon they could meet. Wallace thought possibly by the 13th. Roosevelt thought this too late. They must be got together on the 10th—Friday. Since this was the 8th, Wallace could only say that we would try.

What had been a bright idea had rapidly become a serious job. We made our way through the crowd in the outer office, put off the newspapermen, and climbed into the secretary's old Buick—which Gerard, the Civil Service chauffeur, drove stolidly regardless of emergencies, one secretary being like another to him—and went back around the circle to the department, where Wallace began telephoning within minutes. And, sure enough, the response was nearly complete. All the leaders had been sitting on the edge of their chairs anyway, straining to hear news from Washington. They were agreeable to meeting at once, and no objection was made to ignoring their quarreling lobbyists.

It has been too little noticed that many of our later troubles were caused by the decisions taken during these early days. When we assumed the burden of making choices among the competing schemes, we were indeed asking for trouble. "Action, action now . . . " Roosevelt had said, and the whole nation had applauded. We told ourselves that discussions about farm relief had by now gone on for years and might never really be settled unless we tried one plan and found out if it satisfied the farmers and got the results we needed. Besides, the long arguments had never caused any changing of sides. No one listened to anyone else. But there was one final argument. Spring was upon us. If planting was to be restricted at all, the time we were allowed was very short indeed. If we delayed, nothing would be done for a whole year, and the surpluses would increase.

It is true that we had a rather complete outline of the organization needed to put our plan into effect. But when we thought of setting up several thousand committees, of measuring millions of fields, of sending a check to every family, and making sure of compliance, we could hardly be complacent. What we had to rely on was the well-organized system of county agents who would actually do the fieldwork. As it would turn out this reliance was well founded; most of our troubles would come rather from differences about what to do rather than the doing of it. Administration would never be a serious problem.

We estimated some of the complexities involved in the vast program we were planning. When Roosevelt asked about numbers of employees we told him it would be more than a thousand—a very poor guess, as it turned out. He said we were being extravagant. We had no defensible answer; but we had added up at least three thousand; however, many of these would be the existing county agents. Within months the total would be seven thousand. It was a big country, with some six million farmers.

While we were occupied with these immediate concerns, Woodin, over in the Treasury, assisted by the Republican holdovers, was struggling to reactivate the banking system. He had to damp down the hysteria of the bankers who were flocking to Washington. He decided to issue new notes based on Federal Reserve assets. The bank holiday was runnning out and a new proclamation was got ready extending it indefinitely. When the validation of earlier emergency measures had been completed, Roosevelt held a conference of interested officials, including Wallace. He planned to send a message, he said, authorizing extensive public works and permitting the reorganization of agencies. He would also demand economies, among them reduced Civil Service pay and cuts in payments to veterans. This was the first intimation the politicians had that this new trouble was in prospect. They went away with long faces, as Wallace told me in spite of Roosevelt's prohibition. It was the first time I had reason to feel that the La Follette–Wagner urging about the expansion of relief and public works had been successful. The depression was still deepening. If he was still going to insist on economy, he was at the same time going to expand public employment.

The legislators saw trouble ahead. It made matters worse, evidently, that what would be proposed was only a works program with no mention of direct relief. This would be more costly and would take effect much more slowly. He had also spoken again of his Tennessee Valley project and had added to it a similar proposal for the Columbia basin. It was disturbingly sudden. Still, with approval borne into the White House on every mail, what could legislators do? Democratic leaders of the old type—Robinson, Harrison, Garner, Buchanan, Byrnes, and the like—were being pushed into an uncomfortable situation. After years of lethargy, of irresponsibility, of the no-saying appropriate to a minority, they were members of a majority. No group of legislators can ever have been less fitted to cope with a crisis requiring movement, adaptability and imagination.

Experience in dealing with their sort, it must be assumed, is what determined Roosevelt's slowing down later in the spring. He could hope to get done only so much. The measures to be undertaken seemed to the older leaders wildly radical, and they resorted to underground opposition. There were conservatives who went so far as to regret that their party had won the election. Those from safe districts would have held their seats anyway, and without the responsibility of belonging to a majority. There were reasons why dislike for Roosevelt, which infected them from the first, was for a while not openly exhibited. For one thing, fright had only partially dissipated; but also there was the distressing reality that patronage was actually being withheld. The prospective new agencies would offer many jobs free of Civil Service requirements, but only, Farley intimated, to cooperators.

The congressman who felt able to withstand the demands of the powerful lobbies of those days was rare. He was indeed almost non-existent; but the anguish of being whipped into action against the wishes of processors and bankers was nothing compared to that of reducing the incomes of veterans and bureaucrats. Veterans had traditionally been the most untouchable of all. Government workers were not yet mostly Democrats but they soon would be. Besides, there were those who saw well enough that the program as a whole had glaring inconsistencies.[1] None of us who might have protested had any opportunity to do so, although both Wallace and Ickes were dismayed. Douglas had the legislation ready, and it was sent to the appropriate committees wtih a presidential demand, somewhat peremptory, for immediate passage. There was anguished squirming, but the dose apparently had to be swallowed. If so, it had better be done quickly. The bill was not passed in a few days as the money bills had been; it was not signed, in fact, until March 20; but that was remarkable speed for legislators acting against their deepest political interests.

The corps of lobbyists were somewhat handicapped in those early days by having to deal with many new legislators whose weaknesses had not yet been probed. Blackmail as well as bribery had taken on a highly refined form by 1933; but both required exploring and feeling out. Still the present members, like others before them, had come to Washington with obligations to those who had helped in their campaigns. Their first allegiance was to these; but the lobbyists had many ways of reaching those whose votes they needed.

We considered ourselves lucky. The farmers' lobbies in Washington were divided. The Grange, the Farm Bureau Federation, and the Farmers Union all had nationwide membership and were growing. There were, besides, such less inclusive groups as the cotton cooperative marketing organizations much favored by Hoover's Farm Board; then there were the Dairymen's League, the California Farmers Association, the Farmers National Grain Corporation (holdover from the northwest revolts in earlier years), the Illinois Farmers Association, and several others. Most of them maintained Washington representatives. All of

---

[1] The Economy Act, signed on March 20, fixed the cut at the proportionate drop in the cost of living during each preceding six months, with a limit of 15 percent. The president would proclaim a finding and reduction on March 28. It would be renewed on July 3 and January 9, 1934. On March 28, 1934, Congress, over the president's veto, would reduce the maximum cut to 10 percent from February to July and then to 5 percent to June 1935, when full pay would be restored.

them had determined positions, but they traded with other groups for votes and influence. The result was that congressmen often found themselves trying to meet conflicting demands.

The leaders Wallace called in from back home on March 8 were certainly less venal and more direct than their Washington representatives. It was an affront to send for them and it did risk future enmity, but we thought in succeeding days that we had accomplished our immediate purpose. Those who came to Washington on the overnight Capital Limited out of Chicago did join in accepting our proposal. They announced it next morning with an air of discovery. We allowed ourselves to be persuaded, and made some preliminary exploration of ways to conciliate the more reluctant groups. These were, as expected, the Dairymen's League and the Farmers Union, whose representatives prospered through dissent rather than cooperation, and whose withholding pleased their principals.

The meetings were held in a department hall; and at the beginning I presided, making a short speech recalling our efforts to get together during the past winter, and pointing out the present opportunity. I then withdrew and, as we had arranged, W. R. Ronald, editor of the Mitchel, South Dakota, *Republican,* was elected chairman. This was to nullify jealousy among the organizations, since he was not identified with any of them.

As had been true in December, each leader felt compelled to make a speech for home consumption, and this, together with some conferring, used up the first day and the evening. But we were able to hold them to the omnibus formula we had devised. It would allow us to take land out of cultivation, make marketing agreements with processors, or subsidize exports, whichever seemed best as we got to work. Those of us who had some regard for consumers, or who believed that we ought not to cause rapid price increases lest consumers should balk—I was concerned on the one ground and Wallace on the other—could not agree to the cost-of-production formula wanted by the Farmers Union. We argued that cost of production was mythical anyway. For one wheat farmer it was, say, forty cents, and for another $2.00. (As was presently revealed, the Union had in mind a minimum of $2.25.) And for another thing we should have to choose whether to favor high-cost or low-cost farmers and acres.

The absurdity of price fixing was of no concern to the agitators. They were not interested in settling issues; they wanted them kept alive. But we were really afraid only of John Simpson of the Farmers Union, who, as luck would have it, had not himself arrived for the meeting, but was represented by Congressman W. P. Lambertson. We suspected that this was a device to allow Simpson freedom; and we were not surprised later on when he testified vehemently against our bill at the Senate hearings. But at any rate Lambertson was persuaded to sign the findings of the "committee." Holman and his Grange colleagues behaved as usual, going along in a way that gave notice of eventual withdrawal; and there was a sharp quarrel between the two wings of the beef-cattle industry, the cattlemen of the West against the feeders in the corn country. This last was adjourned for the moment, though it too promised trouble later on.

That night, with the business unfinished, a noncommittal statement was distributed:

The farm leaders were unanimous in their opinion that the agricultural emergency calls for prompt and drastic action. Only a prompt advance in prices of basic farm products, in the opinion of these farm leaders, can restore a fair exchange basis between agriculture and industry and make possible a resumption of normal business activity.

The farm groups agree that farm production must be adjusted to consumption, and favor the principles of the so-called domestic allotment plan as a means of reducing production and restoring farm buying power. . . . They admitted serious, but not insurmountable differences of opinion. . . .

This was substantially accurate, although there had been a good many reservations. Worst of all, as may be imagined, was the reluctance to surrender positions maintained so long and so profitably. Gingerly approaches to compromise were made; but it came hard. Wallace and I, as well as they, had such respect for the disruptive powers of the processors' representatives that everyone was sworn to secrecy, and this helped to keep dissent from being openly voiced. We already had an arrangement for reporting to the president the next morning; and we had no trouble in getting agreement to a statement we would present to him:

Report of a special Committee of farm organization leaders authorized at a general conference called by Secretary of Agriculture Wallace, Friday, 10 March 1933.

Your Committee recommends the enactment of an emergency law, as hereinafter outlined:

That following the preamble setting forth the condition that exists in Agriculture, the measure shall declare, that an emergency exists and that the powers granted to the President under this act shall continue for such period of time as in the judgment of the President the emergency continues.

It shall be the purpose of this legislation to establish the principle of parity of prices between agricultural and industrial commodities on the basis of their pre-war relationship and to approach this parity of prices by stages at as rapid a rate as seems feasible in the circumstances.

Powers to be conferred upon the President and the Secretary of Agriculture, as follows:

One: To lease agricultural land and/or enter into contractual agreements for the control of agricultural production.

Two: To take such action and to make such settlements as are necessary in order to acquire full legal title to all cotton or other farm commodities on which the government has made loans or advances upon such terms as may seem fair and just, and to exchange such cotton or other products with growers for acreage reduction.

Three: To regulate and supervise the marketing and processing of agricultural and competing products in domestic and foreign commerce.

Four: To levy such charges on agricultural products or products manufactured from them as seems necessary to accomplish the purpose of the Act.

Five: In the drafting of a bill to carry out these recommendations, all powers necessary to the successful carrying out of the purpose to be achieved shall be included.

* * * * * *

The Secretary of Agriculture shall in his discretion apply the provisions of this Act to the following farm commodities: Wheat, Cotton, Corn, Hogs, Cattle, Sheep, Rice, Tobacco, Milk and its products.

> *Chairman,* W. R. RONALD
> CHAS. EWING
> U. B. BLALOCK
> CLIFFORD GREGORY
> L. J. TABER
> CHAS. HOLMAN
> C. E. HUFF
> E. A. O'NEAL
> RALPH SNYDER
> W. P. LAMBERTSON
> M. W. WINDER, Secretary
> FRED LEE, Legal Adviser
> M. EZEKIEL, Economic Adviser

We could be excused a certain euphoria when we marshaled the leaders first in our building, then in the White House lobby, and finally led them into the oval office. They stood facing Roosevelt, in a circle, veterans of old wars, experienced politicians, hardened by competition. Roosevelt said, smiling, that he understood they had at last agreed on a formula. He reminded them that this had all along been his condition for making a proposal to the Congress. Unless they held to it there would be no bill, and no action; but if they did the farmers might have quick relief. He said that was not only just but necessary to national recovery.

Not all these visitors were Republicans, but most were, and they had been holding back for traditional reasons. Now they were subdued and even willing to put aside—at least for the moment—their most cherished differences with him and with each other. The presidential power could be seen working. They left, a more companionable group than would have seemed possible. Even Wallace saw the humor in the situation; he also wondered, when we were finally alone, how long the friendliness would last.

Next day we could take some satisfaction in the *New York Times* account, and especially in its last paragraphs, reporting the chagrin of the processors:

As to the proposal that the President be empowered to fix prices and regulate foreign and domestic commerce in the commodities concerned, this feature had apparently been overlooked in the advance speculation on the conference's outcome.

It had been advocated in speeches of certain farm leaders during the past six months and had found its way into the hearings on the allotment bill in the last Congress, but its serious consideration for inclusion in legislative programs had not come until the plan was suggested for extending drastic emergency powers to the President.

The proposal, originated by a small but strong minority of the fifty conferees, was literally "sold" to the entire group by those who drew up the plan in tentative draft, following the record action of Congress on a similar proposal for dealing with the financial emergency.

A bill already had been prepared embodying the plan when the leaders called at the White House and if it is acceptable to the President, it is expected that he will transmit another message to Congress asking for its immediate passage.

How far the administration might go in exercising the powers proposed could only be guessed at, even by those who made the proposal. One of these expressed belief that, under the land-leasing provision, between 50,000,000 and 60,000,000 acres probably would be retired from cultivation.

The surprise with which the conference proposal was received by agrarian observers was also reflected among representatives of millers and other producers and exchange merchants stationed in Washington.

First reports of the plan brought forth many kinds of inquiries for official confirmation, and it was believed by some tonight that it was for quieting any further speculation as to the agricultural program of the administration that Secretary Wallace authorized publication of the memorandum.

CHAPTER 12

NRA and Other Measures

AGRICULTURE WAS NOT my only concern during the early months when the emergency was being dealt with. There were other measures Moley, Berle, and I had worked over with Roosevelt, and we necessarily had to take part in their actual formulation. One of these was the reduction of disorder in business so obviously displayed as the depression deepened. It became the National Industrial Recovery Act; but actually the word "recovery" was misleading; the activation of the economy was attacked in a more immediate way by the legislation authorizing the Civilian Conservation Corps (about which I shall have more to say) and the Emergency Relief Administration. There was also the enlargement of the Reconstruction Finance Corporation and the establishment of the Home Loan Bank for the relief of home-owners who were being dispossessed. These last I knew about but did not work on.

A similar action was needed to extend more generous credit to farmers; but this, it was discovered, could be done by executive order, and such an order was signed on March 22. Henry Morgenthau was put in charge, a compensation for his not having been appointed secretary of agriculture as he had hoped.

With the Civilian Conservation Corps I was involved not only because I had brought the idea to Roosevelt and negotiated its preliminaries with the Forest Service before inauguration, but because as an agricultural official I would be in charge of the Service. It was not thought of in the beginning as including the improvement of parks and other public lands as well as the forests. We in Agriculture expected to have the whole responsibility.

I should say something also of the exhausting negotiations with foreign governments about economic matters. I served with Moley and a few others as part of the group appointed to meet with experts from other nations who were invited to Washington for discussions of the crisis. Prime Minister MacDonald arrived early in April and was succeeded by other heads of government; but they had been preceded by lesser officials with whom we had to deal. What the former allies wanted from the United States was forgiveness of the huge war debts. They had no intention of paying but they were embarrassed to default without negotiation. They also wanted reduced tariffs for their exports and a monetary arrangement they could count on. If our currency was fixed in relation to gold, they could control the value of their own currency and have an advantage in trading.

These negotiations were demanding. They required careful preparation and cautious approaches. Roosevelt entertaining MacDonald could be general and evasive. He could be less so with the French, who were outraged by the segregation of gold and the stopping of foreign trading in the metal. But on April 22 statements of accord were issued, saying nothing about specific agreements but announcing that the expected World Economic Conference would be held in London beginning on June 12.

The delegation to this meeting was headed by Secretary Hull, who was advocating free trade at a time when we were virtually isolating ourselves to deal with recovery without foreign intervention. The troubles that followed when Moley was sent as Roosevelt's special emissary, practically replacing Hull, and then was himself repudiated by Roosevelt's message refusing to make any arrangement about monetary stabilization, I shall not dwell on here. They were fully discussed in Moley's book, *The First New Deal* (N.Y., Harcourt, Brace and World, 1966). This was the beginning of the end for Moley in Washington. What with Hull's fury and his own repudiation after so much publicity, he could not continue. I was luckily excused from going to London, although it had been arranged that I should follow Moley by a week or two. That unhappy incident was something I was glad not to have had any part in.

The National Industrial Recovery Act was not signed until June 16. It had been recommended in a message to the Congress on May 16, and during the intervening month had been the center of chaotic struggles over the draft to be sent with Roosevelt's recommendation to the Congress. These struggles were a continuation of those that had begun as soon as Roosevelt decided to ask for its passage.

The proposed reorganization of industry was conceived as a companion to AAA. That was now on the books, having been signed on May 12. It authorized the shaping of agricultural policy by the voluntary cooperation of the nation's farmers. The recovery act would similarly authorize the shaping of industrial policy through the co-operation of its operating units. This would be done by the making of agreements to eliminate unfair practices among competitors. These practices centered in maintaining indefensible wages and conditions of work as well as unethical competitive practices.

It was judged by Roosevelt after long consideration that the time had come for such an initiative. This consideration had included many discussions with those of us who had worked with him during the spring (the "Brains Trust") and further talks as the economy worsened after the election. It was evident to him that something was basically wrong with the business system. Free enterprise involved freedom to behave in ways that could hardly be distinguished from war with workers; and fraudulent treatment of consumers had become all too frequent a business practice. There was no attempt to find out what goods were needed and should be produced, and this led to mistakes in investment and a waste of resources. The resulting savage competition led to the survival of the most unscrupulous.

There were industrialists who had come to the same conclusions and who could be counted on to support reform. Gerard Swope of General Electric and Henry I. Harriman, president of the U.S. Chamber of Commerce, were names to conjure with, and Bernard Baruch, having been President Wilson's wartime industrial czar, had seen the immense gains in efficiency when the economy operated under a general rule that apportioned tasks and modified competition.

Berle was a well-known student of corporate organization and my own book, *The Industrial Discipline and the Governmental Arts*, now waiting to be published, outlined the organization of a governmental center to establish orderly relations. Roosevelt knew not only from us but from his own experience the progress already made toward such an organization. Hoover had in fact, when secretary of commerce, encouraged trade associations, and although these had never been authorized by law they had done something toward establishing fair competitive practices. Roosevelt had once been counsel for one of these associations—the Building Trades Council—and so was familiar with what needed to be done.

Almost at once after inauguration some of us began to formulate legislation, although we had no expectation that it might be acted on during the special session. As in the instance of our agricultural scheme we thought it might be taken up seriously when the regular session met in January. But when Roosevelt's emergency demands were met so promptly, and especially when our agricultural act succeeded, we asked him whether it might not be possible to ask the Congress to act at once. The lesson of the depression was fresh. The chaos in the business world was obvious. Even the conservative legislators might be moved to accept some reform.

With this, as with other assignments, Roosevelt was vague about delegation. As a result General Johnson considered that, since he had been an assistant to Baruch, the responsibility was his and he shut himself up to work on a draft. When Roosevelt told me that he was ready, I also went to work, enlisting Jerome Frank and John Dickinson, who was now assistant secretary of commerce, as helpers. I heard accidentally that Johnson was at work, and, although he was reluctant, got him to meet with us. We found that we were not far apart and, after Roosevelt urged that we reach agreement, and Moley also intervened, we finally presented him with a recommendation. The draft was sent to the Congress where it met with a mixed reception. Before passage it was drastically amended, the most damaging changes being the deletion of penalties for noncompliance with the codes of conduct. Roosevelt, in this instance, was no match for the lobbyists of business.

When the law was passed as the National Recovery Act, Johnson was appointed to be the administrator. He supposed that he was to have the central responsibility for getting the country out of the depression. That was what was meant by "recovery." But Roosevelt assigned to Ickes the responsibility for the public works part of the bill that would give employment. Johnson was only to supervise the making of the codes that would reform competitive practices and bring about cooperation in production.

Before long, however, Johnson had an idea that would, he thought, give him more direct responsibility for getting things going again. He took it to Roosevelt, who was struck with its possibilities. So he launched the scheme for getting from businesses simultaneous agreements to reemploy the workers they had laid off. His theory was that if all did this at once, the goods made by one industry would be bought by the workers in others. All would be producing; all would be getting wages; and all could become consumers. This, in fact, would *be* recovery.

The symbol of membership was a small poster displaying a formalized symbolic thunderbird. It was called the "blue eagle" and would be awarded to all cooperating businesses for display. Johnson had found an outlet for his evangelism, and he made the most of it. The furor he created was tremendous. It was the chiselers who defeated him. The blue eagles were distributed promiscuously, and there were many who got them with the intention of allowing their competitors to comply while they held back, employing only as many workers as could be got to work cheaply and producing only as many products as could be sold at a sure profit. So within a few months the scheme failed. It did, however, have its uses for others of us who went on during the summer with our organizing efforts quite unnoticed as Johnson held the center of the New Deal stage.

The preparatory work was completed when Roosevelt agreed to the ending of the special session. The legislation he had asked for had all been passed. True, some of it had been damaged by lobbyists, and the changes had sometimes been serious. The recovery act had no less than 100 amendments, mostly ones wanted by those who meant to use it for their own profit. Our agricultural act had not escaped. It, too, had been amended to make agreements with processors less confining. On the whole, however, it did seem that the task in agriculture that lay before us was not badly started. That, I now supposed, would be my central concern. For the time being it was. Not only the Congress went out of session. Roosevelt went out of session, too. He and the country needed a rest.

☆ | CHAPTER 13 | ☆

Early Lessons

T HE FARMERS' ANCIENT enemies, the middlemen, had been caught off balance by the speed with which the farm groups had come around to our proposal. Packers, millers, shippers, converters, brokers —all had Washington representatives, but they had not really been ready for the struggle. The confusion, and perhaps preoccupation with recovery from depression had impaired their usual vigilance; but also the speedy adoption of our legislation was altogether unprecedented. They, as much as we, must have supposed until recently that any action of importance was rather remotely in the future. In spite of all the warnings, they did not realize that Roosevelt considered farmers' troubles to be a central cause of the depression and so demanding of immediate attention. They were cynical concerning political promises; besides, they had always been able hitherto to rely on their allies in the Congress and the department to delay action or to modify it when it could not be headed off.

They had been well served during the lame-duck session a few months before. Their representatives had been responsible for defeating our bill in the Senate after it had been passed by the House. They were informed now, of course, that something impended, since the farm leaders' staffs, if not some among the conferees, owed allegiances running to that. They knew what had happened on March 10 even if the press did not. We still had something of a lead, however, and we had hoped our bill would slip through both houses as another emergency act. We underestimated the lobbyists' permanent organization. As it had turned out, the chairmen of both agricultural committees had held back; and argumentative discourses had delayed passage for two months, forcing us to resort to actions our enemies would deplore effectively. Most of the country's crops are planted, well before mid-May and, in fact, pigs and calves were already born. The plowing up of plants and the slaughtering of young animals would seem much more wicked than just not planting or not allowing them to be born.

We could not foresee all our troubles, and we were undoubtedly inclined, just at that moment, to minimize them. Besides the substantial unity of the farm leaders, we relied also on Roosevelt's buoyant assurances. We had watched with interest as the validation of the gold embargo had passed in a few hours. The economy bill had been delayed, but not for long. And the congressmen had not dared to predict anything but cooperation on the proposals for relief funds they were being asked to approve. We had hoped to be beneficiaries of this compliant mood.

It was about this time that I moved out to the hotel with Wallace. We had a normal April. It was chilly and damp, then suddenly summer for days at a time. He often, and I sometimes, walked down to work in the morning. Even so, we often arrived at the department before most of our helpers. And during these months we were there well into almost every night. We were able to collaborate remarkably well, partly because of these constant contacts.

Nevertheless, I was unpleasantly surprised by Wallace's indifference to what I conceived to be our duty to consumers. Before March was over he had refused to back me in an order of the Food and Drug Administration specifying that when corn sugar (dextrose) was substituted for cane sugar (sucrose) in manufacturing, the information should appear on the label of the products containing it. This was my first experience of other than a consumer's view of food and drug laws. How could so honest a man consent to an officially dishonest act? It was my first disillusionment. It happened also that this incident was closely followed by one involving the tolerance we should allow for the residue of poisonous insecticides left on apples and other fruits when they went to market. Then there was still another difference about rates charged cattlemen for grazing rights on the public range. Such issues caused heat in the secretary's office; and he plainly thought it unnecessary.

Of course I knew that we were being tried out by the bureau chiefs, as all new officials are. The outrages perpetrated by our predecessors were exposed to us as tests of our reactions. Civil servants wait—and hope—for a superior who will support them in enforcement. When one does not, the issue is simply shelved until another appointee comes along. It is sometimes irritating to an official, who is quite conscious of his short tenure in any case, to be challenged in this way by the permanent staff. Their attitude says quite plainly, "You ought to do it; but we'll be here when you are gone and then we'll try again." But Wallace was plainly apprehensive about the political consequences of requiring fruit growers, cattlemen, and others to accept demanding standards.

The insecticide residue was the issue that convinced me that I had been mistaken about the Food and Drug Administration. I shared the fashionable view in consumer-conscious circles that its enforcement policies were determined in the interest of farmers and processors. I soon learned that the Congress had ensured this by locating the agency where all its moves would be controlled by officials who represented farmers rather than consumers.

Our predecessors had thought up an excuse for permitting lead arsenate in dangerous quantities to be left on apples and other fruits and vegetables. They called it a "tolerance"—that is, they permitted a certain amount to remain on the produce without penalty. Former secretaries had conceded that this amount must be reduced bit by bit over the years until the poisons were eliminated, and on one of my first days in office I was asked by Director Walter Campbell of the Food and Drug Administration to give notice that we intended to require long overdue reductions.

Interested senators and representatives soon heard what was proposed, and descended on me with flashing eyes, intent on protecting the growers and shippers among their constituents. My disillusionment with political liberals was increased when my radical friend from the state of Washington—Senator Homer Bone, representing his apple growers—sat himself down in my office and pooh-poohed my concern about lead poisoning. There never had been any proof that people died of it, he said. He demanded to be shown a single case. I had to admit the difficulties in this. It was one of several slow cumulative poisons; and though there was plenty of medical evidence, it was impossible to trace cases to specific causes.

Wallace, with all his responsibilities, could not see his way to afford such gestures. He would need the support I was asking him to jeopardize. Consumers occasionally made a row; but they were seldom any match for the professional lobbyists, and no secretary had ever been impressed. Consumers, I soon discovered, are an amorphous—and silent—mass. There were always, it seemed, things to be done for "the public." And there was never any credit; and often serious *dis*credit in doing it. The theory was that government officials were there to protect the general interest. That was a mistake. There were some. The food and drug people were anxious to meet their obligation but there were many others who found reasons for serving those who would support them—before congressional committees, in the press or back home. The inevitability of this, as things were, ought to have been obvious. A job is more easily kept, progress more easily made, and work more easily forwarded when it earns some reward.

As for myself, I learned after no more than a few weeks why it was that assistant secretaries usually did little more than sit in their offices, play politics mildly, and take an interest in a few projects. Departments could have only one policy-maker. Subordinates were appointed in the routine of patronage, and they owed their jobs to a political mentor. Their superior was usually jealous of them to the extent that jealousy was indicated, and quite content to ignore their existence as long as they kept out of the way. The regular thing, I found, was for each new man to ask for a few specific duties, their extent depending on his ability and initiative. By the time he had familiarized himself with his assignment, the bureau chiefs involved would have sized him up; if he could be used to further their interests in budgetary and like matters he might command a kind of specious deference. If, however, he showed any signs of interfering or managing, the chief would immediately begin to go around him to the secretary and to collaborators in the Congress. After a few embarrassing reversals, most appointees subsided, content with a few official entertainments, certain mild intrigues, and a minimum of routine duties.

This was somewhat different for Wallace and myself. We were more equal than most secretaries and assistant secretaries because of my association with Roosevelt. There really was enough for both of us to do. We had only to work out a cooperative relationship. Concerning most departmental policies, however, the time would come soon when Wallace would want those about him who would neither ask questions nor point out difficulties. The beginning of our differences, I could see later, was in his first refusal to enforce the Food and Drug Act and to protect the range lands. The injustices to sharecroppers, tenants, and farm laborers would come later. These I could not and would not accept, and our parting would become inevitable.

The range-lands controversy was, by then, an old one. It was, in effect, a quarrel between the embattled Forest Service and western ranchers. From long usage the ranchers regarded the ranges adjoining their holdings as theirs to use as they liked. The grasslands were in fact being grazed to the roots by an overload of stock amounting perhaps to 50 percent. Most of the wild animals had been destroyed, many of them by government hunters; and now, shortsighted use had brought us close to losing the entire resource. In much of the West, federal lands were a large proportion of the states' territories, and much of this was within the national forests. Successive raids by westerners had reduced effective regulation by a good deal, however, usually by appeal to states' rights. Stockmen evidently could influence state legislatures even more easily than they could the Congress.

The fee imposed for grazing had always been inadequate for supporting effective land management; yet there were constant demands for their further reduction. During the First World War, and on the excuse of need for an enlarged food supply, the fees had been cut in half, a concession represented as temporary. The expense of maintenance and management had increased as overgrazing had had its inevitable results. These results were not merely a loss of grass; the destruction of cover increased the volume and rapidity of runoff, and this in turn caused more and more losses when there were droughts or floods.

The issue symbolized to the Forest Service the distinction between integrity (as they rather rigidly conceived it) in the federal service, and acquiescence in private privilege.

It seemed plain that the fees ought at least to be restored to their prewar level; in fact there seemed no possible excuse for not doing it. There was a surplus of beef cattle. And the destruction of the range, at half rates for grazing, in order to produce unwanted supplies, seemed insane.

Wallace was quickly shown what it would mean just then to alienate the western legislators. He tried not to embarrass the Service by refusing to order a revision; they held out; and for weeks it was argued over. Finally he insisted on a conclusion whose only virtue was that it introduced some flexibility. It was our economist, Mordecai Ezekiel, who suggested that the fees be varied according to the price of beef;

and he worked out an index for it. We thus got something for the future, possibly, even if nothing in the present.

Perhaps these issues ought to have been put off until the emergency was past. Still they were undoubted wrongs and ought to be righted. We were pushed into old controversies, long unsettled because settlement was so politically difficult. They were left about where we had found them.

If, in addition to setting up a new agency of government for farm relief, we had succeeded in settling all the old grievances in the department we should have been supermen. If Wallace was averse to jeopardizing his political position, I was, for the moment, not discriminating between what was important and what was essential. It was inevitable that the early easiness of our cooperation should, in the course of time, break down; but during the first months, aside from differences about enforcement, we were like separate fingers on a single hand. That hand was the president's. His prestige was rising overwhelmingly. The days for him were no longer than they were for us—not so long, in fact, because with his conditioning, he could slough off insistent and unsettled issues until a way to settle them appeared. We did manage to keep the initiative we had gained by proposing the delegation of agricultural relief to our end of Pennsylvania Avenue. The delay by the lobbyists of our act made severe difficulties; but in the end we had got most of what we had asked for. Then our troubles began, as Roosevelt had said they would. While he was keeping quiet and letting Johnson rouse the country with his blue eagle campaign, we, in Agriculture, were beset by new troubles.

II

The Turn to Administration

☆ | CHAPTER 1 | ☆

Finding Direction

O NCE THE SPECIAL SESSION had adjourned on June 16, and the legislators had left Washington, their demands for patronage met or promised, the newly authorized agencies had to be organized. Among the new people, along with a sense of urgency and awe concerning the immensity of what had been undertaken, there was general optimism. Energy was returning after the discouraged lethargy of Hoover's last months. There were suggestions without end about what ought to be done. Some were fantastic and impractical. Others, however, came from sudden converts, practical men of affairs who volunteered solutions for our problems. Not all of the well-turned-out types filling the hotels were lobbyists in the old sense; a good many were men and women who simply wanted attention for their ideas. Our offices were besieged; but listening did not seem a high priority and actually we talked only with those we could not escape.

There was real question in Wallace's mind and in mine whether enough would be accomplished to stave off violent protests. There was no doubt that people generally had begun to *feel* better almost at once in March. In July, however, unemployment was still increasing and measures for relief were only just being put into effect. A start had been made; but no more than that could be said. Farmers were through with their planting, and young animals were growing. We had to begin our reduction with a handicap we might have escaped if the Congress had not delayed.

What sustained all of us was the buoyancy and optimism radiating from the White House. The Roosevelt confidence had not only permeated Washington; it had reached the remotest parts of the country. This rising expectation made the danger of disappointment more considerable. Friendly old hands in Washington warned us that honeymoons were likely to be short in proportion to their intensity, and there had not often been ones so intense as this.

They were right. The criticism would soon become a campaign, and those of us who were new were the most vulnerable. We were more realistic about this, however, than the old hands thought. We knew how little was being done, and we were fully aware of the probable consequences.

We also knew that the sharpest weapons would be used on those who were most seen in and about the White House. Roosevelt had too much support to become an immediate target. He was a symbol of hope. Enemies would have to close in from the periphery. Confidence in those who were considered to be his "advisers" would first have to be weakened; if possible, they should be discredited. They would be singled out one by one as doubtfully competent. Then ridicule would be devised. The outer defenses having been breached in this way, the president himself would become eligible. This was the regular procedure. We knew all about it, and if we had not, there were knowledgeable well-wishers to warn us.

There was no effective defense. It was inevitable that many privileged people would be hurt by the new measures, and they were well represented, often by Democratic "consultants." The cracks and crannies of Washington were alive with fixers who had only hid themselves momentarily. These would discover ways to assess and turn to their own uses any doubtful activities we might undertake. Even as early as July and August we were experiencing the first of our embarrassments.

We Americans being an enterprising people, it is held that opportunities should be taken advantage of—if necessary, they should be created. This is a very simple notion—too simple for our time. Separate impulses, quite undirected in a highly integrated organism, were responsible for the depression. This very characteristic had caused the system to break down. The challenge now was whether it would be patched up and go on to further crises or whether some way of making foresight and discipline acceptable could be found.

The economy could perhaps be reactivated by extraordinary measures; but it would not keep going permanently unless enterprises could be got to operate as contributors to a stable whole; and from what we were experiencing, we concluded that this was unlikely. The depression, businessmen felt, had been an unfortunate accident, not something inherent in the way they themselves had conducted their affairs. Farmers thought so too. They had no intention of making any changes, and their Washington outposts had been alerted to repel the advocates of control. They wanted a new start made in the ways they were used to.

Once we were engaged in learning our jobs, establishing liaisons, and watching the effects of our efforts, not much time was really spent in such worries. Every day brought problems, and somehow they were dealt with. For this, Roosevelt's support was necessary, and usually we could depend on it. There was nothing we could not discuss with him; and the opportunities were sufficient for the purpose. Sometimes there were talks in the evening; and during the two years beginning in June I was often given nonagricultural assignments. There were not only the matters of policy Moley and I had been working on before inauguration, there were also many committees, boards, and *ad hoc* groups having to do with the now-beginning recovery efforts.

Walter Lippmann was now disapprovingly insistent on distinction between reform and recovery, and accusing Roosevelt of satisfying old grudges against the business community. I thought the reforms necessary—but not now! In fact, I would have liked to see preparations made for more drastic changes than were likely unless Roosevelt took the lead. It was impolitic to say anything like this publicly. Years later, Moley, my closest friend of those days, did not recall that I had argued for at least public ownership of the Federal Reserve; he was even a little indignant that such a suggestion should be attributed to me. When the conservator system had been set up, the banks were reopening, and the reform measures were being debated, it was too late to expect drastic change. The opportunity had passed and would not come again.

One thing pleased me. Roosevelt reversed himself on the work of the department. Instead of wanting to reduce the work, he began to urge agricultural improvements and the betterment of farmers' lives. As for forestry and roads, they were familiar interests. We could do much with emergency funds. I had brought him a useful soil-classification map, another showing a national road plan, and still another showing the forests and parks (although these last were the responsibility of Interior) with a rating of their condition and what was most needed in each. He pored over them and kept them in a drawer of his desk. He developed concern about the eroded areas in the old corn and cotton country, about the overgrazed ranges in the West, about the inroads of diseases and the means for their control, about the overcutting of timber and the failure to replant cut-over tracts, about fire losses and the inaccessibility of many areas in the West. Also, I think he had not realized how many farmers were still a long way from hard-surfaced roads. He inquired about farm tenancy. Its increase in such states as Iowa, Missouri, and Illinois had been so rapid as to mock our pretension to be a nation of owner-operator farmers, each a free man on his own acres. About this, as about so many of our problems, he was inclined to agree that something novel would have to be done, and by some other agencies than the present ineffectual ones.

He had an old concern for conservation. He lectured me about developing town, country, and state forests to provide recreational areas and a timber reserve. He thought they could often serve to retire worn-out land. Also the preparation of these areas for new uses could give employment during the emergency, as the CCC was doing. He proposed preparing parks and recreational areas for transfer to counties and cities, something never before done with federal funds.

He had definite ideas too about the sharecroppers and farm workers. He knew, as so many others seemed not to know, that farmers themselves and their families made up only half or thereabouts of the rural people. The other half lived precariously as dependents, as squatters, or hidden away in remote places on poor and unproductive acres. There were many such in the South, in the cut-over areas of Michigan and Wisconsin, in Appalachia all the way from New York to Alabama, on the dust-blown plains of the short-grass country, and even in New England. Many of these were in Virginia and Maryland not very far from Washington; and several times he went to see them on a Saturday or Sunday, sometimes driving from Washington, sometimes landing from the *Sequoia* and making inland journeys.

He kept track of our progress, or lack of it, in controlling the Dutch elm disease. The infestation spreading from a shipment of imported wood was now loose in the shaded streets of all the towns within a hundred miles of New York. At Morristown a departmental laboratory was trying to plot the epidemiology of the disease and so find a way to check it. He was impatient with the researchers' bafflement.

This was no more than an incident, an unimportant one, perhaps, but the wineglass elm, so stately and graceful, was prominent in the scenes all easterners carried in their memories. Landscapes without those trees in the meadows and along the streets of towns seemed unthinkable. I persuaded him one Saturday to make a short journey down into Virginia and along the completed part of the skyline drive to where an extensive area of what once had been a forest of chestnuts now stood dead and stark, killed not long ago by just such an imported epidemic. Of all the millions in the hardwood forests none had survived. He sat gazing and was appalled. He spoke of nutting parties in his boyhood; we had had those too in my part of New York. He asked about replacement, and I told him the plant explorers had brought back other chestnuts from China and Italy. They were now growing in our introduction gardens. They might prosper, some one or several of them; but none was so fine a tree as our own.

There were many other such problems of husbandry. About some he was ahead of me, except that now I was backed up by the department's experts. When he asked a question and I did not know the answer, I could find it. And usually such questions opened the way for suggestions from the foresters, the pathologists, the entomologists, and the other specialists.

It was in these summer months that schemes were being developed for further-ranging changes than had been thought of as the legislation of the Hundred Days had been fought through. These spread all the way from the shelter-belt forest for the great plains to new ideas in education; from a program of social security to an increase in world trade; from public housing to recreation; from the encouragement of better cover crops in the South to the rehabilitation of the overplowed plains; from the decline of the European empires to our own obligations as neighbors; from Russian recognition to the rise of Hitler. About all these subjects—and many others—Roosevelt carried on an endless dialogue with those around him.

When, by summer, Moley had gone, I had more responsibilities; but I never mastered the art of ghost-writing. It seems to me, looking back, that I had heard or joined in discussion of an incredible range of problems, projects, and proposals. Sometimes I would be asked to look into them and report and then to see what could be done. It was quite certain that he knew what he wanted for the nation. He wanted a people free and self-reliant but educated and informed. He wanted both farmers and businessmen to prosper but not at each other's or their consumers' expense. He wanted the land made more productive and thus more comely. He wanted resources guarded and used with reason. As for how to get all this, or any part of it, he tried to find ways. He seemed to vacillate when he was only considering alternatives and possibilities; and sometimes he had to give up.

Among those who saw and talked with him most often during that summer was Harry Hopkins, who had come to Washington in May. There were others with whom he was equally open—Felix Frankfurter, Bob La Follette, and Fiorello La Guardia, for instance—but they were not so often available. With still others—some of the ambassadors, his cabinet, and the politicians—he had no particular reticences; but he gauged very nicely their limitations. With them he was more apt to try out ideas or proposals in tentative terms.

I learned to watch his approach to thorny matters with those who might help in their settlement or in their carrying out, but whose holding back was all too obvious. With the older Democratic conservatives, for instance, only one of all his policies was really popular—economy. But how badly this consorted with his fertile ideas for changing matters here, there, and everywhere he was constantly reminded. With his imagination and political talents it had been inevitable that economy would give way to contrivance. There was no more need to worry about funds. Roosevelt, the president, persuading his reluctant party colleagues to allow one thing after another to be done—and dragging along an intelligently bitter Lewis Douglas—was something I should never forget.

If he could not get done nearly all that he wanted to do, the marks of that first administration would be on the land from then on. There would be enlarged forests, and greatly improved ones; there would be new public buildings; city streets and country roads would be repaved; then there would be new schools, water and sewer systems, enlarged electric power facilities, and a beginning of public housing. And this is not to mention what happened to and within the American people themselves as they began to gain faith in their futures again, to feel that opportunities were not closed. Nor is it to consider the greatest advance of all, the social-security system he was testing in his mind for acceptability. Gradually, even though the realities of recovery were slow to show themselves, it became clear that the Roosevelt intention was trusted. Some demagogues dwelt on the continuing miseries; but their effect was never really beyond containment in spite of Huey Long's following. The start was slow, but it was understood.

Roosevelt was a man of goodwill; but like all men of goodwill he had to deal with ill will in others. He did it in high good humor and patiently; he compromised with it constantly; he even gave it praise for political effect; but his own sympathies were so apparent and his determination so well recognized that from the very first there was a gathering on either side. His task was to mobilize the latent decency of the majority, whose lethargy needed to be stirred. That leadership was his greatest achievement.

I had begun to absorb the lesson that a democratic leader has to be careful not to expose his intentions. For one thing, he may not exactly get what he wants, and this will cause a public disappointment he cannot afford. For another, he must always remember that plans, once exposed, are vulnerable to an opposition often stronger than the support he can muster. So what I learned by being told or by deduction I could not speak of as presidential intention. I might talk of such things—he encouraged me to—as ones we ought to attain, but I must not attribute them to him. If my association with him carried any such implication, he ignored it. In all my time with him he never repudiated anything I advocated and never even checked my advocacy. True, he often did not assist when it seemed unpolitic; but I had no complaint to make. He had never promised support.

CHAPTER 2

On Being a Helper

W HENEVER I WALKED to the White House from the department, I had the full effect, seeing it across the oval, with gardens in between. What I saw was an eighteenth-century mansion sited and planned for uses far less demanding than the modern presidency. It had been besieged by politicians in the past. Lincoln—after long Democratic years—had had lines of office-seekers reaching out into the street. To relieve the pressure, the first Roosevelt had added a west wing, but even that had not made it an efficient center. Most of the present petitioners were diverted to Farley's office in the Post Office building; and some jobs, at least, had been relegated to the Civil Service. But the oval office was still irresistible to would-be sharers in presidential power. There was no tight security in those days; and access was all too easy. The outer rooms were usually crowded.

The Roosevelt day was planned at his bedside. Those present most regularly then, besides McIntyre with an engagement list, were Stephen Early, Lewis Douglas, and Ross McIntire, his physician. Louis Howe wandered in and out, frail and querulous. The pattern of the day was set in this way, but it was only roughly adhered to. Congressmen had to be mollified; and there were others who could be useful in some way who must not be offended. About the ranking of visitors, or the working out of deals and compromises, we—or some of us—knew what was in the wind sometimes; but often we could only guess.

Roosevelt was his own manager, not only in party matters—with

Farley acting as lieutenant and with Charles West coming to play an undefined role as emissary to the Congress—but also in all the necessary maneuvering to see legislation through, establish the structure of administration, and persuade the public that all was in order. When I was told to see someone, to prepare some data, or to make an inquiry, I did not always know what it was for. Roosevelt regarded it as his own responsibility to put things together, and he never delegated it; but, because he was so successful, he would sometimes demonstrate how it was done. Of his more mysterious ventures, however, it could only be guessed what he was up to. When Harry Hopkins' status as a confidant became secure, he joined with me in the guessing game. He was an inveterate gambler. There were times when we had a whole book of bets on the results of processes we were not allowed to know enough about to understand. If many of those involved could have known that their jobs or their policies meant a dollar either way to Harry or to me, they might have been less insistent on getting our attention in the belief that we had influence and could be got to use it in their interest.

It was clear enough to us that we were not to have any influence, except in those matters we had to do with as administrators; and even in these we were expected not to take advantage of our other relation as confidants. We would have been useless if we had engaged ourselves in any but the most detached way. Harry only tried to find out what was wanted. I tended to pry; and there were things I thought ought to or ought not to be done. Harry expressed no such opinions except as to relief and its associated activities. I must have been more irritating than he; but then I sometimes got explanations or defenses.

Ray Moley was still occasionally around during the summer, but after his final resignation in September, was less and less seen—and I was taking his place, with Hopkins following along. Neither of us wrote speeches or messages; he was no better at it than I. Besides, he had a job of enormous size as he proceeded to set up his emergency relief organization. So the preparing of memoranda for addresses fell more to me; but actually Ray was depended on for writing, and even after he left Washington he was often called back.

The White House day began at nine or ten o'clock, when Roosevelt, still in bed, had finished breakfast and skimmed through several newspapers. As soon as he sent for them, McIntyre and Early were ready with schedules and comments; Douglas furnished his version of the way things were going, and whoever else was on hand added his bit.

Dr. Ross McIntire came in at some stage and had a look at his charge. Usually there was a half-hour then of conversation, half-humorous, half-serious. It was a time for telling stories and incidents concerning friends and enemies. Roosevelt's informality was taken with reserve; but he was not above telling stories about one of those present, especially embarrassing ones. They usually ended in laughter I should have thought could be heard all the way to Pennsylvania Avenue.

As I became notorious, I was treated to the characterizations of me by Frank Kent of the *Baltimore Sun,* Mark Sullivan of the *New York Herald-Tribune,* John Boettiger of the *Chicago Tribune,* or others of the fraternity, all with presidential embellishments. The burden of it was that I was the Machiavelli of the New Deal. I was pictured as leading the president into courses he would otherwise not even have thought of. I was at one and the same time a scatterbrained theorist and an influential and determined plotter. Enlarging on Frank Kent was Roosevelt's way of telling me that he knew well enough what was going on; but I am sure he thought I needed lessons in political behavior.

My answer was that things practically never went the way I wanted them to and that what I was blamed for I had usually objected to. I protested that I was the object of unfair attributions; but my protests in that company were lost in persiflage. It was amazing how quickly I had become a target; it was suspected that I had had more to do with New Deal policies than anyone could have had. It was evidently feared that I might produce others even more startling and that I might have a good deal to do with their operation. It was believed that I was influential in checking the infiltration of special-interest representatives as administrators and in recruiting the new personnel. This threat to the usual procedures was bitterly objected to. Roosevelt knew all this, but none of his political credit was used in getting me out of trouble. That was up to me.

This was true of Hopkins too; but he had a much better chance to offset the attacks sure to be made on the relief and works programs. After all, they were useful assets to local political machines. He was frankly accepting the advice of party bosses on appointments. This, I argued with him, was a mistake, because it would alienate the senators and congressmen who were often the local bosses' rivals. Besides, he would have a terrible set of administrators, and it was to the Congress that we would have to look for successive appropriations. He could not see, however, that he had any choice if he was to get relief going quickly; and he felt that his vast corps of dedicated social workers would keep the politicians straight. Actually, his troubles were never comparable with mine. He was, at least, the head of his organization, responsible only to the president. I was only an assistant secretary, and after AAA was well started I was excluded from its councils. I should have to struggle for every concession I could wring from that organization.

Because I served on so many boards and committees and was a memmer of so many informal groups, I was in a position to supply much information, some of it important, some not so important, but to Roosevelt, as to myself, for some reason, interesting and even vital. Much of every day I spent in the Budget Bureau, in Interior or Commerce, on Capitol Hill, or with Hopkins; and I seldom had a meal not arranged for conference purposes.

Of one thing I became certain: Roosevelt had an area of intentions a good way below the surface. That surface was all charm, inquiring comment, or display of fascinating detail. He was careless about operations. Beneath, however, there was a stirring; patterns were forming and decisions were materializing. It was plain that there was an organizing center and that everything was arranged around it. What went on that was easily visible was what gave him momentary satisfaction; but there did exist, I was certain, a general strategy. The tactics did tend to harden, to become fixed, one by one; but then there were inconsistencies, and even if these did not bother him much, real conflicts. Some were not easily resolved. They often caused confusion until a resolution occurred.

For one who guessed when the resolution of conflict was about to occur it was fascinating to see it showing itself here or there, at this time or that time, as daily activities went on. Those who might be hoping to obstruct must not have the advantage of notice. Those who had contrary intentions, however, were shrewd too. It was a contest between professionals. Others could piece small evidences together and make patterns. They mostly had to do it from the retailing of gossip by those who stood close but who were innocently unaware of what impended. Obstructors did not need hard information. They always suspected more than they could prove; but they were frequently correct. Sometimes they forestalled what otherwise would have been done.

From watching I learned a useful rule. When special interests in contact with the government, and with much to gain or lose from official decision, become anxious, they tend to panic. They will not wait for revelation of what they believe to be hostile intention, but will create a stereotype to work with. Because they prefer not to show their own concern they will always try to involve other, more defensible persons. In ways first subtle, then not so subtle, Roosevelt was pictured in the conservative press as being against "the American way of life." It was soon being said that he tended to "socialism" or that he was "unreliable," "impractical," and so on. One of the favorite criticisms was that "he did not know his own mind." The relation of this to the process of resolution was close. Sometimes it was quite true that he did not yet know his own mind. He had not yet fully decided; but oftener he was simply determined not to let others know it until the time to act had come.

There would be nothing involved or tortured about this if every product of the patternmaking process had been approved by those who had interests to serve and access to the media for shaping public opinion; but that can never be true of a president or of those who share his responsibility. Unless, that is, he believes that the public good is an additive construct, and that the encouragement of private interests comprises the public interest. Roosevelt did not.

Success in manipulation has a stimulating effect. It develops latent ingenuities. There is temptation to go on. How many of these rejuvenating successes Roosevelt had in those early days can be understood just by looking at the record. The tides of support became irresistible. They originated in public confidence that he was making a good try. One after another he brought projects into the open, and many of them were so widely approved that opposition was stifled or overwhelmed. The failures were quickly forgotten.

So we had a president whose responsibilities were well weighed, who was judging nicely the forces moving in and around him. In bed in the morning in an old sweater, cigarette in its long holder, newspapers scattered about him, he spoke of his immediate plans. There were thick folders of papers to be discussed with the small group of his intimates. Then he was helped out of bed and into his clothes—often old and worn but carried well on his wide shoulders, shirt soft, tie quiet. All done, he was rolled to the lift and down the corridor to the oval room. Progress along the way gave him a chance to savor the air, have a glance at flowers and trees, perhaps a bed of daffodils or a magnolia coming into bloom, before he settled down behind his desk for five or six hours. About eleven the visitors began to come. The first one interrupted the signing of a commission or the study of a report. Roosevelt looked up, then, and turned on the famous charm for whoever it was. He began the talk, and likely enough went on through the attack of fidgets apt to seize a petitioner who had calculated how he could put his problem in the precious minutes he might be allotted. As he listened, conscious of passing time, and Roosevelt rambled, the visitor knew he ought to memorize the talk in detail; but often enough it seemed to him afterward a blank, impossible to record. He was lucky if instead of a quarter or half an hour to discuss his business he had five minutes left before McIntyre, worried about the schedule, interrupted, and, in all conscience, he had to leave.

Roosevelt had a positive dislike for saying no. Visits were likely to be unsatisfactory in this way. Many an important personage emerged with a pleased look and awakened, as he walked across the outer reception room, to uncertainty. Had he, or had he not, had an answer? He could not, for the life of him, tell. He had seen a pleasant man in a pleasant room, windows running down to the floor, bringing the lawns and gardens close, walls hung with naval prints. Behind the president's shoulder there had been the flags in their standards and on his desk the litter of statuettes and mementoes; but concerning his mission the visitor could not be sure.

In a side room, unseen by visitors, was Missy LeHand, typing last night's late dictation or parceling it out to Grace and Paula Tully. Missy was an ease-maker, sweet and witty and knowing. If the visitor knew how things went in the White House, and knew the way to her office, he stopped to speak with her; or perhaps he saw Louis Howe. But mostly he had to face the gathering group of newsmen in the outer lobby at a disadvantage, not being at all sure what had been the result of his visit. In any case by custom he could not quote the president. Invariably he would be invited to tell what had gone on; it was a part of the newsmen's ritual to ask; but they knew the rules, and indiscretions were rare. For a politician it was something to have it reported that he had got to the inner office. He was expected to make a story if he could. But the quizzical faces around him told him well enough that they were aware of his bafflement.

I learned how to make out well enough. I seldom underwent the ordeal of interview, simply because I went out as I had come in, by the way of the lower floor and the door to West Executive Avenue but when it was useful, or when I was there with Wallace on department business, or with an official group, I prepared for the newsmen as carefully as for the president. I could get published anything I had to say. The comment about it, or the setting it was given, might be—usually was—prejudicial, but still I could count on certain effects. Occasionally I was briefed by Roosevelt himself; he found trial balloons useful, and he knew well enough that I was becoming a sensitized agent.

☆ | CHAPTER 3 | ☆

Peek and the Lawyers

W HEN THE SPECIAL congressional session had adjourned Roosevelt went off to sail a small boat with his sons along the coast of Maine. Arrangement was made for newspapermen's accommodation; but the situation was strange to them. They were keeping track of an experienced sailor; but even a landlubber could see that there were risks, especially from fogs and sudden squalls; and it involved, in any case, an interlude of isolation no one is really ready to grant a president.

There was no doubt that such cruises were therapeutic. All through his youth and early manhood Roosevelt had been a player of strenuous games; now his useless legs limited his movements. In a sailing boat he could regain something of that athleticism he had lost in 1921. Judging the moods of the coastal seas and the handling of such craft had been familiar to him from boyhood. To set off toward an unseen port in chancy weather merely required the practice of seasoned skills. Also, such vigorous vacations confirmed an already strong public impression of courage and virility. This was the kind of man it took to surmount the nation's troubles. His performance at the helm of the *Amberjack* had that effect.

In Washington the situation remained uneasy. The economy was still stagnant. Unemployment relief would improve with Hopkins' coming; and our payments to millions of farmers for crop reduction would be made quickly. We hoped that by fall there would be noticeable economic lift.

Nothing would come of the London economic confernce. And I, for one, was less than amazed when the president on July 3 sent his "bombshell" message. He was, at that time, on his way back down the coast aboard the cruiser *Indianapolis*; and none of us who had had anything to do with the preliminary conversations in Washington was with him. The political utility of his action was understandable; but I would have counseled a change of a sentence or two of the message if I had been asked, especially those chiding the European nations for not having balanced their budgets. It would have been better to suggest joining in a recovery program; and that could still be done. I prepared such a statement with Jerome Frank's help, and tried to persuade Roosevelt to send it when he got back to Washington; but it was too late. He wanted to forget—and have others forget—the conference and its futility. He had other things in mind, and he was certain that the foreign leaders meant to use him for their own purposes if they could.[1]

Ernest Lindley, writing on July 3, described the effect:

The Conference reels. Europe explodes with resentment and wrath. Mr. MacDonald speaks of Mr. Roosevelt as "that person." The American public cheers the repulse of the foreigner. In a laudatory article, Mr. Keynes says Roosevelt is "magnificently right." "Magnificently left," remarks Moley . . . The American delegates are lost. Hull, according to one correspondent, is "a stricken man."[2]

The harm had been done. There was no further possibility that international action of any kind could be counted on to affect our immediate crisis. We had to look to ourselves. It would doubtless be different in the long run. We might achieve freer trade and so create markets, for our agricultural products especially, but it would take some time. We had better forget Europe and think only of what could be done at home.

This had been evident enough, anyway. Those who had hoped to dispose of our surpluses by dumping them in markets abroad had got recognition in certain provisions of the Agricultural Adjustment Act;

---

[1] The so-called "bombshell" message was a reproof to the conference for being "diverted by the proposal of a purely artificial and temporary experiment affecting the monetary exchange of a few nations only . . . When the world works out concerted policies to produce balanced budgets and living within their means, then we can properly discuss a better distribution of the world's gold and silver supply to act as a reserve bank for national currencies . . . The conference was called to better and perhaps cure fundamental economic ills. It must not be diverted from that effort."

[2] *The Roosevelt Revolution* (New York: Viking, 1933), 211-12.

so had George Peek's favorite prescription—agreements with processors to raise prices. But neither was regarded as of much account in the crisis. We were preparing to limit production. Since, however, the act had been passed so late it had been agreed that there was no alternative to plowing up growing cotton and slaughtering pigs before they grew up into hogs. Wheat would have to be disposed of somehow after harvest. Now, in July, we were in the midst of the plow-up campaign; and the pigs had been slaughtered. We were being excoriated by the opposition. It was a field day for publishers who had been cautious about attacking Roosevelt. They could really let themselves go about those little pigs; and one enterprising reporter said that the southern mules were refusing to follow the unnatural plow-up commands; and an Iowa editor had to remind the Chicago *Tribune* that pigs were not raised to be pets.

Now the consequences of having Peek as administrator of the AAA became apparent. I had long ago recognized that what I regarded as realism was subject to correction. I was too inclined to like people; and this led to mistakes. I usually guarded against this with some determination; but I have to admit that, in an access of sentiment, I did not object when Wallace proposed Peek's appointment. He had worked long and hard for farm relief, and there was a general feeling that he was entitled to recognition. He would carry Baruch's approval of our work: and he had in fact organized and run a large farm-machinery factory. I was consulted, and I had plenty of chance to offer alternatives.

In an early series of conferences among all of us, it had really begun to seem that we had generated a dedication, perhaps even a willingness, to cooperate in what we had collectively agreed on. How mistaken this was can be seen from Peek's contemporary notes. We should have seen that he was maneuvering for a position he hoped would presently enable him to oust Wallace from the secretaryship and install himself in that office. I must say that I recovered very quickly from my attack of sentiment and did warn Wallace of what I sensed was being prepared for him; but by then we had created for ourselves a powerful enemy. Peek not only had a promise of noninterference from Wallace and Roosevelt, something no subordinate ought to have, but at once proceeded to buttress himself in every direction for a coming struggle. His mentor, of course, was Baruch, who had continuing influence among legislators. The agricultural bureaucracy in the states felt indebted to him because he was entrusting them with enormous responsibilities and with the powers necessary for carrying them out.

Baruch's other protégé, Johnson, was operating across the mall in the commerce building, as national recovery administrator. Having Johnson and Peek in charge of the two principal posts in the emergency administration must have gone some way to compensate for not having a cabinet post. His suite at the Carlton served as a convenient command center. It seethed with activity, and had objectives all its own. They were not necessarily Roosevelt's.

It was Peek's operational guide—as it was Johnson's, Jesse Jones's, and others of their sort scattered throughout the government—that the business system as it existed was a natural and necessary arrangement and that government ought to serve it. It was not unusual for Chamber of Commerce meetings, trade conventions, and similar gatherings even then to bog down at some point into soggy, almost tearful, self-praise. The depression had presented difficulties; it needed to be explained; and there had been a rapidly spreading public hostility to the business establishment for a time. Some of it still persisted; but the rehabilitation was proceeding in Washington with sickening success.

Roosevelt, having more or less accepted the necessity for restoring confidence, was now advised that he must award businessmen positions of responsibility. On the whole, that is what he did; but as they knew well enough, he did not share their exaggerated conclusions concerning either their abilities or their selflessness. Since they sensed that he was not committed, they demanded more and more evidences of his compliance. They wanted what they could not have: solid proof that he meant them to take charge. What still annoyed them was the continued presence of such people as Henry Wallace, Harry Hopkins, Frances Perkins, Harold Ickes, and a few others in the administration, including myself. We were not many and there were among us all degrees of willingness to follow Roosevelt's lead in accepting the tutelage of business representatives in our midst; but generally we were not the dependable sort they liked to deal with—and could usually find among the bureaucrats as well as the legislators.

As the emergency agencies were organized—AAA and NRA—they were taken over by business battalions. Not many upper-level policy positions in either administration were occupied by disinterested public servants of any sort. NRA might not be any of Wallace's affair or mine —Johnson made it clear that such was his opinion—but we did not acknowledge yet that any institution with real responsibility for recovery and reconstruction was a matter of indifference to us. This would lead to some sharp differences; but we had our own immediate problem in AAA.

Peek's appointment had been a strategic error that would plague us until it was corrected. As he began to set up his organization he turned sector after sector over to old associates. Many of them were processors, the natural enemies of the farmer, and gradually the whole top level of the administration became an agribusiness outfit. The only public-minded officials in the lot were Jerome Frank and Victor Christgau. They were so alien in that crowd that their tenure was obviously uncertain.

Victor Christgau was a lame-duck farmer-laborite congressman who needed a job; and Frank was there because of a series of mistakes. Like many others in those days who thought the change from Hoover to Roosevelt in Washington meant that at last the special interests would be purged from government and public-minded citizens would be given a chance to be useful, he had told Felix Frankfurter that he would like to join up. Because he was extremely well recommended by everyone who knew him, Frankfurter directed him to us.

We needed a department solicitor. Here, Frankfurter said, was an able and energetic lawyer who ought to be a welcome change from the kind who usually served in such posts. We were attracted to him and, with the president's consent, offered him the post. A mix-up in identities kept him from that appointment. Roosevelt, recognizing the injustice, had suggested him for general counsel of AAA, not yet organized. When it did come into being, Frank had been working with us for several months. He had resigned from his firm in New York and was acting for us as a kind of general consultant. It was quite undeserved good luck for me to have found so able a counselor. In spite of being more experienced, he insisted on taking directions from me, as perhaps was proper, since I was responsible, and presently I learned to give them freely. They needed only to be general ones. He went on to elaborate them for himself. He was, in one way or another, a formative influence in shaping both the NRA and the AAA—as well as many other measures. He was indefatigable in argument, he was a thorough workman, and he was extremely persuasive. It was not long before I felt that I had multiplied my own effectiveness many times merely by having him as my second.

When he became general counsel for AAA, however, he assembled a group of young lawyers some of whom, as it turned out, added to our difficulties. It was possibly as competent a group as had ever been got together in a government agency; but most of them had no rural background. This irritated the Peek men and those in the field who had been trained in the agricultural colleges. There were easily ridiculed *gaffes*. There began to circulate a series of stories, partly true and partly invented, illustrating their ignorances. This tended to exaggerate Frank's own urban origin, and eventually this affected me because our association was known to be an intimate one.[3] Neither Wallace nor I actually saw much of those young lawyers, but we knew they were around and became familiar with their faces as subordinates to Frank in many conferences.

Many of them, however, emerging from their law schools into a disorganized and competitive society that was degenerating rapidly into chaos, were critical of democracy. Some were even attracted to communism. Frank, like myself, believed collective measures to be necessary; but this seemed to these severely logical and disillusioned younger people to be hopelessly futile. But we thought our departures from orthodoxy important, especially compared with the Brandeis-Frankfurter progressive program. We did not believe the restoration of business competition was adequate, and we were convinced that the business-government partnership, as it was being developed by Peek and Johnson, would not succeed. Brandeis had let Roosevelt know that he was opposed and we had visited him during the spring on several occasions to argue the matter. We had come away each time more convinced that he was hopelessly unrealistic. He was patient and painstaking in his effort to make a disciple of Frank as well as me; but he was quite unwilling to listen when we offered our alternative.

So Frank and I were beset on one side by disillusioned helpers who were certainly extremist believers in disciplined state organization, to the extent, as we thought, of submerging the individual completely; and on the other side by many more traditionalists who were convinced

---

[3] Some of this is reflected in Russell Lord's *The Wallaces of Iowa* (Boston: Houghton Mifflin, 1947). Lord is possibly the best source for an understanding of the strange character and brilliant mind of Henry Wallace. His book is especially good for this period at the beginning of AAA's administration. The farm problem, the various approaches to its solution, and the successes and failures of those of us who worked at it in those days is given a full and fair treatment. Lord was present as an observer of all the events of this period. He was at the moment attached to the information division without regular duties; but he was kept busy, along with John R. Fleming, writing Wallace's speeches and pamphlets explaining what it was we were trying to do.

believers in enforced free enterprise. Then there were the Brandeis people, the most active of whom were the two I have spoken of who were already in Washington—Thomas G. Corcoran and Benjamin V. Cohen. They had been assigned to the drafting of the reform acts promised by Roosevelt. They were also busily assisting Frankfurter in his recruiting activities. Wherever legal staffs were being enlarged they were ready with candidates.

Their convinced opposition to the introduction of collectivist organizations would be supported by the later failure of NRA; and Corcoran's personality and ability would presently make him a White House favorite. Cohen was a behind-the-scenes worker. It would be said by commentators after a few years that Corcoran and Cohen had succeeded me, as I had succeeded Moley. They were credited with the second New Deal as we were credited with the first. That was an oversimplification, of course; but there was in it a good deal of truth. We created the NRA and the AAA. They wrote the banking-reform legislation and that regulating the security markets. I still thought these needed to be done but that they ought to have awaited recovery. If activity was not quickly resumed, nothing else would have any importance, and we ought not to be distracted by lesser issues. I was not entirely convinced about this, of course; when the reforms were those I was most concerned about—such as the food and drug legislation—I was quite willing, I am afraid, to believe they should be pushed even if recovery was admittedly a first priority.

Among Frank's young men were several who later had some notoriety. One of these was Alger Hiss, of whom it has to be said that he was regarded by his own colleagues as hardly radical enough to be acceptable. This opinion I recalled afterward when he was accused of having been a Communist. If he actually was a party member, he was so far underground that even his close associates did not know it. He seemed to them, they said, to be mostly interested in his own advancement. And this opinion seemed to be confirmed when, a little later, Frank was "purged." Most of his associates left instantly in indignation; but Hiss stayed on to serve in AAA, which the others felt had been taken over by "the interests."

One of the most useful of Frank's helpers was Lee Pressman, who afterward became general counsel for the Congress of Industrial Organizations and who, when interrogated years later, admitted having been, for a while, a party member. Pressman had a special legal capability, and Frank often assigned him to work with me when I had drafting problems or regulatory complications. He did a good deal of work for Hopkins too, enabling that careless administrator to maintain the fiction that he "ran his show without any damned lawyers to complicate things." It was true that Hopkins never had a legal division in any of his successive relief organizations; he did, however, have numerous experts in administrative law of one sort of another—for instance, Corrington Gill—who worked out his procedures. When it came to drafting proposed regulations or to judging the effect of competing legislative proposals—there were apt to be sudden floods of these on Capitol Hill—he needed help. Pressman supplied it. Often he spent weeks together on Hopkins' problems.

Since the revelation—made by Pressman himself—that he was at that time a Communist, I have wondered what, if any, difference it made. Communists could not have been under suspicion of being helpful to any enemy. It was only later that there developed the tense feeling that Russia was a challenging world power. There was an active anti-communist sentiment; but there was more contempt than fear in its composition. Russian imperialism had not been as yet—and would not be for decades to come—identified as a serious challenge. During that whole year, when the London conference was over, foreign affairs were hardly ever discussed in the press. The progress of Hitler and Mussolini was noted; but Americans were concentrating on their own troubles, and this was true of those who were working in Washington.

☆ | CHAPTER 4 | ☆

New Dealers
and Communists

THE QUESTION NATURALLY arises whether becoming a Communist to any degree—that is, as a full party member or as a fellow traveler—represented, for highly intelligent young men, simply a reaction against the injustices of American life, such as they had seen all around them during the twenties when they had been growing up, and now in the depression, or whether it was something deeper and more serious. That something would, I suppose, be the conviction that the totalitarian system was a better way of organizing society than was possible by holding to democracy. That they might feel this way was, to me, an appalling possibility then as it is now. There was a lot to be done, some of it drastic; but the prospect of control by a self-appointed elite seemed to me worse than what we had.

There was something in the experience of these younger people, along with the disbelief in our society's capacity for regeneration, that had made it possible for them to anticipate a communist state with approval. This was not my first experience with this willingness to depart from the democratic tradition. I had had students in my Columbia classes who had argued for the communist ideology; and I had made the disagreeable discovery that one of the instructors in my own group in the college was going that way. I had had to refuse him renewal of his appointment, not because he was a Communist—I did not actually know then that he was—but because he was neglecting his teaching for party duties. I probably would not have recommended his separation merely because he was a party member in the circumstances of those days; but the reason I gave was not credited by the little band of the faithful on our campus, or so they pretended. They were able to make something of an issue; and I was in the strange position, for one who had been through struggles for academic freedom on his own account, of being denounced for violating its principles. There had been a few days, just at the time when I was transferring to Washington, when the university had been in an uproar, with mass meetings on the library steps, student strikes, and all the other familiar phenomena of such agitations. One of these gatherings had been passionately addressed by Diego Rivera, the Mexican painter. This naturally commanded abnormal headlines and contributed to my general notoriety. The artist knew neither me nor Henderson; but this seemed only to allow him more freedom. For several days the issue commanded headlines and space in all the New York papers.

I made a public statement saying that I took full responsibility and that Henderson had been released for neglecting his work and not because he had peculiar views; but this did not have as much effect as I thought it should have had in view of my record. And certainly the small group of activists was able to foment considerable disturbance. There was in this the usual complete disregard of issues, and the deliberate distortion of facts.

A number of those who had denounced me in the most immoderate terms in the speeches on the library steps owed me something. Some of them I had befriended (a few I had seen through difficult situations with loans never repaid); and all of them knew that I had defended their rights to dissident views and had sponsored their campus organizations. Out of this personal experience I reached the conclusion that I would never again work with any Communist if I could avoid it. To do so would be to risk betrayal in any clash of loyalties. If I had had any reason to think that our young lawyers were signed-up party members, I would have refused them employment. Their first duty would be to another cause; they would indeed have been dedicated to the overthrow of the government I had sworn to uphold—as, of course, they had too. I hoped to see it changed; but so did most people, in one way or another. That, however, was another thing.

Was the education I had been helping to dispense at fault? I did not think so. The mark of our teaching was a skeptical appraisal of social operations. If we concluded that they did not work well for the purposes we believed in, there were ways to change them so that they might. So, at least, we thought. It seemed to me that succeeding generations of earnest students might be persuaded to realize the possibilities in this kind of effort. And the Roosevelt administration was the agency for more changes, and more rapid ones, than had been possible for a long time. Their abilities were being utilized to the full. What more could they ask?

That many of the dissidents asked a good deal more was afterward evident; and those of us who were older, and so more involved in shaping the changes then going on, ought probably to have sensed the discontent in some of the younger minds around us. We gave them more to do in every day than they could get through. We discussed ways and means at length; we even assessed implications; but we assumed that what was being done, or what could be done, was approved by all those engaged in it. That some of them must have thought our ameliorative efforts futile we had not realized. So much criticism came from those who thought we intended far too much that it seldom occurred to us that there were those who thought it far too little. It would have made no difference, I presume, if we had. What we did, our younger colleagues helped us to do well; and we were not aware of any withholding. Then, too, there must have been very few of them; many more saw the possibilities as we did.

Among these last was Abe Fortas, who was an able workman and who later on became undersecretary of the interior and was Harold Ickes' right-hand man until 1945. After that his legal career and his unaccountable mistake as a Supreme Court justice are well known. There was also Paul Porter, who afterward would serve usefully in many posts, among them the chairmanship of the Federal Communications Commission and head of the wartime Office of Price Administration. He lifted the spirits of all those with whom he had dealings, something welcome in those grim days. He was, in fact, seldom employed as a lawyer; his political talents, seen by everyone when he had charge of publicity in the Democratic campaign of 1940, were already apparent in 1933.

There were others; and, as need arose, we called on outside help. Thurman Arnold (later a federal judge and author of *The Folklore of Capitalism*) and Wesley Sturges (later dean of the Yale University School of Law) were among them. The School of Law at that time was a center of lively legal learning, and we regarded it as a better resource than most other such institutions. Robert M. Hutchins had lately left his post as dean at Yale to go to the University of Chicago (for a twenty-year stay), but the Hutchins influence persisted. Adlai Stevenson was also one of this group, but I could not afterward recall ever having known him.

I have dwelt at this length on the younger men in our aggregation because so many of them, during successive Democratic administrations, had positions of responsibility; and because, even while they were yet so subordinate, their talents enabled us to accomplish extraordinary things.

Wallace had a message for the country in those days, and he was delivering it in person. His opportunities to speak were many, from coast to coast, and he made use of them to let people know what it was we were trying to do. For as cotton began to be plowed up and all those little pigs were slaughtered, we knew well enough that we would be pilloried as proponents of scarcity and destruction. Then too there was a real challenge from the farm states themselves as Milo Reno and other demagogues denounced us. Farmers were still all too ready to believe that some way other than crop limitation ought to be found to renew their prosperity; and Wallace knew he would have real difficulty in persuading them that their cooperation was necessary to recovery—and to their sharing in its benefits.

☆ | CHAPTER 5 | ☆

Cabinet and Executive Council

W HEN WALLACE WAS AWAY on these missions and I sat for him
at the cabinet table, I was between Claude Swanson of Navy
on the right and Frances Perkins of Labor on the left. Across from me
was Harold Ickes and, at the foot of the table, Vice-President Garner.
There were several with unimpeachable conservative affiliations. George
Dern of war, former governor of Utah, was a progressive; but Hull
and Garner were suspicious of all that was going on. They had no chance
to protest in cabinet meetings—or at any rate did not intervene—but
their disapproval was obvious. More dissent, of another kind, came
from Frances Perkins. She was incorrigibly loquacious and often voiced
objections or advanced ideas. Wallace or I often came armed with
memoranda from Ezekiel or Louis Bean, protesting that recovery was
far too slow and that the economy drive was creating unemployment
while relief funds were being spent to cure it; but we also learned that
this was not the place for attempts to argue matters of policy.

The meetings soon became less cordial than they had been at first.
Even Roosevelt's geniality seemed forced. It was quite evident that the
vice-president understood little of what was being done, and what
he did understand he was against. He was not likely to expose himself to argument with Frances Perkins or Henry Wallace, prepared as
these two always were with overwhelming facts and figures; but he
was bewildered by the multifarious activities all around him and he
did not like it. For the moment he was going along; after a short time
he no longer pretended to approve.

117

Roosevelt had no intention of encouraging differences to show themselves—none, at least, of any importance. Almost always, I believe, from Wallace's reports and my own observations, he did most of the talking himself. He spoke generally of the state of the economy; and it was to these summarizings that Wallace and Perkins were most apt to take exception. His account of accomplishments was so far from reality that we conspired to furnish him with a statistical office. This was duly done by executive order on July 27, 1933. The Central Statistical Board consisted of the secretaries of interior, agriculture, commerce, and labor; the governor of the Federal Reserve Board; and the administrator of NRA. Their supervision was, of course, nominal. Isidor Lubin's long and valuable service began when he became the director. We appealed to him whenever questions of fact arose. It limited Roosevelt's more optimistic interpretations of what was happening.

Often cabinet meetings began with an incident related by Roosevelt himself. Sometimes these seemed relevant, but occasionally they did not. Always, however, they served to make a beginning, and afterward there was some loosening of stiffness.

Looking around the table, at my first meeting, I thought a very high price indeed had been paid for conservative cooperation in the Congress; but I recalled the old maxim that when you possess power you must reward your enemies and punish your friends—an enemy might be won over and a friend could not afford to oppose; but to have enemies in the inner circle seemed to give them unnecessary opportunities for obstruction, and that was beginning to be something to worry about.

No one could say, however, that rewarding and punishing had not been effective so far. The Congress had very rapidly yielded to the president on emergency measures; and in the strategic spots he had a few of his own men for the administrative job ahead, although there were others whose loyalties were suspect. His maneuvers to keep Baruch out of the cabinet had succeeded. If, as he reminded me once, Baruch "owned" sixty congressmen, it had taken some bargaining to avoid making him secretary of state. Fortunately Hull had a recognizably superior claim as an elder statesman with a long record of service to the party and with definite internationalist ideas. Still, Baruch had to be kept quiet, and it was largely for this reason that Peek and Johnson had been appointed. Roosevelt obviously hoped that they would be amenable and competent; but it was a considerable risk. Johnson seemed more reasonable than Peek, who had already demanded freedom from Wallace's supervision and the right to deal directly with Roosevelt. In July, however, Johnson began to show the same determination to escape direction. He was supposed to be a subordinate of the National Recovery Board; but this was a responsibility he ignored from the first, as Peek ignored Wallace and me. Baruch and his men represented the vast power of business; the question was whether it would prove to be too much for Roosevelt. There was reason to fear that it might as the staffing of AAA and NRA began and as policies began to be shaped.

By July, Hull was back from the unfortunate London conference. His opening speech there had in effect denounced economic nationalism; but since economic nationalism was a fair way of describing what Roosevelt was establishing he was pursuing a dissenting line. We were isolating ourselves from foreign influences, and Hull was retreating into a sour sulk as the program developed. But he was waiting for his chance; and, of course, it would come as the recovery petered out. He could then go on with his program of international *laissez faire*, and also go on consorting with others who shared his views. These included the Brandeis followers.

At the moment there was no effective opposition to the enlargement of relief and public works. Even Garner was for it, and Farley was positively enthusiastic. But that did not mean that there would not soon be a change. Presently the backwash of stories from the field would begin to be whispered about the Capitol corridors—relief was too generous; people doing public works were worthless loafers. Hopkins would have to counter growing criticism. He would meet it by repeated reorganizations and apparent changes of policy: the Federal Emergency Relief Administration would be succeeded by the Civil Works Administration and CWA by the Works Progress Administration. But the opposition would grow; and the worst of it would be represented not by Republicans but by conservative Democrats. They were already grumbling when he had hardly begun.

The truth was that in these early days there were four centers of furious activity in Washington: AAA, NRA, RFC, and FERA; and none was directly represented at the cabinet table. This was not quite true of AAA; Wallace, as secretary of agriculture, was nominally Peek's superior; but he had made the concession demanded by Peek for direct dealing with the president, so even Wallace did not always know what was going on. None of these differences were argued out in the cabinet. In reflecting on this situation a year later—after experience as a code administrator for NRA—Lindsay Rogers, as an experienced political observer, was inclined to suggest, as had others before him, that parliamentary government on the British model might be better than our system. The cabinet would then be a committee of the Congress, and therefore better able to commit it to permanent policies. Certainly it was true that the crisis had centered vast power in the president, and it could fairly be described as undemocratic. Also, the president was less effective than he should have been because the cabinet consisted of a fixed number of heads of old departments from whose control a good deal of government activity had escaped.

This cabinet weakness would be temporarily corrected by setting up the Executive Council (by executive order on July 11, 1933). In addition to the cabinet the following were named as members: the director of the budget; the administrator of national recovery; the administrator of agricultural adjustment; the administrator of federal emergency relief; the federal coordinator of transportation; the governor of the Farm Credit Administration; the chairman of the board of the Reconstruction Finance Corporation; the chairman of the board of the Home Owners Loan Corporation; the chairman of the board of the Tennessee Valley Authority; the director of the Civilian Conservation Corps; Louis Howe, presidential secretary; and the assistant secretary of the treasury. The executive secretary was to be Frank Walker.

This agency was intended to appease those who felt left out when the cabinet was meeting; but if it made the new administrators happier it worsened relations with conservative congressmen. The emergency powers had been granted only grudgingly and with limits of time. This showed suspicion of presidential intentions. The Congress had adjourned until January, but conservative members were not wholly satisfied with the patronage arrangements, and this, added to their dislike of New Deal policies, made them hard to deal with. When the Council was set up by executive order to represent the functions actually being carried on, such presidential novelty was regarded with suspicion. Those newly added were the ones least trusted—Hopkins, for instance.[1]

This point concerning executive leadership in the American system had been argued by numerous political scientists, of whom Lindsay

[1] The Council list included Lewis Douglas, Hugh Johnson, George Peek, Harry Hopkins, Joseph Eastman, Henry Morgenthau, Jesse Jones, John Fahey, Arthur Morgan, Robert Fechner, Louis Howe, L. W. Robert, and Frank Walker. It should be noted that this group proved unwieldy and was transformed, again by executive order, into the National Emergency Council on November 7, 1933, with a smaller membership.

Rogers was only one. Usually it was left about where Woodrow Wilson had left it in 1907. Indeed, Rogers referred to a certain passage from a Wilson text:

Leadership and control must be lodged somewhere; the whole art of statesmanship is the art of bringing the several parts of government into effective co-operation for the accomplishment of particular common objects . . . The nation as a whole has chosen him [the President] and is conscious that it has no other political spokesman. His is the only voice in national affairs. Let him once win the admiration and confidence of the country and no other single force can withstand him, no combination of forces will easily overpower him . . .

The President is at liberty, both in law and conscience, to be as big a man as he can. His capacity will set the limit, and if Congress be overborne by him it will be no fault of the makers of the Constitution—it will be through no lack of constitutional powers on its part, but only because the President has the nation behind him and Congress has not. He has no means of compelling Congress except through public opinion.[2]

The opportunity to observe, and have some part in the attempt being made by Roosevelt to furnish the leadership spoken of by Wilson, was an exciting one. The drawback was the focusing of so much attention on myself. The notoriety I had first experienced before the election as a member of Roosevelt's "Brains Trust" was building up. It was being added to by the furor about the "Tugwell bill" providing those much-feared controls over the manufacture and sale of food and drugs; by editorial resentment concerning the supposed influence of a "theoretical professor"; and by the distrust of the businessmen who had learned of my resistance to their capturing of the strategic places in the recovery agencies. This was a combined opposition I had no means for softening, and so I did not try. I could only point out that I was not even a member of the expanded cabinet—the Executive Council. Once adopted, however, such a stereotype is not easily given up. It is impervious to argument and independent of fact. I was trapped. I decided to make the most of it. I had been given a certain notoriety. I would use it.

[2] The Rogers book was *Crisis Government* (New York: Norton, 1934). The Wilson quotation was from *Constitutional Government in the United States* (New York: Columbia U. P., 1908).

CHAPTER 6

Trouble in AAA

T HE ORGANIZING OF AAA was well under way by midsummer and the developing policies were becoming clear. I had no choice but to oppose much of what was in prospect. When the first marketing agreements with processors were being made, Jerome Frank and I proposed that, in return for exemption from the anti-trust laws, the processors should allow public examination of their records and some scrutiny of their price and wage policies. They categorically refused; and Peek saw no reason for our demand as long as farmers got more for their products. In his view the consumers could look out for themselves. They were not our responsibility.

Wallace, however, had been persuaded that AAA ought to be provided with a consumers' counsel—not a difficult decision for him before the pressures began to be felt, since he saw beyond farmers' interests to those of the country as a whole. His early speeches had been explicit. Agricultural adjustment was justified not only because it would make farmers better off but because the economy could not recover unless farmers had higher incomes. He argued that agricultural products had to be bought by someone; and this could only happen if consumers were able to buy.

It happened that Frederick C. Howe, who was venerated by all younger liberals as a warrior in many old battles, was drawn to Washington. He had been an associate of Tom Johnson's in Cleveland, and had since written several vivid books, one on Denmark as an example of national maturity, but also *The City, the Hope of Democracy*, widely read by younger liberals. His *Confessions of a Reformer* was to be classed with Steffens' *Autobiography* as an account of struggles with the business system. Howe was interested in Roosevelt as a progressive; and since he was a surviving embodiment of the movement for reform we had read about as students, what could be more fitting than that he should have a part in our effort? He was still a persuasive liberal. He seemed an ideal person to represent consumers' interests. Above all, as Wallace saw it, his presence among us would be a guarantee that farmers' gains were not to be at consumers' expense.

So far urban congressmen had not opposed farm relief. This was partly because at the moment they were accepting Roosevelt's program, but also partly because we had always presented our efforts as a necessary part of a general scheme for recovery; agricultural improvement was to correlate with renewed employment for industrial workers.

This recognition of consumers, we soon found, was an empty gesture. It was all right to talk about, but when it came to implementing it, those who took it seriously were regarded in AAA as traitors to the farmers' cause. Howe was given a title and an office, but was soon excluded from policy discussions. There were, however, a few epic fights over specific issues before he began to be left out. Peek and his assistant, Chester Davis, still felt that their best chance of doing something for farmers was to persuade the processors to pay the farmers more; and they were setting about it through the agreements now being drafted. If Howe persisted in objecting to these increases being passed on to consumers—and he was supported by me and then by Wallace—their whole scheme would fail. Some of these agreements, with the alternatives drafted by Frank and his assistants, were hotly disputed.

Wallace, however, soon began to weaken. He had to deal not only with the processors themselves, but with the farm leaders alerted by Peek and Davis. It was their thesis that Frank and I, persuaded by Howe, were reformers who were using this occasion to secure radical ends. Our demands, they said, had nothing to do with increasing farmers' incomes, the first business of the AAA. They simply proved what had been suspected, that we were "against the profit system." Peek remarked, with the air of having said something profound, that he had nothing against this system if the farmers could get in on it. That benefit the processors would concede if they were allowed to raise their prices at will and take what they considered to be a fair margin for themselves. This, Peek felt, was "the American way."

We thought it only reasonable that the agreements should not benefit the processors unduly; and that could only be determined by an examination of their books. We had seen the catch in these agreements from the first, of course, and had opposed giving the processors complete freedom. Peek's forthright statement of intention was something we had expected, and, so far as we could, we felt compelled to prevent the turning over of farmers' relief to their traditional exploiters. To grant exemption from anti-trust laws without any commitment to regulation seemed to us a retreat from many years of reformers' efforts.

By now Wallace had his own staff, headed by Paul Appleby, who was soon supplemented by C. B. ("Beanie") Baldwin and James D. LeCron—pretty much an Iowa outfit, although Baldwin came from down in West Virginia. All of them were inclined to side with me in the issues I have described. But the opposition was strong and determined, and all of us who gave them trouble were asking for their active enmity. For this purpose it was convenient to single me out as the head devil with the rest grouped about me—Frank, Howe, Ezekiel, and Wallace's assistants; and, indeed, I was often forced to play the role prescribed for me. The issues as they came up were seldom settled short of a general meeting in the secretary's office; and quite often I was needled into a forcible statement of our position. It became more and more Wallace's part to sit in judgment. There were some difficult decisions. Concerning the largest of the agreements, and the exclusion of sharecroppers from their landlords' benefits, Wallace took the matter to the president. Peek insisted, when he could, on making Wallace responsible. Naturally both Roosevelt and Wallace found this annoying.

So far as I was concerned, Roosevelt recognized that the identity created by my detractors had a certain utility. However subversive they tried to make me appear, there was some suspicion that it was being done for other motives than the protection of American ideals. Roosevelt actually said to me after one outburst that my critics were really his critics. I asked how that could be when I so seldom prevailed when decisions were made on controversial issues. That, he said, was because he was allowed much leeway. The progressives must know that he got as much as he could out of the deals he had to make. He had many struggles going on and he had to give here and there. My value was that I represented an uncompromising attitude. He said not to worry about the publicity.

Conversations about this took place in unusual circumstances. I especially recall one in October. He had invited me to lunch alone with him at his desk, something that had symbolic meaning, not missed by my detractors. I was by now sophisticated enough to realize that my presence was not without its uses to him. The progressives were unhappy, and were becoming outspoken about it. They had achieved their long struggle for relief and public works; but they did not like the way AAA and NRA were beginning. Also it seemed to them that the wolves were being set to watch the sheep in other places than AAA and NRA. For instance, they saw Jesse Jones expanding the Reconstruction Finance Corporation to save big businesses, especially financial ones; but they saw very few reforms being exacted in return.

I had almost the same moral support from Wallace as from Roosevelt. He was caught in a familiar dilemma: he could do the right thing or he could do a less right one. He was not really consumer-minded, or disposed to consider workers' rights. He was an Iowan, and he was sensitive to farmers' wrongs. Those of workers or consumers were intellectual concerns. Still, he did have a conception of the economy as one whole. He saw the need for pursuing, through the jungle of our current struggles, the far and retreating light of public interest. Bringing it nearer was easier for him to defer than it was for me, but his purpose was clear.

I still thought, as I reviewed our complex difficulties, that it was a privilege to be able to work, as I was being allowed to do, for causes I believed in, elusive though they were, and compromised as they often were. The president—and he alone—represented the whole. And he was well aware of his responsibilities. That he saw trouble coming was shown in some of his casual conversation—hard to credit now in view of his long incumbency yet to come. For he began to talk of what he would do when his term was over. It was not yet clear that a new constituency was forming. He was preparing himself for eventualities. He spoke this way with Harry Hopkins too. We must have heard a dozen outlines of adventures, usually novel ones, as possibilities for his retirement. He saw chances to expand his farming ventures in Hyde Park and in Georgia—where, on the rocky soil around Warm Springs, in a part of the country he loved, he was trying to grow crops and breed up a herd of beef cattle. This had little chance of profit; but he talked also of a venture corporation to start new industries, such as chemical synthetics and improved metals. He spoke of how far behind Germany, for instance, we were in these matters, and of the significance this might have if we should ever be drawn into war.

The exercise was fanciful. He had no reason to doubt that there would be a second term; but politics is notoriously chancy, and those who risk it always have to be prepared for the worst. So it was natural for him to consider alternatives, even though at that moment his support was beginning an irresistible surge. It was considerably later that he made those arrangements for an editorship of *Collier's* which eventually came to light, but in these early days he did speak of the need for an "enlightened" newspaper or magazine.

This reminded me that my commitment to Columbia was still one I had not abandoned. I had not yet decided that I wanted to. I was having troubles. I would have to do something about my impossible situation as a nominal, but helpless member of the AAA council. I met with them but no longer had much to say. I should either withdraw or demand more consideration. Farm workers, sharecroppers, and, indeed, small farmers were being neglected. The organization was astonishingly efficient for having been put together so rapidly; but the way it was going left a good deal to be argued about. I could see that I would gradually be excluded, since all I had to say was in opposition.

It was different in the old department. I was now accepted by most of its scientists and administrators and recognized as a defender in difficult times. Besides, by now, their old projects for expansion were being incorporated into works projects and were regularly being approved. There was genuine satisfaction in these activities. It was about AAA that I had serious reservations. It was becoming popular among the farmers who counted—the more efficient ones; and this was an asset Roosevelt could not afford to forego. He, like Wallace, seemed to me to be convinced that the poorer half of the rural population must be left to the mercies of the more prosperous half. Perhaps this assessment was unjust; but in pessimistic moments I felt very accusatory. My situation might very well become untenable if I kept on saying what I felt.

CHAPTER 7

Problems of Organization

T HE EXECUTIVE COUNCIL, and its successor organization, the Emergency Council, did not prove useful to Roosevelt. In one capacity or another, sometimes as Wallace's substitute, I attended many of their meetings during the next few years, and I can recall only a few discussions of the sort it might have been expected would take place. Doubts and differences were not cleared away. Coordination was less noticeable than competition. Stated meetings of all the active agency heads may have made them better acquainted with each other; but coolness and suspicion were all too apparent.

We gathered in an anteroom, each coming to the executive wing in his own way. Our secretary's office had only two cars, and one was usually engaged in Mrs. Wallace's affairs. The other had to be held for the secretary's possible occasions. I had no transport to these meetings as I did when I was summoned for other purposes. So more often than not I walked. The Capitol stood at the end of the plowed-up mall on the right and the Lincoln Memorial on the left, with the Lee House just visible across the river on the heights. During the summer and fall it was hot and I arrived at the White House in an unbecoming state; but whenever I could find the quarter-hour it took I went that way.

Since the Council meetings were large, the room was crowded; and when the president was wheeled in, silence fell on the company. He started talking as he came through the door. Sometimes he began lightly, sometimes with a story he had just heard; less often he had a particular project on his mind and said something about it. There was, therefore, some direction given; but resistances could hardly be overcome in this way, and it would be a serious matter to offer anything approaching rebuke in so large a company. These were able and ambitious individuals; but some dissented from his policies and some were empire builders. If it was dissension that the meetings were meant to prevent they had very little such effect.

There had always been a question whether cabinets—and the Executive Council was, after all, merely an expanded and formally instituted cabinet—were meant to give counsel to the president or were merely staff meetings of departmental administrators. Theory had tended to run in favor of consultative status. Washington, for instance, had expected advice from Hamilton, Jefferson, Knox, and Randolph. Later presidents had found their department heads too specialized to be of use in the general decisions they must make. But political scientists had persisted in urging the cabinet's usefulness, and the public liked to believe in collective wisdom. Presidents had usually complied, as Roosevelt did. But if at the beginning they thought it would strengthen their decisions as well as their image, they soon found this a mistaken theory. During their early days some presidents had made commitments likely to be embarrassing later, about "seeking counsel," "being guided by advice," "finding good men and depending on their collective wisdom," and so on. But they uniformly discovered that the advice they needed could not come from busy administrators.

Besides having large departments to manage, secretaries had other disqualifications. They were often chosen because they represented factions to be placated and kept in some kind of amenable humor; or they were selected from among influential legislators, who, it might be hoped, would incline their remaining brethren to support for the president. Neither of these turned out to be qualifications for disinterested advice.[1]

---

[1] Harold Ickes' impression, as recorded in his diary of February 28, 1935 (and published in *The Saturday Evening Post*, June 5, 1948, p. 16), after the cabinet meeting of that day, was similar to mine concerning President Roosevelt's experience: "Only the barest routine matters were discussed. All of which leads me to set down what has been running in my mind for a long time, and that is just what use the Cabinet is under this administration. The cold fact is that on important matters we are seldom called upon for advice. We never discuss exhaustively any policy of government or question of political strategy. The President makes all of his own decisions, and, so far at least as the Cabinet is concerned, without taking counsel with a group of advisers. On particular questions he will call into his office persons directly interested, but it is fair to say that the Cabinet is not a general council upon whose

The Executive Council was a recognition that the old cabinet had not been useful, only traditional. If even this enlarged body did not serve a consultative purpose, it was not altogether because its members were political appointees or because they were former legislators. Some were neither—Ickes, Frances Perkins, and Wallace, for instance—but they were still intent on their own administrative affairs and in accumulating power but not in being helpful to the president.

Roosevelt had an interest in overhead management. What had formerly been merely an interest had now become a real need for finding better ways to get done increasingly demanding jobs and to prevent squabbling among those who were doing them. This was true of his cabinet. The enlarged councils were attempts at improvement. For Roosevelt, however, as for all modern presidents, the difficulties were too formidable. Neither served any good purpose.

A larger governmental reorganization became associated in my mind with the whole problem of the president's constitutional duties—with policy-making and its execution. Roosevelt opened this subject several times, continuing conversations we had carried on in Albany. It had seemed easier then than it did now, because, as he came closer to it, all the reasons for not making changes became more insistent and all the vested interests more vocal. He had been given power, in the Economy Act, to shift agencies about, and this authority would run out in a year; but he was hearing from legislators who had associates among the bureaucrats. It soon became clear that nothing was going to be done in this way; and reorganizing would not begin, in fact, until he appointed the Committee on Administrative Management during his second term and had, in their *Report,* a comprehensive scheme for guidance. Even this, however, would not solve the impossible constitutional problem. The Framers had made their president both a chief of state and an administrator; besides, he had become the leader of a party. No individual could be all these at the same time—not successfully.

For me, however, this experience was educational. I learned something of how decisions were made. I also discovered how difficult it was to carry them out. During Roosevelt's time there was, I think, a good

---

advice the President relies, or the opinions of which, on important matters, he calls for. Our Cabinet meetings are pleasant affairs, but we only skim the surface of routine matters. As a matter of fact I never think of bringing up even a serious departmental issue at Cabinet meetings, and apparently the other members follow the same policy."

deal of improvement; but it would come slowly. He showed more inclination to add agencies for all the new tasks than to assign them to already existing agencies. He was obviously afraid they would not be undertaken with any enthusiasm. The old departments were pretty much allowed to go their way, with the excisions accomplished by Douglas before he gave up.

What was involved in this—and was spoken of in a tentative and inquiring way then—was the larger question of democratic leadership. Roosevelt was beginning to be called a "dictator" by those who were dissatisfied with his policies. It annoyed him. There was never a more convinced democrat; but he was a realist. This came, as he liked to say, from his Dutch caution as well as long experience with politics. I asked, when he first spoke of it, if something else was not involved. He may have been more affected than he realized by his eight years in the Navy Department and his four years as governor. He was being more the administrator and less the executive than he imagined. I recalled his accomplishments in the Navy. In those days he had had just about nothing to do with policy; that had been attended to by President Wilson and Josephus Daniels. It had been his job to see that ships were built, were kept in order, and carried out their missions. He and the admirals seemed to have succeeded. In New York, as governor, he had been submerged in day-to-day problems. Besides, it had been politic for a presidential aspirant to repress larger inquiries. He had overcome his reluctance to express opinions on national matters only gradually and under the compulsions of the depression. In the months before his nomination he had belatedly applied himself to the problems of policy; but his conclusions were less certain than he made them seem for public effect.

If he had asked for unusual powers when he became president, it was because he was uncertain and knew that he might have to experiment. Those people who called him a dictator, he said, betrayed a kind of wish for one; but what a democracy needed was leadership, not discipline. Dictatorship was easy compared with leadership. He hadn't watched Mussolini and Hitler for nothing. They got and kept popular approval; and they could do nearly anything they liked. This led them to imagine that they had a kind of infallibility. This would get worse and they might make fatal mistakes. In contrast, when he was getting ready to act he had to have general agreement that what he was about to do was something a good many people would say ought to be done.

This did not mean that he never tried to persuade. He did that all the time. There were matters that had to be simplified. People could not understand. He used the example of monetary policy. He could convince people that he meant well and could get permission, it might be said, to do things; but they couldn't tell whether these were the right things. What did most people know about public finance?

He worried this theme. Take the fireside chats. They were education. He had said before that a president must be first of all an educator. Whether or not he really understood it when he first said it, now he was sure it was true. He found himself asking people to believe that he meant well. He was saying that he knew best and they must give him confidence—something they seemed only too willing to do. He found himself making admissions about experimentation, saying publicly that policies might not work but that he would try something else if they did not. That was honest. He had to admit that what people mostly wanted, and what a politician was tempted to give them, was something different: reassurance. It was better politics to act as if what was being done was the only thing to be done; that it was sure to succeed. It was sad to say that failure was not usually held against even the most mistaken politician. It might be by a few critics; but most people wouldn't listen to criticism if they had once given their confidence to a president.

He went on to speak—not once but several times—of the dilemma involved in this; but I can testify that it always came out at the same place. He wanted people not only to have economic security but to have minds of their own. He wanted his behavior to be directed by demand. This was the reason he was so annoyed—and spoke so often—about the poisoning (his own word) of communications. For people to furnish direction they must be able to make up their minds; and to do this capably they needed information. In our circumstances they were apt to make up their minds mistakenly, and this was because they were given twisted facts. They were worse than just twisted. They were shaped to serve ends—the ends of those who owned the newspapers and radio stations.

We didn't have to be mealy-mouthed about this, he said. Look at the reporters around here. You ought to hear—well, of course, you have heard—what they say about their own situation. Most of them want to be honest. Not one—well, maybe a few—can. They have to follow orders. With most of the newspapers—about 85 percent—against him and all he stood for, he was able to go on persuading most of the people that what was being done was honestly meant. But it had to be done against serious odds.

I should say that he had quite remarkable success in being what he wanted to be—an educator or leader who brought people nearer to approving what he did rather than just consenting. What his predilections of this sort had to do with the problem of the cabinet, with overhead management, with policy-making and execution, is fairly obvious. The governmental machinery was ponderous even then. He thought it could be made less so. If what ought to be done could be threshed out by experts—the very difficult and complex things—and if their conclusions could be made far more apparent and obvious as the best policies; and if this could be conveyed simply, perhaps strikingly, to the public, one part of the problem would be solved. Then, as to execution: that was what the charts he was obliging me—and others— to carry around were about. It was an agreeable exercise for him just as the other—the why of it all—was less agreeable because it was elusive. He liked to finger those papers, make marks on them, add and subtract, let his imagination run to what they meant for getting things done. He saw in them the translation of policies into reality. He saw people getting from government what they had a right to expect.

I have read in some historians' accounts of Roosevelt's methodology that he did not like charts and designs of this sort. They assume this, I suppose, from a previous conclusion that he was an inefficient administrator. That, I find, is almost universally believed. It is certainly not true that he disliked paper representations of different arrangements. He pored over them with unflagging interest. As to his administrative skills, I should object that he was the first president to meet problems of such scope and volume as to choke government almost into paralysis. Something had to be done. It was better to have done it experimentally than to have clamped another complex organization on the government before the issues were really clarified and it was known what would succeed.

His reluctance to come to the point of acting, of really reorganizing, was partly his new concern for the whys, which carried with it a certain feeling that machinery was less important than it had once seemed to him and so not worth the serious controversies certain to follow from drastic change. Partly, however, it was the feeling that if he got it just right, after long experimentation, the sense of rightness would stifle any trouble the vested interests might start. He had an enormous respect for rightness; and he did not yet have the feeling that he could see it. So he continued to speculate, to weigh the functions and to assess the opposition.

But the government grew; it had to. At the moment new agencies were simply being added as new jobs were taken on. The list of "alphabetical" agencies was becoming formidable. It was clear that, not too distantly, a time would come for recasting; but that would be when the emergencies had been overcome.

There were moments in working with him when the feeling of centrality was very strong. There seemed at such times to be a shaping going on. Moreover, the purposes seemed suddenly to become clear. It was possible to visualize a unified nation, its parts working cooperatively for agreed ends. When that had been accomplished, the divisive forces would be weakened, special interests would be sunk in larger ones, and a whole people could be thought of as going forward into a better future. That there were not many such moments, however, must be admitted.

For the most part Roosevelt was struggling to subdue those divisive forces and to establish areas of agreement. And in the midst of such efforts there were not many opportunities for speculation or even for assessment of progress. What there were for me came when I had some special reason to feel his conviction that we were an energetic and resourceful people, capable of anything. I had the same feeling sometimes when I talked with Jerome Frank, with Hopkins, or with La Follette. There were not many others—or if there were I did not know them. Wallace, who had once been one of us, was now a little difficult. The pressures on him were formidable; and he was giving in to them more than his mind approved. His struggle with himself was painful and tragic. Harold Ickes was lost in a vast administrative complex, happily lost, and not questioning the outcome. But my three best friends were never lost; they never would be. On the American destiny and the means for realizing it they were always clear. It is a great satisfaction to recall how, each in his own way, they contributed something to what, looked back on, would be recognized as a really creative time.

☆ | CHAPTER 8 | ☆

Communicator

W HEN I RECALL the many speeches I made and articles I wrote during the next few years, I must conclude that something important seemed to depend on my educational efforts. Of course, I was needled by persistently waspish opponents; also, my notoriety furnished a ready audience. Partly, I spoke and wrote in self-defense, perhaps, but more, I think, because of my belief that changes had to be made and that progressives should keep on saying so; at any rate, I did undertake to defend the new regime.

On the whole it seems to me not to have been done too badly. Wallace was doing his part too, but had different audiences. At the moment mine was a larger one. He more and more devoted himself to a way out of agriculture's difficulties. His *America Must Choose*, to be published by the Foreign Policy Association in 1934, was the culmination of an effort begun in a series of speeches in 1933. Should we be isolationist or a cooperating part of the world? America never did choose, really, and Wallace, by making an exposition of the dilemma, did not choose either. We were making adjustment in the agricultural program to domestic requirements for farm products; but it would always be painful and very difficult politically. Farmers thought there must be a foreign market. Wallace was unhappy; but he was also realistic. Cooperation among nations would have to wait, but it was not to be given up permanently.

Some of my articles and speeches had to do with agriculture; but more of them were about the whole New Deal. Perhaps I thought that if I kept on presenting a logical version of our efforts they would gradually become logical. Actually there was still much confusion and warping toward the version of our mandate preferred by those who were in charge of operations. My exposition drew protests from Johnson, Peek, Morgenthau, and others as I went on; but none from Roosevelt. I concluded that he was not displeased; and as long as that was so, I saw no reason for not persisting. Occasionally he let me know that I was being useful.

A certain number of the public addresses and articles were gathered together and published a year later as a book.[1] As I look through them now, they rate good marks for effort. Of course, I may be inclined to regard the figure of myself as an active public figure with some tolerance; but I can see well enough at a distance that what I was trying to do, both for myself and the program, was impossible. I knew well enough that an opposition was gathering; but I saw no alternative to proceeding with all flags flying. We might not survive the broadsides being prepared for us, but there would have been a hot engagement.

My addresses must have been hard to listen to, and my articles hard to read. They seem now to have been relentlessly academic; but there was a very general wish to know what all the activity in Washington was about. This need was not satisfied by the fireside chats or anything else Roosevelt said. He was asking for confidence and appealing for trust in his leadership, as it was his duty to do, but he was not explaining things in detail or even how they fitted together; nor was he dwelling on what was to come. If he had, it would have limited his freedom of action. Also his enemies would have been forewarned and able to check him more effectively. What I said, or what Wallace said, did not commit him, but did suggest a certain confidence that all was not improvisation.

I did not hesitate to point out implications and possibilities, to show how necessary it was that, in administration, strict public purposes should be adhered to, and to indicate that responsibilities and disciplines must be accepted by everyone involved. It was this last—what must be given up to get what was wanted—that was most impolitic. Neither Roosevelt nor anyone else in the administration was tough enough about this.

This tendency, perhaps naturally, grew more marked, but the second fireside chat on May 7 was somewhat more descriptive. Employment

---

[1] *The Battle for Democracy* (New York: Columbia University Press, 1934).

was being given to young men in the Civilian Conservation Corps. The Tennessee Valley Authority was being set up, and mortgage burdens for farmers and homeowners were being relieved. Public works were being planned to give more employment, farmers' incomes were being raised; for workers there was collective bargaining and shorter hours of work. He explained why all this was necessary and went on to say:

We cannot ballyhoo ourselves back to prosperity. I am going to be honest at all times with the people of this country. I do not want the people of the country to take the foolish course of letting this improvement come back on another speculative wave. I do not want the people to believe that because of unjustified optimism we can resume the ruinous practice of increasing our crop output and our factory output in the hope that a kind Providence will find buyers at high prices. Such a course may bring us immediate and false prosperity but it will be the kind of prosperity that will lead us into another tailspin.

There was some discussion about the inclusion of this passage. It was an unpleasant reminder of a need for restraints. He knew well enough that farmers and businessmen were not persuaded that they—each of them—would have to accept discipline. When they did recognize the general need, they hoped that in practice the limitations would constrict someone else. Chiselers were soon to become a serious problem, one foreshadowed even then. In the end it was they who broke up NRA and nearly ruined AAA. Resistance to rules would grow, and ways would have to be sought for control, because regulations would not be respected.

The larger corporations would shape things in their own favor; and the farmers—although in agriculture we had a better mechanism for merging individual interests in the interest of the whole—would always be restless, and sometimes rebellious, under restriction. NRA would simply have resulted in a corporative state if it had gone on in the Johnson way; and agriculture would never have reached an adjustment of production to consumption except for a series of unexpectable circumstances—droughts which reduced production in 1934 and 1936, and ultimately the vast demands of war.

Roosevelt would indeed become softer as the emergency grew less grave and as resistance rose. He hesitated because he judged that he could not afford further political risks. Then too he was always finding it necessary to give something to get something more important. And in these circumstances it was difficult to insist on fixed objectives. As

136

fall came on, he wanted—he had to have—majority acceptance of his leadership. This would yield a power which could be brought to bear on those who were reluctant to cooperate. He was trying to enlarge his popular support and still hopeful that recovery might be substantial before winter. In a statement at the time of signing the National Industrial Recovery Act (on June 17) he had felt able to state the position of the government in hard terms. The act, he said, after explaining its purpose, "is a challenge to administration."

We are relaxing some of the safeguards of the anti-trust laws. The public must be protected against the abuses that led to their enactment, and to this end, we are putting in place of old principles of unchecked competition some new government controls. They must, above all, be impartial and just. Their purpose is to free business, not to shackle it; and no man who stands on the constructive, forward-looking side of his industry has anything to fear from them. To such men the opportunities for individual initiative will open more amply than ever. Let me make it clear, however, that the anti-trust laws still stand firmly against monopolies that restrain trade and price fixing which allows inordinate profits or unfairly high prices.

This statement was useful as a text; but in my expositions I said repeatedly that respect for the rules was necessary since I felt so strongly that this was where the dangers were. The blanket codes for industry and the reemployment agreement employers were being asked to sign would almost certainly neglect the necessary controls. They meant to compete in any way that would lead to lower costs at consumers' and workers' expense. On the other hand, prices ought not to protect the highest-cost businesses in any industry. To do so would be to encourage inefficiency and to allow "inordinate profits" for the efficient units. "Fair competition" was a difficult concept to define and even harder to enforce.

In general, NRA was dealing with the sector of the economy where prices ought to be kept low, just as AAA was dealing with the sector where they ought to be raised. But this was not a uniform rule; and it would require skill and determination to guide the self-government movement toward balance. The industrialists wanted the codes; but unless a firm and steady governmental pressure was exercised, the melee of code-making would end by allowing the monopolizers to fix prices without restriction. The effect would be just the reverse of what had been intended.

This process did begin, and at once. In arguing as persistently as I could against the reemployment agreement and against the weakened codes I was acting for Wallace as a member of the Industrial Recovery Board; our opposition was effective, and ultimately Johnson—embarrassed, and not wanting criticism—persuaded Roosevelt to stop our meetings. The board would then be merged in the National Emergency Council, successor to the Executive Council, but its usefulness in requiring Johnson to process the codes more in accord with the public interest was ended abruptly.[2]

In agriculture the result of a similar attempt to check exploitive policies was that processors got exemptions from the restrictions of the anti-trust laws in return for mere promises to raise farmers' prices. A few of us put up a better fight than did the public representatives in NRA; but the conclusion was much the same. Those who objected were handicapped because insistence on public regulation could be made to seem, unlikely as such a contention was, to be against the farmers' interests. This struggle was a bitter one; and it led finally to a series of embarrassments for the administration, quite unnecessary if we could have persuaded Roosevelt to enforce the rules he had at first laid down.

It was in this struggle, and its corollary ones—including those for food and drug reform, liquor control, conservation, and so on—that I earned my reputation as a troublemaker. I doubt if I ever hoped for a whole victory; but I certainly hoped for more than I got.

Having devoted assistants was one compensation. By fall, in spite of the attacks coming, it seemed, from everywhere at once, I had reason to be thankful for the support of my associates. Two of these, Russell Lord and John R. Fleming, were especially helpful. I ought also to say that Milton Eisenhower, as director of information for the department, put at our disposal the resources of his whole division. He had

[2] This merging would occur on December 19, 1933. The action appeared to include NRA along with other agencies in the National Emergency Council. Actually the Special Industrial Recovery Board had not been meeting or performing supervisory functions for some months. A note explains this in the *Public Papers* but is not very revealing: "The Act itself did not set up any specified form of administration. It authorized and directed the President to designate such officers and employees as might be necessary . . . The functions of the Special Industrial Recovery Board were never very clearly defined and in the course of time the actual day-by-day administration centered more and more in the Administrator and the President." That was certainly the case; but the reason for it was that the administrator felt so strongly the board's critical attitudes; and because the president chose to support him rather than the board. He was in a hurry to complete the code-making. To protesters he said that when this was done we could go back and revise the codes.

been director under Wallace's Republican predecessor, and might have been expected to look rather sourly on the Democratic regime. Actually, like many other Republicans in the department, he had been irked by the restraints of past years and willingly lent his experience and talents to our cause. He and his assistants ran some risks in doing this; they might well have been punished for their cooperation if the Republicans had won a national election at any time soon and had reverted to the old policies. Neither Wallace nor I could have conducted the campaign of the next few years without their cooperation. A little later I had the help of John Franklin Carter (better known as Jay Franklin), whose ability as an expositor I have seldom seen equaled.

One effect of my many arguments, public appearances, and articles was curious. Personal attacks on me multiplied. I was said to be an unreliable fellow who wanted to destroy the values of American life. This rose to a kind of climax, later, when the *New York Herald Tribune* published a lead editorial with the caption "Rex the Red." But this was only a more conspicuous example. In hundreds of newspapers daily, the stereotype was being fixed. The *Herald Tribune*, the *Chicago Tribune*, and of course, the Hearst press gave the lead. The smaller newspapers followed. This daily devotion of paper and printer's ink to my character and personality made me better—if not favorably—known than any of the cabinet members. My counterthrusts did something to disrupt and distort the stereotype; and much of the indignation that poured out daily complained of my perverse behavior. I did not speak or act as I was supposed to do. Therefore I was dishonest—and all the more dangerous because I dissembled.

There were public men all around who never wrote a word of what they said. I made an adaptation of the method Roosevelt used, except that I reversed it. I wrote the drafts myself. After I had done my best with them, my collaborators checked my facts, questioned my conclusions, and suggested more effective illustrations.

Presently what seemed a providential opportunity offered itself. It would, if it succeeded, allow me to penetrate the opposition. Before accepting it I talked about it with Wallace and with Roosevelt, who was amused by the possibilities. We were talking across his desk in the executive office. I had again been asked to share his office luncheon. It could be taken as a kind of notice, as I recognized, to those who were telling him that I was either dangerous or a political liability. It was, as he said, just as well, in all the maneuvering he had to do, that there should be kept in mind his affiliation with the progressives I was coming more and more to represent. This representation was involuntary; it was haltingly assumed on my part, and I knew very little about its possibilities. Still, I was learning.

It had been my duty, assigned long before inauguration, to gather support from these progressives. He needed it if the pressures from the reactionaries were to be resisted. For a president can only cautiously abandon neutrality between fixed opinions on great issues. He must be sure, as he moves from the center, that what he is risking is worth what he is gaining. This was a lesson he had learned, in his day, from Wilson, who had longed for more unity and discipline among progressives and all too often not found it; indeed his leadership had never been acknowledged. Now his first Democratic successor was feeling the same lack.

I was a convenient ambassador. Somehow I had been so provocative as to become a symbol, and symbols are not only targets but may be rallying points. Although the old-line Democrats represented by Garner, Byrd, Robinson, Harrison, Rainey, and others of their sort were annoyed by the newcomers, and me in particular, it was quite otherwise with Wagner, La Follette, Johnson, Cutting, Wheeler, Norris, and Black; also a few governors like Floyd Olson in Minnesota and Philip La Follette in Wisconsin. The conservationists had accepted me as a partner; the group around Harry Hopkins were allies too; there were many people out in the countryside needing help, and no one else in the department had any interest in them. I even had some support on the other side—Gerard Swope, Henry I. Harriman, and a few more of the business leaders did not regard me as hopeless. We had worked together on NRA. There were many among the leaders of organized labor who regarded me as a friend. For Roosevelt it was useful to have me doing what I could to keep together these largely maverick, but nevertheless potentially like-minded, individuals and groups. Their cause did center in him. Their support could save him from having to make an unwelcome compromise.

As this idea was explored, I detailed the reasons why I was an unlikely catalyst. Roosevelt said these things were not matters of choice; they happened to a person, or they did not happen to him. It is true, he went on, that your enemies have set you up, but it would be foolish not to take advantage of their labors.

Then I told him the opportunity that had been offered me. It tickled him. And, I had to admit, it *was* very pat—very pat indeed—if it could be worked. John Fleming had begun it. He had met, somewhere, Monte Bourjailly of the King Features syndicate; and Bourjailly had said to him, in effect: this fellow Tugwell has got to be so notorious that maybe we could use a column written by him. At any rate, John brought the idea to me, and of course the opportunity was irresistible. Could it be that we could thus infiltrate the enemy? Would the newspapers allow their sense of news to overcome their fixed idea that I was an enemy? It seemed unlikely, but it just might work.

CHAPTER 9

New Deal Expositor

THE CATALYTIC JOB was useful even if it never developed into anything significant. Roosevelt often departed from progressive policies to please the conservatives. It was his responsibility to decide when compromise was necessary; but the progressives tended to be inflexible critics. They were, in fact, in a continual state of protest: too much was being conceded to the southern reactionaries; there was too much stress in the western states on building up regular Democratic organizations at the expense of their own. They might have Republican origins, but they had supported the Roosevelt candidacy. He owed them more than he was willing to pay. They had other grievances: relief was too meager; assistance, through RFC, to banks and businesses, was too generous; NRA was fostering monopolies. All these and other annoyances were repeated over and over whenever they got together. I shared them. I always tended to suspect compromise. Moreover I thought Roosevelt was strengthening his opposition dangerously; but it was his responsibility to decide about both practicality and timing. He wanted this concession from the whole group; and he expected me to do what I could to get it.

He did not ask them to accept passively all his decisions. Besides, things often did not go their way because they had not won sufficient backing. The conservatives were stronger—far stronger—in the Congress; and they had almost a monopoly of the press. He judged that it would take a long time to overcome the effects of agricultural and industrial disaster. If AAA and NRA, together with other agencies, such

as the Home Owners Loan Corporation and the Farm Credit Administration, were not quickly effective, the failure would make other projects
impossible. He wanted to commit businessmen to NRA, to show the
southerners how much they had to gain from AAA, and to allow the
effects of hunger, cold, and the fear of dispossession to fade. He had told
me once in Albany that he might end his administration without a
Democratic party but with a progressive one. It had to have a majority,
however, whatever its name. It was that majority he was after.

He did not demand that the progressives stop calling for the actions
they believed in; but he thought they ought to acknowledge that his
aims were the same as theirs. He wanted their support even if it sometimes came hard. When he did have to make compromises he would
like less criticism from them than he was getting; and he was getting a
good deal. It seemed to him that they ought to understand even when
they did not approve.

There was nothing formal about this. It was not even anything new.
I was friendly, at least, and in many cases something more, with most
of this group. I was somewhat alien among them, in a way, because
they were elected politicians and I was not. Still, the president had won
a notable political victory and his helpers were given credit for participation—too much credit, but the misapprehension could be useful.
Old progressives—Johnson, Wheeler, Wagner, Norris, Black, Nye, and
others like them—were not resentful about "upstarts" as the more regular
party politicians were. Bob La Follette, Ned Costigan, Bronson Cutting,
and Homer Bone were closer and I saw them often. These were not
silent men; they were continuously talking and writing. So they had
influence.

I naturally saw less of the older legislators; but still I saw a good
deal of them. Bronson Cutting presently quarreled with Roosevelt, and
a little later he was killed in an airplane crash. The elder statesman of
our political faith were Burton Wheeler, who had been the first La
Follette's running mate as a Progressive in 1924; Hiram Johnson, who
had been a running mate of Theodore Roosevelt in 1912 and who had
a long record of progressivism in California; and Senator George Norris
of Nebraska. Johnson and Wheeler were especially annoyed because,
in their view, years and services entitled them to much more consideration than they were getting. They looked with suspicion on Farley's
political activities, and it was true that patronage in their states more
often went to regular Democrats than to their followers. Sometimes
it went to their enemies. Roosevelt interfered when he could, and on

great political occasions made a point of honoring them in spite of Farley's objections. But they harbored a latent jealousy and were not easy cooperators. Still, they were very kind to me.

Some others had to be dealt with in different ways. Charles McNary, the Republican leader in the Senate, came from Oregon, and so had progressive leanings and was willing to forget his partisanship when forgetting seemed called for. He was the minority Senate strategist and counseled his colleagues that times were not propitious for unreasoning opposition. He had always favored farm relief and had been the senior author of the successive McNary-Haugen bills; but further than that, when he was consulted, he acted far more as a progressive than as a Republican. He was, in fact, an unacknowledged ally.

Then there was Long of Louisiana. He became more and more raucous and bitter. He was at the height of his notoriety and was in process of moving from his regional base onto the national scene. The doctrine he preached was what some newsman called "boondocks radicalism." It had traces in it of all the demagogic appeals in American history. He would betray any cause if it suited him; his machine was corrupt, and his objective was not really the one he presented so stridently. In the depression atmosphere, when so many families were suffering and when recovery seemed endlessly deferred, his appeal was heard eagerly, just as Milo Reno's and Father Coughlin's were. He could not be ignored any more than the others could; and he had a large following. Roosevelt, even before inauguration, had asked me to see what I could do with him, and for a while I tried. I saw him a number of times in the bizarre circumstances he favored; but I had little luck. He could not be argued with or conciliated. He would not work with anyone; he did not even listen. He had a jargon suited to his supporters, but it was impossible to translate it into rational terms. He meant to carry his bid for power to disgruntled masses, and there was every likelihood that he might succeed in creating such a disturbance as would be at least embarrassing. Where it all might have ended if he had not been assassinated it is hard to say. Returning prosperity would probably have damped down his appeal; but Roosevelt never minimized his effect while he lived.

Since my notoriety resulted in opening so many opportunities, I gave my best to the weekly syndicated articles. These went on until newspaper publishers after six months simply stopped using them. I never had more than twenty papers, and these gradually dropped my column. So the amusing possibilities the effort seemed to hold did not develop. When my list narrowed down to a half-dozen there was nothing to do but quit. My notoriety could not outweigh my predilection for academic discourse, I suppose; but naturally I preferred to think that publishers' distaste for the New Deal was to blame.

1933 is usually thought and spoken of as a year when reformers were on the offensive with a popular leader and with a compliant Congress. The truth is, however, that those who wanted changes were few; moreover, they were divided between those who wanted the deferred reforms of the old progressivism and those who felt that a more unified and collectivist nation had become necessary. For myself, I would like to have seen public ownership of banking, insurance, power, transportation, and communications, together with extensive equalizing welfare measures. If Roosevelt had not entered on his first term with a depression to fight, and therefore with recovery as his first objective, some part of such a program might have been accomplished in his honeymoon period. Only a few of my progressive friends felt that the time had come for these measures. La Follette, Costigan, and Cutting did; and, under other circumstances, the older men such as Wagner and Johnson would doubtless have approved. As things were, nothing really remedial would get done.

A certain support for public ownership of utilities had appeared from time to time in progressive campaigns. But we were tormented, when it came to that, by the Brandeis dogmas. Someone described the situation as a contest between individualism and collectivism, and that was fairly accurate. Brandeis and Frankfurter had old connections with Roosevelt; and their lieutenants, Corcoran and Cohen, regarded me as a dangerous influence. They would be, from about this time, about as unhappy about me as the business interests were.

I explained to Roosevelt how strong this revulsion had grown, and even this early I warned him that he was losing those who ought to be singleminded in his support. He minimized the danger. He could claim that both groups were on his side; but he underestimated the devotion of the old gentleman on the Supreme Court to the breaking up of big business. Brandeis was a tireless opponent, and his followers were not averse to creating a picturesque Tugwell who looked a good deal like the one assiduously worked up by Mark Sullivan, Frank Kent, Carlyle Bargeron, and certain of the others among the columnists and Washington correspondents in response to their publishers' demands. Roosevelt would find out about Brandeis when the court got its first chance at NRA; but that demonstration of stubborn traditionalism would not happen until 1935.

Both Frank and I often tangled with the champions on the other side of this argument, from the old justice down to Corcoran and Cohen. We had NRA and AAA as examples of collective effort; and if these stood up in administration and gained public support, we would have something more than arguments on our side. Brandeis was in a strategic position; but it was not at all clear yet that he would prevail with his fellow justices. What we did not sufficiently appreciate was the possibility of a classic union between individualists and monopolists. It seemed to us that, in NRA especially, we were doing what Hamilton had counseled for the nation in its formative years—trying to bring the country's powerful industrial leaders to the support of the national interest. It seemed possible that with their participation we might create a collective economy.

It will be hard for anyone in the future to explain why NRA failed, why it was rejected by the court, and especially why Roosevelt accepted the decision as final and made no attempt to amend the law and go on. The gradual growth of trade associations seemed to have prepared for the giving up of the antiquated trust-busting policy. Self-government for industry had seemed reasonable enough if done under public auspices. Nevertheless it would be abandoned. Among the reasons for failure, the most important was certainly the turning away from careful code-making and the blanketing-in of numerous industries, ill prepared and sometimes unsuitable. What was worst, however, was that so many businessmen took advantage of their new privileges and gave nothing in return.

Another reason for failure was that NRA was quite unsuited for the labor reforms it was required to effect. These ought to have been made separately under such an act as was later passed regulating hours, fixing minimum wages, abolishing child labor, and so on. What was called for was concentration of all Roosevelt's prestige and Johnson's administrative efforts on the crucial issue of government-industry relations within a concept of partnership. Instead, in return for concessions in what really were extraneous, if desirable, gains to labor, the government's senior partnership was bartered away. The codes became little more than charters for escape from regulation; and innumerable small businesses chafed under the legalized domination of their more powerful competitors.

At the end, only those who had been able to use it quite improperly would be sorry to see the finsh of NRA. The public would lose nothing by its abolition in its final condition—except, that is, the possibility of its being rehabilitated. AAA would survive rejection and, after its re-writing as a conservation measure, go on into a far more useful future. But the task of subduing the now recovered and aggressive big business-men and establishing a genuine integration was an undertaking Roose-velt would not assume.

NRA, as well as the marketing agreements of AAA, were, it will be understood, substitutes for public ownership; and I believed that public ownership would be inevitable if they did not succeed. I myself would like to have seen all the great industries brought under codes and, at least for the moment, the smaller industries neglected. The progressives were uncertain what they preferred; and there was never any clear agreement even on a compromise program. Among the older progressives, resentment boiled up; and before long Wheeler and John-son were opposing the president on everything. The younger men were dissatisfied with the slowness of reform as well as with the inadequacy of welfare measures; and they were alienated by codes allowing favors to business but requiring no sacrifice in return. Obviously the senior partnership of the government, spoken of when the act was being pro-posed, had been dropped. Punishing friends and rewarding enemies was all very well, they said, if it did not involve adopting the enemies' policies. When the first approved codes allowed price fixing and the allocation of markets, the progressives protested. When Roosevelt told them that after the code-making was done he would turn to revisions, they were skeptical.

Roosevelt, however, was blamed and not me. I was regarded as being badly treated too. From the first they had been suspicious of NRA, and now they felt that their suspicions were thoroughly justified. They felt so strongly, however, that collective bargaining and fair labor practices were overdue that they were inclined to think NRA justified for this reason alone. On August 5, Senator Wagner himself assumed the chairmanship of the first National Labor Board, created by executive order under the NRA act. That this resulted from the many disputes arising under the reemployment agreement is the information con-veyed to posterity in Roosevelt's *Public Papers*. Actually it was made necessary because employers were refusing to comply. There was trouble about this in many places, but especially in the South. Wagner, of all the progressives, was the most amenable, the most selfless, and the most willing to assume burdens. This labor assignment was a thankless task for a senator. Actually the Labor Board was responsible for businessmen's hostility; but Roosevelt spoke approvingly of it and when industries made concessions he was inclined to approve codes which for other reasons ought to have been rejected.

I tried loyally enough to defend what was being done. True, some of the new administrators and counselors considered my explanations of their work to be exposés rather than defenses, and sometimes I heard from them directly or indirectly. Especially Peek and Johnson, with whom I most often disagreed publicly, regarded me as a nuisance. They were, however, steaming ahead on their own courses; Johnson, by early fall, was causing tremendous furor with his reemployment agreement, and Peek was deep in dealings with the processors. Both seemed to have Roosevelt's support. They had failed to note that he often seemed to be approving inconsistent policies at the same time, and that resolution would come when it became clear to him which was failing and which succeeding.

My speech-making that summer had one pleasant setting. I was invited as a local celebrity to address the Federation of Bar Associations of Western New York. If I had wanted to be cynical I should have remarked the number of prominent citizens who had suddenly discovered that they were old family friends, and the number of local politicians who were ready to recognize my possible usefulness. I was happy that one of my heroes, the liberal and learned Cuthbert W. Pound, who was then chief judge of the New York State Court of Appeals, and who would have graced the Supreme Court itself, appeared as my sponsor at the meeting on the campus of the University of Rochester. I had had occasion to study Judge Pound's opinions, and it pleased me to recall his consideration in a correspondence when I had been much younger.

There was no doubt that there was a hearing to be had from the country. In spite of detraction, there was genuine and widespread interest. And in the newspaper fraternity there was understanding, even sympathy. Ernest Lindley was always wise, informed, and helpful. His *New York Herald Tribune* was editorially hostile; but he had known Roosevelt even in Albany. His paper's reports from Washington made a running account of the first year's events, much more so, for instance, than those of the more voluminous *New York Times*. This, of course, was because Lindley was trusted by us. To a lesser extent, perhaps, Richard Wilson of the *Des Moines Register* was kept fully informed. His relations with Wallace were close, as would be expected, since they were fellow Iowans; and Alfred Stedman and Roy Hendrickson, midwesterners, seemed sometimes to know more about our operations than we did ourselves; but of all the columnists, Raymond Clapper was the hardest-working and most careful. Heywood Broun belonged in New York rather than in Washington; but he visited us once in a while. He was in a special category—the dean—among commentators. Of all of them he was the only one who supported food and drug reform personally and in his writing. His advocacy was regarded as a kind of quixotic venture among his fellows, who were generally too sensible to share his risks.

The newspapermen in Washington seemed not to resent my syndicate venture. Indeed they gave me a good deal of advice about it. I had so much approval that I found myself in danger of revising my fixed opinion of reporters—that they were entirely unprincipled when it came to getting news. In early New Deal days they made no secret of their liking for the president. As a result, the stereotype being fixed by Mark Sullivan, Frank Kent, Henry L. Mencken, and other outright dissenters, who, of course, carried more weight, tended to escape and to take unexpected shapes. Actually, there was a good deal of sympathetic, even if bootlegged, support. I was pictured as at least interesting and colorful, at best a sincere crusader, at worst a mistaken but earnest reformer. The stereotype of an irresponsible radical became somewhat skewed.

The Washington Scene

IN 1933 WASHINGTON had not yet begun its manic modern expansion. The streets were not so crowded, there were slums but not bulging ones, the suburbs had not reached far out into the hills of Maryland and Virginia, and Alexandria and Georgetown still had much of the lazy antique character they were about to lose. The countryside, heavily wooded, with tangled underbrush and vines, could be reached in a few minutes. The light soils to the east and south had been exhausted by hundreds of years of corn and tobacco cropping, and much of it had gone back to woodland. It supported only a few impoverished farmers but, in Virginia, out toward the Blue Ridge, there were lush grasslands; and these extended up across Maryland. This was the horse country where wealthy estate-owners had their seats. A few of these shared the Roosevelt noblesse and joined in the New Deal activities. One of these was Mary Rumsey—a name prominent in the society of earlier generations. Another was Averell Harriman, her brother, who was later to have a long career in several administrations, and to be governor of New York. Mary Rumsey was active in NRA as consumers' counsel; her charm and energy went a long way to soften the sharp differences within that organization as the codes began to be shaped.

Harry Hopkins envied the life-style of the horsy set. He was born, he said, to be a country gentleman, lacking only the fortune needed to keep up the appurtenances. He spent a good deal of time with friends of this sort not only around Washington but on Long Island, in Florida, and in the West. He loved racing, could never resist a card game, and was able to abandon the problems on his desk with astonishing completeness since the whole load of hunger and cold in our paralyzed land had been laid on him. He and I shared many of our troubles and successes; and he was always trying to carry me off for weekends with his friends. Why, in spite of his ability to escape, he should have developed that disease of harassment, stomach ulcers, and in a dangerously aggravated form, I have never understood. I have thought since that he cannot have carried his responsibility as lightly as he seemed to do.

There was another place down in Virginia where Jerome Frank and I liked to go. It was not up to Harry's standard, but it pleased us better. This was Howe's small modernized farmhouse. More usually we were—or thought we were—tied to town. For a time during the fall we lived in a house on a street just off Massachusetts Avenue. Like so many Washington houses it had a livable garden, much used in the hot months. There were frequent gatherings there in the evening. On one especially warm evening, we entertained André Maurois, who was curious about our doings and, as his description afterward showed, our personalities. These mixed groups almost always included journalists of some category and people from various government agencies. Aubrey Williams, Corrington Gill, Leon Henderson, Howard Hunter, and others of Harry Hopkins' people, and Harry himself, were often there. Also various people from "up on the hill"—our progressive friends mostly. There was nothing secret about what we thought; and whatever we thought seemed to get itself into print, usually as authentic inside information.

Not enough has been said in the accounts of this time about the amenities of the city where we worked. It was, to begin with, curiously designed. Everyone knows this and gives L'Enfant credit; but commentators have neglected the unsuitability for modern uses of his system of avenues centering in circles. It illustrated the dangers of building frameworks for future cities whose size and uses are unknown. More than other American cities, however, it was protected from commercialism. The height of its buildings was limited, and in other ways growth had been forced into the L'Enfant scheme. That design would torment later planners who must accommodate several times the population and more than several times the street traffic; but in 1933 these problems had not yet become bothersome. It was a spacious and pleasant city with a southern flavor.

There were outdoor eating places in half a dozen converted country houses; but there were also hotels with outdoor terraces. Extravagant bonuses of landscape were added to luncheons on balconies over the wharf where the Chesapeake oyster and fish boats tied up, or when we took the few minutes required for the journey to Hains' Point where Bolling Field and the War College furnished the main items in the cross-river landscape. The Potomac grew on us. Here, below the falls, it merged with Chesapeake Bay. It was often muddy and was not really extensive enough to cool the city much, but walkers used its shores as though they were on country paths. At that time the system of parkways leading outward had not yet been built. There was only the Mount Vernon highway; but it was an example of things to come, a proud accomplishment of the Bureau of Public Roads.

One of my duties, until our solicitor found a way of relieving me, was signing the hundreds of contracts for road construction my predecessor had warned me about. This led to curiosity about standards for construction, methods of planning, and the establishment of priorities. Thomas McDonald, the chief of this bureau, was assiduous in educating me, and through me, Roosevelt. We supported McDonald and in doing so made some changes that could begin within sight. It was at this time that we began to think and plan not only for Washington's communications with the hinterland but for those of other cities as well. And we went some way toward changing the preoccupation of the state road departments with scattered roads and toward planning a system of national highways.

Like that of the forests, of resettlement, of the attack on erosion, and of the rebuilding of government properties, this duty relieved somewhat, because part of the job was close by, the feeling of detachment and remoteness, of never seeing the results of paperwork, so tormenting to higher-echelon officials. I always felt sorry for bureau chiefs who were so tied to their Washington desks. They propitiated legislators and wasted time with lobbyists, when what they wanted most was to be in the places where the real work was going on. When a research worker or a field administrator took up duty in Washington, his special interests had to be submerged in those of the whole organization.

W. W. Stockberger, our departmental personnel officer, had been a botanist and had thus given up a scientific career. And most of the bureau chiefs had made a similar hard choice. They sometimes retreated to their laboratories or to field stations where they could again get their hands on the satisfying tools of their trade; but they knew how unlikely it was that they would ever catch up. There were some, of course, who were born administrators. I tried to find them and in some cases succeeded. This was certainly true of Lee Strong, Knowles Ryerson, and Ferdinand Silcox. But, of course, McDonald was there both before and after me, shaping, through one presidency after another, and one Congress after another, the nation's highway policy.

My companionship in this capital summer included growing friendships within the department. I tried, as they knew, to understand the scientists' problems, and to further their work. I gradually learned their traditions and sought ways in our current pressures for economy to save what was essential in what they were doing. Most of them admitted that their organizations were inefficient. For one thing, they were scattered all over the country, an arrangement necessary when there was fieldwork to be done in various places. Citrus-fruit problems had to be studied in California, Florida, Texas, or Puerto Rico. The deserts had problems to be solved, and the short-grass country had under way range-management and dry-agriculture experiments of immense importance. So it went. But it did seem to me that not every bureau needed to maintain a national field organization; and I tried to reduce overhead and establish decentralized administration. I had in mind a departmental branch in each of the great natural regions; but this needed detailed examination and the help of those who had experience.

There was satisfaction in dealing with such matters so much in contrast with the more baffling ones of politics and policy. I never had any scruple about asking Roosevelt to see the people who were doing the real work. Gradually he acquired some knowledge of what was going on at Orlando in Florida, at Indio in California, at Mandan in North Dakota, and in the many other places where our people were at work. After that summer I heard very little from him about getting rid of research and not much about reducing our activities.

By late July, many of the preliminaries for the Civilian Conservation Corps had been cleared away and Camp No. 1 at Big Meadows, Virginia, was well into its operations. The early conception of the corps had been enlarged, and it had been settled, after much negotiating, that the Employment Service of the Labor Department would do the selecting, that the Army would manage the camps (calling in its reserve officers), and that the Forest Service (and to a lesser extent the other land agencies) would direct the actual work. In this summer, when things were just beginning, no one was very happy about the various compromises; but the scheme, however unsatisfactory, was in effect.

A joint committee was in charge to iron out difficulties; and Robert Fechner, a Boston labor leader, had undertaken to administer the whole. Because the corps was a special interest, and because he wanted to give it support, Roosevelt decided to visit, with appropriate publicity, Camp No. 1 as soon as it was in full operation. So on a pleasant day in August I found myself riding with Ickes to meet Roosevelt—who had come to nearby Harrisonburg by railway overnight from Hyde Park—at Big Meadows for a sort of dedication. There most of those who had been through the organizing struggles of the past months were gathered for lunch with the foresters and reserve officers. We found the president in high spirits. He elaborated a scheme for a multitude of little forests—town and county woodlands. He agreed that we ought to plan a scattering of lakes—little lakes at the heads of rivers and on small streams created by simple dams—where wildlife could find refuge and where recreation facilities could be provided for literally millions of people. It was pleasant to enlarge these themes. Ickes was especially elated. He saw the parks he cared so much about taking on new life. The Indian reservations too could benefit. Even General Malone, who was present, conceded that service in the camps might be good for his reserve officers. It was a day of bright sun, a cool breeze, and companionship in a job well begun. What we saw here made other accomplishments seem possible.

Louis Howe was bored by these fancies, as he called them; he was always bored by anything but politics, and he never enjoyed country scenes. He had managed at the cost of exhaustion to reach this rendezvous. He was a little weaker every day, a little thinner, and shorter of breath. But he insisted on staying close to Roosevelt and keeping others away. There was never a suggestion that his services were less wanted. It could not be denied that he made unnecessary complications whenever he undertook to interfere; but Roosevelt, at least, treated him with consideration. His position in the White House was still jealously maintained.

Farley was attending to politics vigorously; and Louis no longer supervised him so closely, although he occasionally asserted his generalship. By now, he seemed to have made up his mind about me, after having been so withdrawing until inauguration. He now recognized that I existed. I often consulted him, and in general tried to see that he knew what was going on. Sometimes he gave me a wintry smile, and once in a while expanded. He was feeling that the corps we were now visiting was more his creation than anyone else's; and he would not have missed this visit on any account. Somehow I found myself in the car with him and the president as we drove, after lunch, about the area to be improved. As we traveled, he remarked, as we passed some horses in a pasture, that he had always wanted to own a racehorse. The president joshed him about this. We all knew his weakness for the races and his complicated relations with bookmakers—he made his bets regularly, as Harry did, and did not do too badly. What the president said was that if he hadn't wasted so much on the horses in one way he might have been able to spend it in others—he might own a whole stable. Louis was indignant. He was ahead, he said, on his betting career, and anyway it was just as legitimate as gambling on stamps or naval prints —and a lot more exciting.

This ride was like others that summer and fall. Roosevelt talked of all the fine things to be done with the public-works funds, not only to change and revivify the land, but to improve the convenience and amenity of communities all over the country. He spoke, as he had before, of the penchant the Treasury architects had for making monuments of public buildings. He had persuaded an Atlanta contractor, L. W. Robert, to take charge of that work, and Robert knew, he said, what he had in mind. All the new buildings—post offices, customs buildings, and so on—must be modest and appropriate to the region. There was no reason why a post office should be on the town or city's most expensive property or why it should try to look like a state capitol. It ought to be suitable for the business it had to do and not necessarily on Main Street. I reminded him that some post offices were housed in buildings also used by other agencies. Many were shared by Forestry, Public Roads, Plant Quarantine, and the Weather Bureau. Still, he said, they might furnish an example. No skyscrapers, he specified, and space—a park—around each one. He thought it especially important that the architecture be regional. There ought not to be a single stereotyped federal building.

I have often wondered in later years what the country would have been like, after twelve years of Roosevelt, if it had not been for the wasted efforts of war. That predilection for construction and improvement might have done much more in the pattern of the CCC, the PWA, and the WPA. Even the abortive effort to resettle displaced farm families might have kept them from descending on the cities in future years. It is a useless speculation. We were in for deep troubles, troubles which in those days we thought we were averting.

Summer Excursions

Rooseveлt was diverted to foreign problems when domestic pressures eased a little in late summer. When he spoke of Europe's situation it was with misgiving. He had immense respect for German power. Italy, he thought, could not be a menace, but Germany could. And Hitler, as he was beginning, seemed likely to mobilize all the nation's resources. I told him something of the way my old teacher Simon Nelson Patten had viewed the German spirit before the First World War and how he had contrasted it with the British attitudes.

Patten had thought the Germans were making use of science, technology, and administrative advances, and were concentrating them for national purposes; the British, devoted to individualism and resistant to planning, were likely to lose strength, to dissipate it in competition with each other. This was reflected in their economic theories; and these were the ones we had adopted. Roosevelt thought there was something in it. The Germans had a genius for organization and the French and British were right to fear them.

This suggested one of our unresolved issues—whether he meant to move toward an integrated national economy or meant to favor traditional free enterprise. He seemed to be doing both, and the inconsistency promised embarrassment. The codes gave industries freedom from the anti-trust laws—only, of course, when fair standards had been agreed to—but it was a move toward integration. On the other hand, the RFC was resuscitating businesses of all the traditional kinds and followers of Brandeis were conspicuous in the new agencies.

I could only suppose he was being tentative and experimental. If NRA succeeded, integration would evolve; but from the first this seemed problematical, largely, I thought, because the codes were faulty. The principle of selectivity was being lost; the codes tended to be permissive; their so-called authorities were badly organized; and preparations for enforcement were being neglected.

The depression was refusing to disappear. Since recovery was obviously lagging, something more must be done. Unemployment must be further reduced, and debtors must be relieved of more burdens. In such circumstances, it was hard to argue for the slow and orderly reorganization of industry under the codes. Besides to Roosevelt, as to others, "cartel" was a provocative word; and it was being said that something very like the German cartels would result from the way things were going.

The truth was that since the National Industrial Recovery Act had become catch-all emergency legislation it was being used for various other purposes than industrial reorganization. Actually the emphasis was being placed on gains for labor: shorter hours; the elimination of child labor; and especially the legitimizing of collective bargaining. The codes had scant protection for consumers and none for scarce resources; but worst of all they had few of the provisions necessary for the integration they were intended to accomplish.

About the many public works projects there could be more satisfaction. There was that August day I have spoken of, for instance, when the president met us at the Blue Ridge camp. This was in Ickes' territory, being a Park Service project; but Wallace was there, and so were General Malone and Robert Fechner. The luncheon was served on a rough board table. Roosevelt sat at its head. Ickes was a little worried about the Army's participation, and he said afterward that the apple pie had been inferior. Perhaps it had been, but Ickes was critical of most enterprises run by others.

Looking at the photographs taken that day I am confirmed in the impression that it was a good day for Roosevelt. There were deepening lines in his face, but his smiles could more accurately be described as laughs. And why not? The way ahead was not yet clear, but there was action. The taking off the streets and out of the poolrooms of hundreds of thousands of young men was under way. The first of them were gathered around him at Camp No. 1. They were to have the experience of living and working in the forests and parks. They would be better men because of it; and the land would be better because of their contribution. He said he wished he could spend a couple of months there himself. In the background of the photograph, standing close about him, the boys of the camp, a couple of young army officers, and a forester or two were evidence of one hope becoming reality.

I was less satisfied on other such occasions. But they had their lessons too. The trouble with me was that I had got to feeling that arguments were being lost that I ought to have been more effective in arguing. Robert B. Smith in a column he called "The Daily Mirror of Washington" said at that time:

Professor Moley has been displaced by Professor Tugwell as the most discussed member of the brains trust . . . the spotlight is beating upon him as fiercely as it did upon Moley a brief season ago.

Some rather exaggerated stories of his influence are being written, but there seems to be little doubt that he has had much to do with the formulation of the recovery program in its newer aspects . . . Moreover, the Professor has an extraordinary talent for clear expression and is able to explain the New Deal more lucidly than any other member of the Administration, as he demonstrated in a recent magazine article.

I presume this was the kind of comment anyone would have liked to see. At any rate it was selected by the keepers of my papers to cheer me. The magazine article referred to was one I had written for the *New York Times Magazine* for July 16, 1933. It was called "The Ideas Behind the New Deal," and was mostly a defense of the wide powers transferred to the president in the emergency. One paragraph said:

We have just passed through several terrifying years. But these years did teach some lessons. Even the hard-boiled American industrialists and bankers are for the moment repentant. They have begun to ask anxiously for direction. Consider how hardily our businessmen . . . insisted on walking into the old dilemma of an exhausted purchasing power; consider how completely they then commanded our common fortune; consider how, in ungoverned allegiance to the eighteenth century dogma of free competition, they nearly wrecked us; and possibly you will find cause to wonder at industry's sudden change of heart.

I had gone on to contend that the beginning was good even if it did involve two startling innovations: the granting to the president of emergency powers, and the recognition in NRA that concentrations in industry could be legalized and controlled. I spoke of "an epochal passage of the powers from the legislative to the executive," and the recognition that in modern society, free competition led directly to depression. "In the third decade of the twentieth century we are resolved to recognize openly that competition in most of its forms is wasteful and costly." But further than this, "we now say that larger combination as a principle should prevail under new conditions, conditions which assure just distribution of the wealth they develop." This was, of course, the senior-partner doctrine. I was alone just then in openly making the case for integration under government auspices and saying just as openly what the policy required in the way of discipline. Obviously I still hoped Roosevelt would commit himself to policies neither Peek nor Johnson would implement if they could avoid it.

This was an issue of immense consequence. On it depended the fitting into democratic forms of the agreements and codes; otherwise they would be intolerable. But this was only one of several such issues I had become involved in and felt I must be candid about.

We had all of us been working at high tension for some months now, Moley and I for many months. We had been the only reliance for odd jobs in the interval between election and inauguration. Moley was gone now to a new and less demanding employment. But I had had no relief and was obviously tired. Roosevelt noticed it and suggested that I get away from Washington. "Go and see what's happening," he said, "see what they think of us. See what our people are doing. We've been talking about a lot of interesting things, but we don't see much of them."

"Presently I will," I said. "Hay fever will arrive toward the end of the month. I can get away from it out west."

"Good," he said. "Meanwhile, we'll have a really long weekend and never mention business."

So on a hot Friday afternoon we set out for Quantico, where the *Sequoia* was docked. The president came down to the garden door in his wheelchair; he was so gay that even wispy Louis Howe caught the mood and produced a quip or two. Missy, chic and shining, whispered to me as we stood on one side while Roosevelt was hoisted into the car, "How does he do it? We had a simply awful day. But anyway we're not taking any papers."

The fountain was playing and the trees were limp in the afternoon heat; but as we went down the Mount Vernon highway in the open car we stirred up a travel-breeze. Roosevelt spoke of the airport as we passed. "Some pilot is going to overshoot that old field," he said, "and I don't want it on my conscience." There would be a new airport and I knew where it would be. He pointed out the place and went on for some time talking about dredging for fill and the best positioning of runways. He liked the riverside site because the approaches would be free of interference.

We spoke then of a larger frame for Washington's growth. There ought, he said, to be an outerbelt, ten or fifteen miles from the White House—a great circling parkway. From there the avenues could simply extend inward to connect with existing ones. The departments could be grouped along this parkway, so that their communications would be easy. Agriculture and Interior could be near or adjoining the Beltsville center out in Prince George's County, in Maryland. War and Navy could be on the level ground down close to Mount Vernon. "And," I said, "there ought to be a country White House up on the high ground over the falls of the Potomac." This kind of talk did not come under the head of business. Louis was not interested; but Missy was.

"Is any other head of government anywhere tied to the center of a capital?" she asked. The answer, of course, was no.

It was play, just as the multitude of little forests and lakes was play; but only half-play. Because this president believed that in all the maze of political maneuvering he could find the resources and talent to carry out physical reconstruction of many sorts and in many places. He thought—he always had thought—that people were better when they were not only well fed and secure against illness and old age but also when they had country sights to see and natural interests to pursue. He had never had to do any work with his hands, but he had been strenuous enough as a young man. He still missed it now that he was a prisoner—a prisoner both of his crippling and of the White House. He was nevertheless cheerful, as he had been at Albany in the old governor's mansion; but although he had learned to live in confinement, he had devised many ways to escape. He could see more in an hour's drive than anyone I had ever known. He noted crops, woodlands, streams and livestock. To ride with him was to be deluged with talk, half-practical, half-fanciful. He was always speaking of the vast work to be done. There were airports, parks, playgrounds, dams, post offices, schools to be built—and houses. We must build better houses for the slum people—both city and country. We must build millions of them— and he had notions about ways and means. But the rural housing was just as bad. We must have a program to improve it.

There was very little ceremony at Quantico. The marines were used to the presidential passage by now. But there was a smile for the guards, a handshake for a few officers; and soon we were settled on the after-deck of the *Sequoia*.

I had one reservation about these naval outings. The food was terrible. In fact the food was pretty awful wherever the Roosevelts were, except at Hyde Park, where his mother's management prevailed. This may have been because it was a hearty family and consequently not very discriminating; but maybe, also, because Eleanor was not interested. This might well go back to her strangeness in kitchens and to her seldom having had a home of her own even after marriage. The White House was bad enough in this respect, but the *Sequoia* had a Filipino mess crew, navy-style, and the cook seemed not to know how to prepare food without frying it. I mention this because of what happened the next day.

That night we anchored and sat on deck, the president reminiscing with Louis about navy experiences. Next day we landed at Easton, and from ten until four in the afternoon visited some half-dozen historic Eastern Shore country houses. I cannot recall what houses they were; but all of them were representative of plantation life in another century. It gave Roosevelt a chance to display his amazing knowledge of architectural detail and to point out the differences between this country and the Hudson valley. It was very hot; and when we passed through a small town on our way back to Easton, he told our driver to stop in front of a drug store. He asked me to go in and see if they would bring out ice-cream sodas. I asked the proprietor if he could scare up something for the president of the United States and his party. He would have been incredulous if it had not been for the motorcycle police; I rather expected a retort such as someone in the Food and Drug Administration had given Mrs. Roosevelt when she had called to ask about something. She had said, "This is Mrs. Roosevelt," and in a flash was answered, "And this is the King of Siam. What can I do for you?" But the druggist did produce chocolate ice-cream sodas for everyone, not without some fluttering and delay, but competently. Naturally most of the nearby population was gathered around before they were consumed. The president's car was being crowded, something the Secret Service men did not like too well but often had to put up with on such trips; and besides, harm was to be looked for at scheduled places, not in a Maryland village chosen at random for a stop.

Roosevelt liked his brimming ice-cream soda and insisted on having another. We went on our way then, and got back to the *Sequoia* in good time. We settled down on deck again after showers. On the table within easy reach of the presidential hand was a large silver bowl of dark-red cherries, just from the refrigerator, frosted, irresistible. Roosevelt ate a good share of the bowlful. Then, of course, we had a greasy dinner.

Next morning when I came on deck, only Missy was there, looking tired and white. "How do *you* feel?" she asked.

"As good as could be expected," I said. She managed a smile; she knew my reservations about the Roosevelt food.

"Well," she said, "the president was the sickest man you ever saw last night—he's still sick. It frightened me half to death when McDuffie called me—and no doctor along. I really thought he had been poisoned; but then I remembered the chocolate sodas and the cherries . . ."

"And the dinner," I put in.

"Anyway," she said, "that's what it was. But don't expect to see him today." Nevertheless by lunchtime he was having milk toast on deck; and by Monday morning, when we docked at Quantico, he was his usual self again.

III

Battles—
Mostly Lost

CHAPTER 1

Public Works and the NRA

T HERE WERE THOSE to whom the vast—for that time—expenditures beginning to be made by the government were of interest because they promised recovery; but there was far from unanimous belief that recovery would be furthered in that way. There were fewer objectors than there had been recently, and they were no longer able to determine policy; but a considerable number of businessmen were not converted, and a larger number were still merely skeptical. If public works and relief did not show results quickly, there would be formidable demands for return to economy, deflation, and a balanced budget.

Many senators or congressmen were among the skeptics; and it was all too evident that there were others in the cabinet and elsewhere in the administration. The most strategic position occupied by one of them was, of course, the directorship of the budget. Lewis Douglas was more and more open in his determination to restrict spending for relief, and to obstruct the public-works programs. These attitudes could be masked by his duties, because any budget officer must reconcile the requests coming to him with what he has been told there is to spend. But Douglas' intention was too clear for disguise, even if he had wanted any, and all of us who believed in the reconstitution of purchasing power as the starting point for recovery recognized him as a common enemy.

Roosevelt himself was the source of the inconsistency. Expenditures of one sort continued to be reduced while those of another sort were being expanded. He was reluctant to give up his campaign contention that the Hoover administration had been extravagant. He had spoken so confidently in his Pittsburgh speech of a 25 percent reduction in government expenditures that he clung to it as though he had some special information. The speech had had a rhetorical flair characteristic of Johnson, who had drafted the speech, and so it was remembered. Roosevelt had seemed to say that all bureaucrats were a nuisance, and that there ought to be fewer of them.

Among the projects I hoped would turn Roosevelt away from this hostility, was the Beltsville center established some years before but never expanded. Several of our bureaus carried on experiments there. Animal Industry had several herds of cattle, sheep, and swine, and a large poultry-breeding operation; and Plant Industry was improving crops, introducing new ones, and finding new ways to protect the ones we already had. A farm was always something to bait Roosevelt with, and Beltsville's animals, and especially its pastures where imported grasses and feed crops were being tried, would almost certainly catch his interest. I had in mind a general enlargement of these experiments—in fact, the creation of a genuine national research center. We might even move the whole department there except for administrative offices.

One serious difficulty was that there would be political opposition. Congressmen are always vigilant about securing federal appropriations for their localities and preventing any activity from being discontinued. The agricultural stations associated with the land-grant colleges in the various states were well seated and, of course, were supported by federal grants. They would be very quick to oppose any suggestion of a competing national center, and their representatives would be responsive to their concern. Such a project could probably not be undertaken at all if the Congress had to be asked for approval. But it might be done with allotments of emergency funds. Presidents do, after all, represent the national interest, not those of localities.

I had only to convince Roosevelt that the research to be done, with all the bureaus cooperating, would never be done in the smaller state centers, each having highly specialized problems. There was the difficulty that the Cornellians had indoctrinated him so thoroughly in the virtues of their college and the dangers of Washington dominance that his prejudice would be hard to overcome. Beltsville, however, was only ten miles from the White House, and that made it a convenient objective for late-afternoon drives. It was easy to convince him that there were general projects no state would be interested in undertaking.

As things were, there was not much to see in Beltsville except extensive fields and a few buildings. It had to be imagined what an expanded center would be like. Roosevelt's first remark was about the land. It was part of the old corn-tobacco economy, exhausted from many generations of cropping. This did not matter for such a purpose as I had in mind. Perhaps it was even an advantage, since it was just such areas that needed rehabilitation.

When the Special Board for Public Works actually began to have projects to be passed on, Ickes turned to me for the processing of the federal projects. In fact Turner Battle (assistant secretary of labor) and I did practically all of this first job ourselves. The projects had been divided into two large categories, one being applications for funds of various agencies of the federal government, the other being those of cities, states, irrigation districts, power or housing authorities, and other local bodies. Selecting the federal projects was more difficult than we at first anticipated. For one thing, although nearly every agency had long-deferred improvements to suggest, specific estimates had not actually been made. Also, when they were made, they were usually timid ones. The bureau chiefs had learned, they thought, that modesty was wise. So we had, just at first, to fall back on simple construction—a building here or there, the reconstruction of a laboratory, the improvement of grounds or experimental gardens. We gradually persuaded the bureaus to plan and ask for really adequate facilities. There was as much trouble with our people in Agriculture as with others. In every part of the country there were stations where the most diverse kinds of experiments, demonstrations, and regulatory activities were carried on. Nearly everywhere the facilities were run-down and insufficient. Laboratories were housed in frame buildings little better than shacks, and fieldwork was done with the most primitive equipment.

As the projects began to be submitted, a few bureau chiefs in the department responded to encouragement, and this gradually spread to others, so that before we were through they were all hoping for substantial modernization of the departmental facilities.[1]

The case of the War Department was interesting and complex. The

---

[1] Perhaps I should explain that the Special Board for Public Works consisted of the secretary of the interior, chairman, the secretary of war, the attorney general, the secretary of labor, the director of the budget, Colonel George R. Spalding, and Assistant Secretary of the Treasury Robert. The Special Industrial Recovery Board was similarly composed. Statements concerning these appointments may be found in the 1932-33 volume of Roosevelt's *Public Papers*, edited by Samuel I. Rosenman (New York: Random House, 1938).

military establishment was incredibly scattered because of political influence in the placing of posts which, fixed, were almost never given up. The result was that forts established in the Indian or the Spanish-American wars, and now useless, were still maintained in a kind of shabby existence. This made modern equipment difficult to use, even if it had been available. It was impossible to undertake large-scale maneuvers which would be essential if a war should ever be in prospect. We tried to raise the whole question of rearrangement, urging on the generals the possibility that in such a comprehensive program they ought to be able to do what they told us privately was necessary. Secretary Dern undertook more ambitious planning, but although we refused appropriations for the most obviously unsuitable and ill-placed posts, not much was accomplished.

With Interior's bureaus we had no difficulty. The national-park planners were the easiest to deal with. Also, Robert, in the Construction Division of Treasury, having charge of federal buildings such as post offices, customs houses, and the like, was doing better than his division had done before. He knew that Roosevelt would support him. As Battle and I completed lists, we took them to the Special Board for approval. There were discussions, usually pointless, sometimes absurd, about detail; but practically always they were accepted. Then, however, they had to have presidential approval. After several delays from formal transmission, I suggested to Ickes that it might expedite matters if we got the president's approval first. He countered by suggesting that I undertake to do it. It was not proper procedure; but we were not being too formal in those days, and so, for many of the lists, I did just that.

Some of my most amusing recollections have to do with those lists. I usually had some on hand whenever he had a little time. As he bent over the sheets, his mind darted to Texas, to Montana, to Georgia. His knowledge of the country came into play, along with his predilection for detail. He often demanded more information—and I had to go and get it. It led him to think and make judgments about the kind of work going on. He made notes to talk to this and that person, and asked to have them brought so that he could ask for explanations; and occasionally he embarrassed those who did not know all they should—although no agency head can know operations in detail, and perhaps ought not to.

This brought me so lively a concern with fieldwork, and such preliminary knowledge, that I had, from then on, a never-failing interest. My pursuit of it during the next few years brought me a fair mastery of departmental affairs and of those in Interior, and some other departments as well. There were few of our outposts I did not visit at least once. Presently, also, I began to make contacts with Hopkins' field people, and his social workers accepted me as one of themselves. I was often able to do them a good turn, just as I was able, sometimes, to intercede with Ickes or others in the interest of some project under their jurisdiction, or to use my place on the board to argue for funds they might not otherwise have had.

Roosevelt sometimes needed to be circumvented. At first he was convinced that most of the projects were being inflated by the bureaucrats and took to making percentage reductions with a red pencil. Recollection of one occasion is specific. It was on the afterdeck of the *Sequoia*. He had been induced to give my lists an hour or two; and it seemed an appropriate time to argue about his method of reduction. Papers, maps, and project estimates were scattered over the deck, and he turned from one to the other. He spotted several which seemed unreasonably expensive for what was to be done, or perhaps, as I insinuated, he had little interest in that particular activity. That day he made reductions of 10 or 20 percent. I told him that these would require replanning and reestimating and that this would not only cause delay but would cost more than his reductions would save. He was unmoved. After that he got estimates boosted to allow for presidential deductions.

This procedure of consulting the president first, did, however, make things markedly easier in the meetings of the board. There was an obvious reluctance to show any curiosity about matters the president was known to have approved in advance, and Ickes was glad to have a remission of the board's inquisitiveness about matters beyond its competence. As time went on, there arose some competition for the allocation of funds; but this was considerably reduced by our screening efforts. The truth was that there was enough for every agency if we accepted only the projects already planned in some detail. There were always those who, even when they had nothing ready, thought they ought to have a reservation of funds; but we paid no attention to such claims, and, with Roosevelt's approval, our lists were quickly processed. Sooner than might have been expected, minor rehabilitation work was going on all over the country.

Not only projects came before the board; there were also matters of policy. Very early, Douglas set out to prevent the works appropriation from being spent at all, or, at least, to wring from it every reduction he could manage. He insisted that the deflationary spiral had come to an end and that "the necessity for injecting an artificial factor into the situation" no longer existed. He thought, therefore, as he said at a meeting of the board on July 1, that "the brakes should be put on." We should stop federal projects; and cities, counties, and states should be discouraged from making further submissions. I countered: "The suggestion is that we should not spend what is provided for in the bill, and the reason for not doing it is that recovery has already come, or will come if we stop now. That seems to me possible; I do not think it is probable yet, and I do not think that we ought to frame a program on that assumption." The board members merely listened.

Douglas went to Roosevelt with his complaint. He also had another. He said we were encouraging the bureaucrats to resume their extravagances. His arguments, however, were not received as he had hoped. He got the bland reply that what we were doing had long needed to be done. The whole federal plant, he was informed, was dilapidated. This reversal was distressing for Douglas but did not notably reduce his enthusiasm for economy.

There was a certain comic atmosphere quite apparent in the meetings of the Special Board. It included several cabinet members but other agencies at interest were included. After the first meeting, however, cabinet members were seldom present; they were represented by assistant secretaries—such as myself—or even lesser officials. All were uninformed, and most had an interest only in their own projects. There was, consequently, some bargaining about the division of funds available; but since all were new in their departments and were more politicians than administrators, what they had to say was regarded by Ickes, who presided at the meetings, as an unnecessary nuisance.

The National Recovery Board had a similar composition of cabinet members and was presided over by Secretary Roper of Commerce who took the duty seriously. He was an old and experienced politician who was secretary of commerce because Roosevelt would not appoint a businessman. General Johnson, as the administrator of NRA, was presenting codes for approval with what seemed to me horrifying implications of price fixing without supervision. Roper was perplexed about his responsibility.

Nothing could be done with Johnson. He did not listen. Roosevelt listened, but made no real concessions. I wrote memoranda, made statements, and was generally a nuisance at meetings of the board. A few of the others shared my concern, and it soon became evident that a confrontation with Johnson was imminent. It often seemed to be forgotten that a question of high policy for the nation's economy was involved in what was to be done by NRA. If the effort failed, we would have lost the opportunity to emerge from the era of chaotic competition and begin one of what Van Hise of Wisconsin had called "concentration and control." The old progressives, still populists at heart, were watching closely to see how the arrangements for establishing relationships among industries were being made. They regarded the origins of the scheme with suspicion and openly predicted that what would emerge would be a system of unregulated cartels with no restriction on the exploitation of consumers. If this could be avoided and the original principles of countervailing powers and the senior partnership of government could be established, we might enter the new era. We would not let Johnson lose it for us if it could be prevented.

CHAPTER 2

Ickes, Hopkins, and Douglas

MY EXCHANGES WITH DOUGLAS went on for some time, he continuing to insist that since the National Recovery Act was wholly permissive, and since the economy was improving, further emergency expenditures were unnecessary. Ickes was naturally on my side. The climax of this controversy came rather unexpectedly at a meeting of the Special Board in an argument about what the rate of interest should be on loans to cities and other local authorities. The issue was quite clear; it was whether we were to reduce the public works program.

My progressive friends had not considered the sums to be spent to give employment large enough; and it was beginning to appear that they were not likely to be spent quickly enough either. Municipal and other improvements would create a demand for steel, cement, lumber, electrical equipment—all that sort of thing—and workers would have to be employed in making them. If there was anything at all in our theory that such works were useful in relieving the victims of depression, this was the time to demonstrate it. We were late; employment should have been enlarged at once when the emergency had begun. The lateness made the effort more necessary; and it would have to be a greater effort. We were failing. Douglas was wrong: the depression was not over.

What interests me now is my reasonableness. I seem not to have exchanged angry words with Douglas on this occasion; but we had hotter arguments in private, some of them in the White House, and our mutual hostility had some newspaper airing. Douglas did not prevail; but his resistance continued. And because my side of the argument had strong support, our relations worsened. The creation of purchasing power was our only ready means of reversal. I said this in my syndicated articles, in others for magazines, and in speeches. I could—and often did—point to the twelve millions of men still out of work. Many were now being given relief jobs or assistance; but they would again be destitute if all this should stop.

I contended that we ought not only to go on with our current projects, but also to adopt a permanent policy of maintaining an adequate shelf of works to be resorted to when trouble appeared imminent. This would not prevent depressions; but it was a way of attacking them at their outset. I had thought that if, through the codes of NRA with the government acting as arbiter, we could achieve substantial balance among industries; if agriculture was kept from future sinking spells; and if, in addition, currency was managed so that the dollar represented equal buying power over long periods of time, we might achieve a relatively stable situation. It was not likely that we should do it with more than an approximation of success; but when there was failure the government ought to intervene. Of all the means for checking decline, public employment was the readiest.

This was not an inflationary program; it was restorative—a distinction it was unexpectedly hard to explain—and this was where I differed from my New Deal associates, or most of them. If I had dared I would have advocated the lending of funds without interest to municipalities. I did suggest it to Ickes, who agreed in principle but thought it impolitic. I finally proposed 3 percent after having lost on every half-percent upward from none at all. It was to this that Douglas made a really indignant objection. He wanted at least 4½ percent. As I read the transcript of the meeting my language seems moderate;[1] but probably that moderation was owed to my previous knowledge that 3 percent had been agreed to by those who counted most. I had done some politicking on my own.

On another issue there was difficulty with Frances Perkins. She was treated contemptuously by the conservatives and by labor leaders, particularly by John L. Lewis, who used his heaviest ham-actor style in denouncing her whenever he could. Hopkins and Ickes respected her lifelong work to improve the condition of the disadvantaged; but they

---

[1] Also referred to in Ickes' *Back to Work* (New York: Macmillan, 1935), 26.

were impatient with her desire to be the central character in any discussion. She was naturally talkative and was sometimes voluble about matters outside her competence. This running on and on led others to underestimate her. In one very serious matter she would influence a decision of immense importance. This concerned social security. The worst of this controversy would occur nearly a year later, but argument was already beginning among ourselves and it could be seen how the positions would be taken. We—Hopkins and I—wanted a national system giving equal protection to all. She, following the Brandeis theory, wanted it done by the states, each according to its own preference. We imagined what would happen in the most backward states where local politicians were in charge. These were the places where national assistance was most needed.

In the present issue before the Public Works Board she had the same orientation. She herself attended several times to insist that federal projects should be stopped and the funds allocated to local governments. This, of course, was an extension of the Brandeis principle of localism; and, because it was so distant from its source, I did not at first recognize it. When I did, I challenged her on strictly practical grounds. There she was weak. Federal projects could be started far more quickly than those of the local agencies. We had urged her departmental people, like others, to produce more imaginative plans. She said in a board meeting on June 29:

It is the local projects that raise the standard of living of the communities and therefore create the wealth out of which later income will flow. In connection with purely Federal public works, they [meaning Turner Battle and myself] came over and said: "You can get a whole lot of new immigration stations built." All right, we can, if that is desired, and we should treat ourselves to a lot of new immigration stations; but that will not increase or improve the standards of living in the places in which they are located.

This went on at some length. I was prepared to argue that federal agencies not only gave work and created a demand for materials, but led directly to an increase of productivity. It seemed to her "ridiculous" to rehabilitate immigration facilities although they were agencies of her department. It did not seem appropriate to argue whether immigration control ought to be effective. Presumably its regulation was an accepted policy; if so, the more efficiently it was done the better. She gave way reluctantly.

We were on easier ground when it came to public-health projects, the control of pests, and such matters. For these the cost for each employee was low, since a minimum of materials was involved. These low-material projects were devised later in vast number by Hopkins' successive works organizations. It was true that they did make a given amount of federal funds yield more direct employment; but they were not multipliers as construction projects were. As to that, except for the argument that it was more moral to make work than to give relief, relief ought to be favored; it was even cheaper. In the succeeding years there would be a good deal of confusion about this, involving acrimonious controversies between Ickes and Hopkins, and with others chipping in from time to time. But it was Roosevelt who made the decisions, and he always pressed for an economical program—that is, one furnishing maximum employment for the dollars expended. He was relatively unwilling to accept the multiplier effect. The result was a diminishing emphasis on defensible projects and increasing emphasis on merely "cheap" ones.

The truth was that his policy could be argued for only on political grounds. Decision was, however, a presidential prerogative. Roosevelt was always sensitive to criticism about spending; but it is hard to believe that carping would have been any less if more useful things had been done. He was continuously assailed; but he got what he had the courage to ask for anyway. It is my opinion now, as it was then, that he could have got much more. The works projects were sure to be criticized; but the criticism was more effective after Johnson, having been relieved of his job as NRA administrator, invented the term "boondoggling" in an attack on Hopkins. Johnson was not alone. Hopkins was always being attacked, even though his procedures improved greatly as he went along.

My agreements with Ickes tended to make us friendly, not only in official matters but in others as well. It will be recalled that he was secretary of the interior and administrator of public works because the progressives had recommended him. He had been quite unknown to Roosevelt until Senator Bronson Cutting had refused the secretaryship and suggested him. I could be of some use to him because of the awkwardness he felt with Roosevelt. Being given the enormous works program to administer, he was anxious to make a creditable showing. He had been a Chicagoan who had supported many good causes but had no administrative experience. When he had assembled his own engineering staff, he began to be impatient with the Special Board; and presently he persuaded Roosevelt to let it die. While the board lasted, we met formally with Ickes in the chair, projects being presented and transcripts being made. Our meetings were held in the office of the old Interior building; it was gloomily paneled, and had a long director's table. Colonel H. M. Waite sat at Ickes' left with the files of projects and their substantiating data.

Ickes regarded himself, as Walter Lippmann was later to remark, as "a proprietor in the nation's estate."[2] As proposals were processed for improving that estate, he almost visibly expanded. He was sometimes irritated by petty objections, but was usually genial and relaxed. His suspicions were abated; he forgot his perennial grievances, and sometimes he positively beamed. He was stirred by the thought that improvements were being made and that he was the agent of the betterment. He regarded me as an ally, and indeed I tried to be.

The contrast between Ickes and Wallace amused Roosevelt when I described the works meetings. Ickes measured at least fifty inches around and was of no more than average height. He was fifty-nine years old and might have been thought beyond the age of driving ambition; but it was not so. He was acutely conscious of being the only cabinet member with authentic progressive credentials and felt strongly his responsibility to those who had been sponsors for his unexpected selection. He valued the power he had and wanted more. He never gave an inch in controversy and produced on occasion the most cutting characterizations of those he disapproved.[3]

Because his checking and spying did seem endless, he soon became known as "Honest Harold"; and presently his caution slowed works so painfully that it became clear that they would not do much toward alleviating unemployment for some time to come. Roosevelt, recognizing the situation, reallocated a considerable amount of his funds to Hopkins, who might have been careless about accounting but who actually gave work to millions without delay. Ickes was furious; but there was nothing he could do.

Wallace was so different from Ickes and they were so competitive

[2] In a daily newspaper column at the time of Ickes' death in 1952. Ickes had retired from the Truman administration in indignation over the appointment of Edward C. Pawley to the Navy Department, who threatened, as he believed, another Teapot Dome scandal over oil reserves.

[3] It was he who later spoke of Wendell Willkie as "the barefoot boy from Wall Street," and noted, in another campaign, that Tom Dewey had "thrown his diaper into the ring."

that my intimate relations with both caused some difficulties. Each did have to be respected for a genuine desire to do his best for the cause we were serving; but each was suspicious of the other's conviction that he could and should succeed Roosevelt. Wallace had only slight interest in administration, but was at least as knowledgeable as any of our departmental scientists about their work. More importantly, he represented the agricultural power group, now having for the first time a decisive part in policy-making. After long frustration with Coolidge and Hoover, they meant to push their claims, with Wallace as their front. This was something Roosevelt fully understood. When pressures were being used in directions he wanted to go, he always gave the pushers encouragement. No one knew better how to use the force thus built up—or how to frustrate it if it became a nuisance. Ickes did have the progressives to. push for him; but their power was hardly comparable to that of the farm lobbyists with their well-developed bipartisan techniques.

If Wallace was an awkward manipulator, he was so earnest and so intelligent about what needed to be done that the persistent and conflicting demands of the farmer-politicians caused him a good deal of anguish. His integrity was impervious to seducers; but there were selfish impulses seething around him and sometimes he was inadvertently used.

Ickes' trust in me ran to the length of allowing me to manage the delicate negotiations concerning old differences between Agriculture and Interior. An unfortunate quarrel, going back to the Taft era, still rankled. Gifford Pinchot had convicted Secretary Ballinger of being party to the plundering of resources and, with Theodore Roosevelt's support, had seated forestry firmly in the Department of Agriculture, where it would be safe from the Interior corrupters. Ickes convinced himself that Ballinger had been the victim of a Pinchot-Roosevelt conspiracy and constantly maneuvered for the return of the Forest Service to Interior. It made sense, of course, as an organization matter. All other public lands were in Interior's custodial care—including the ever-expanding national parks. Wallace was not emotionally involved in this as Ickes was, and if the forestry supporters had left him alone might have consented to some arrangement. He was not an empire builder. Ickes thought he might bring about a new orientation for Interior as manager of all the public lands. He had it in mind that Interior should be called the Conservation Department. In spite of my official responsibility for Agriculture, he often talked freely with me about this ambition.

At such times I was embarrassed, as I shall relate, being also in the president's confidence as well as Wallace's; but during these early days of the public-works effort, there were none of these reservations. Considering that he had never been an administrator before, Ickes had very clear ideas. In the event, his organization would turn out to be efficient even though slowed by his investigative operations. These became more annoying as requests for funds piled up. No one "got away with anything" in Ickes' administration as they did in Hopkins' successive organizations; but by themselves his projects, except for the federal ones, contributed very little to immediate recovery; and recovery just then was the overriding consideration.

Ickes had much the same kind of attitude toward the vast resources under his protection as secretary of the interior as he had in his other administrative capacities. These resources belonged to the American people, not to any few of them, and as long as he was responsible he would not allow them to be exploited privately. It irked him that his hegemony was not extended to its logical limits; and he was furious whenever it was suggested—and it often was—that the forests might not be safe from predators if they were transferred from Agriculture to Interior. He thought that the contemporary generation of foresters was hypocritical. He knew that they were continually compromised in Agriculture because that department so often favored lumber, sheep, and cattle interests. It was notorious that forests were overgrazed, many of them being used as pastures by what he referred to as "cattle kings." He longed to consolidate all the land and resource agencies and to set himself up as their guardian.

It had to be admitted that such an arrangement would be fitting; but the foresters could not overcome their old prejudices, and perhaps they had a justifiable fear of succeeding secretaries. However, they could not argue that their situation in Agriculture was a very happy one. They resorted to lobbying, to dangerous liaisons with their natural enemies, and refused open discussion. This maddened Ickes. But he was never quite able to move the president, although, as I knew, Roosevelt leaned toward doing what Ickes wanted. Every time he approached it, however, he was faced with some twenty or more senators from the cattle and sheep states who had less than no interest in public resources and a very active interest in cattlemen's ranges. They knew how to handle the agricultural bureaucracy. Then there were the lumber men, who did very well with contracts for cutting in the forests. Take it altogether, there were formidable opponents whenever any move was suggested.

Ickes expended enormous energy on this issue. His insistence was annoying to the president. Consequently he was never in the position of one who could give advice, perform coordinative services, or assist with the Congress. He was not an easy collaborator. He had grievances; he was beset; he wanted comforting. As I look back it seems to me too bad that this righteous and determined man could not have had a more intimate relation with Roosevelt; but it was obvious that he did not really grant the president his position, together with its prerogatives. He wanted things his way and no other, and Roosevelt was, sometimes, in his mind, very nearly an ingrate for not giving way.

For long periods Roosevelt avoided seeing him, just not being able to bear such insistence. It was often my fortune to see him at such times and to be deluged with the embarrassing flood of his grievances. On occasion I sought to intervene, to work things out, and a few times I succeeded. As I look back, however, most of this kind of thing fades into insignificance before his complete dedication. That, in a public servant, I have learned, is the highest possible virtue; and in Ickes it was unwavering. He will be best remembered for this by all those who knew and worked with him. He deserved the simple epitaph— faithful public servant.

Affair with the Land

W HEN I SUGGESTED to the bureau chiefs that I might visit our facilities in the West, they deluged me with suggestions. It was soon apparent that this first exploration would have to be short and selective. I wanted most to grasp the sweep of our work, to understand the controversies whose echoes were so loud or so faint in Washington. Also I wanted to see where the piles of paperwork I dealt with daily came from. Many of the problems were technical: how it was possible to control some of the invading pests threatening the forests, groves, and orchards; how to further the adapting of imported plants and animals to American conditions—stocks more productive or more disease-resistant than the natives; how far gone with overgrazing the ranges were; how the numerous irrigation systems worked; where road communications were needed to open new territory or make it more accessible.

Within these general categories I had been made aware of many fascinating possibilities. Also I was coming to see, under Wallace's tutelage, one vast potentiality as another evolved in my own mind. His pondering about the future was leading him to conceive startling improvements in the whole rootstock of life. Genetic changes induced by man and engineered for general use could, if determinedly pursued over a long period, transform every living thing—tree, crop, and animal. Much of the fundamental work could be done at Beltsville, where the researches could be centered. They could then be put to use

Affair with the Land

in the colleges, the research stations, and the extension services. He
finally became as enthusiastic about Beltsville as I was.

My own favorite concept for the department was one of unity,
growing out of its remarkable diversity. We might, somehow, if we
could keep the end in view, and if we could devise the administrative
technique, create out of the now heterogeneous but enormous organization a splendid integrated structure. Agriculture could enlarge its first
purpose of feeding and clothing the nation, and making the products
of each region and locality part of a reservoir. The public domain could
be improved and made accessible to everyone. Talk about these possibilities was a kind of compensation for the daily desk work we had to
get through and the endless conferences and consultations.

As we listened to the individuals with whom we had to deal, so
many wanting things for themselves or for those who had sent them
to us, it was hard to keep any kind of hold on public purposes. They
did not recognize any and would have been annoyed to discover that
any such consideration controlled our reactions. Wallace sometimes
spoke of such matters; in fact, he was frequently criticized as an impractical dreamer, a mystic. He was even regarded with some reserve
by people in the department. Very little philosophy had crept into the
training or invaded the minds of our earnest workers. They thought
only of small gains on nature, ones of use to their immediate clientele;
they did not consider whether devotion of this kind would add itself
to other similar efforts. That parts of it might cancel out other parts
was not an idea they had ever entertained, even now that we had had
a decade of surpluses in agriculture and were in the midst of a national
breakdown. It would be difficult to alter this attitude, and it would
never be done without the shock of suggestion and of proposals for
action, however much these might be resented.

Wallace's long-run contribution was to be just this. In his eight
years as secretary he would influence the whole agricultural hierarchy.
When he was through there would be measurably more willingness to
regard the nation as an integrated whole and agriculture as a con-
tributing part of the organism. AAA helped with the more prosperous
farmers. Wallace would gradually gain confidence and enlarge the
country's confidence in him. Steadily he would press upon farmers and
agricultural leaders the national issues they must help to solve.

It was already clear to us—and if it had not been clear before my
western trip, that experience would have made it so—that we had been
needlessly vulnerable to the troubles of the years just past. Until the

181

war, now fifteen years behind us, the great plains had not been so extensively broken to the plow that drought could cause disaster; nor had the ranges been so overgrazed that the inevitable prolonged dry spells of the weather cycle could have devastating results. On the level stretches of the plains, plowing and overgrazing opened the soil to wind erosion; when the rains came again the land was ridged and barren. It was even worse where there were slopes. There, what soil the wind had left would go with the water during the next wet spell. Reconstitution would be a difficult and expensive business—more difficult and expensive than its potential productivity warranted. The work would take years, perhaps generations.

Much land ought never to have been plowed; it ought even now to be returned to the public domain for controlled grazing and its settlers given assistance to begin again somewhere else. There were areas where measures against wind and water erosion could be undertaken at once; but the problem was vast, and our preparations were still in the arguing stage. Worst of all was the stubbornness of those who had come to the plains, established homesteads, and been hopelessly sunk in debt and a fruitless struggle with their unrewarding acres. They were used to hardships, to living through droughts and deprivations. They always looked for better years after the lean ones. They would not believe that they could not survive.

Exploration made me more than ever anxious that we should get on to our preventive and correctional measures; but we needed funds to purchase exhausted lands and to resettle the people who were now on them and who would again try elsewhere. It could be seen that what we ought to do about the millions of acres between the hundredth meridian and the Rockies would always give way to more pressing matters. If there were funds to be competed for, preference would go to using them for the relief of farmers, rather than to rehabilitation of the land. As long as drought and flood held off, and those who were caught in recurring disasters were being somehow taken care of, living in constant fear would seem preferable to any drastic change.

As I went up, down, and across the plains all I had heard about the situation from our specialists was confirmed. The soil, even in a good year, as this was, showed through the grass; the wheat was thin and had short stalks. Nothing looked as it should in farming country. The people were thin too; but there were enough of them so that rescue from their situation would be an enormous enterprise. Horse and mule power had kept cultivation from pushing far out on the plains. The limit was set by the ability of the land to produce provender for the animals as well as crops for their owners. Mechanization was far from complete, even with the remarkable combine, but the machines were rapidly replacing animals and now there was another push to a new frontier, even more risky, and even at best less productive. It depended on oil for machines and not grass for animals.

The prairies seemed limitless. They were sometimes gently rolling, sometimes flat, but they rose steadily from the Mississippi to the mountains. In all the mile-high country, rain *averaged* less than enough to make a harvest; the Rockies caught it on their western slopes. The native cover—buffalo and wheat grass—had survived even in these conditions. They had a short growing season, then cured in the sun as they clung to the soil. And if their roots were not disturbed, they formed a rippling blond mat and kept the land from blowing in the hot August winds. Overgrazing tore roots away and was bad enough; but plowing ripped away an immemorial protection. The nakedness might never be covered, so delicate had been the ecological balance when the grasses were evolving.

Those of us who were concerned with the land did not love the plowers of the plains, not very much the cattlemen, and not at all the sheep and goat runners whose flocks cut to pieces such roots as grazing cattle had not consumed. Outside the fraternity there was prevalent indifference—something we could never quite understand. We tended to exhort and grow shrill. We had our way a little—a kind of concession to our passion. In our generation it would not be much; but that would not be for lack of earnestness or trying.

To administer the higher levels of conservation was to exist face-to-face, day after day, with those who were, in our extreme language, plunderers, and to try, one after another, the promising means for checking the exploitation. The only adequate weapon, as we all knew, was the infection of larger and larger numbers with our own concern. This was the more difficult for taking place mostly in Washington. The shaping of administrative agencies, the persuasion of reluctant legislators—these were carried on without the possibility of demonstration. Only once in a while were even those of us who were officials released to the open. These were called "field trips"; but they were renewing experiences, really, because out there our luckier colleagues consorted every day with nature, enjoyed her moods and grandeurs, her secret complexes and the tragedy of her violation. With pride they would share with us, for the interlude, their struggles in the good cause of protecting nature from their fellow men. The best ecologists I have ever known were field men who never rose to the higher echelons. There did seem at the moment certain corrective measures we could take. The worst lands could be retired from use and farmers encouraged to resettle; the abuses of usable land could be reduced; forests could be expanded. These were the possibilities. The specifics of such a program would reveal themselves if commitment could be made to its beginning.

Roosevelt was sympathetic and receptive when I reported to him. He had known the plains for a long time and worried about their settlement. It was one part of the national estate that seemed to him needlessly being destroyed. It was the cities that seemed to him hopeless; but when I consider, after many decades, that the plains continue to be overused, that droughts are still recurrent, and the farmers continually in trouble, our accomplishment during the New Deal years seems pitifully small.

CHAPTER 4

Containing Trouble

B Y EARLY FALL only hesitant improvement in the economy could be detected. The price level had risen by something like 20 percent; but that meant a rise in the cost of living, and so was about as much a problem as a solution. Eight percent of the rise had been in the single month of August. Against that there had been a 55 percent increase in payrolls, so that general purchasing power must be gaining. But the five millions who, according to Johnson's rhetoric, were to have been reemployed by Labor Day had turned out to be less than two millions. There had been an upward trend in business activity from March through July; but at about the end of that month decline had set in and was still continuing. The spirits of all New Dealers were declining, too.

Even in agriculture there was a suspicious softness. Farm prices had gone up when AAA promised a reduction in the surpluses; but it was a speculative increase, and they were falling again. September wheat in Chicago was eighty cents. The ten-cent cotton we had hoped would result from the 30 percent plow-up was far from realized: 1933 had been a productive crop year; nature conspired to increase the holdover, and it looked as though the strenuous efforts to reduce had been defeated. Arguments that if the reductions had not been made, cotton would have dropped to two cents, were not impressive; only actual results counted. Farmers began to have serious doubts about the help they had been promised.

The trouble in the corn belt was even worse. The killing of little pigs had not removed the threat of another surplus year, and prices were going down. The new Farm Credit Administration was providing some relief by preventing foreclosures and enabling farmers to pay off old debts, but such operations take time and results were as yet not impressive. With prices for their product falling, and those for what they had to buy rising, there was ugly talk all over the farm country—plenty of it; more, perhaps, than there might have been if nothing had been tried. True, the checks for compliance with AAA regulations were going out in growing volume; but they did not take the place of earned money in farmers' minds. Altogether, it looked as though a new crisis might be in the making, only less serious than that of March. Presidential boldness had faced that one down; but boldness would not suffice to meet another. Something more must be done even though new projects were under deep suspicion after the fiasco of Johnson's reemployment campaign. The blue eagle posters on factory walls and in merchants' windows were fading and torn. Many had disappeared.

Rising consumers' costs were partly the result of the codes. On this, all of us in Agriculture were agreed. Peek, Wallace, and I were to have moments of common endeavor during the next few weeks. It seemed possible that our accord in this respect might become a general alliance; but there was too much hostility already, and too many on both sides of our difference with an interest in its maintenance. The parity between industry and agriculture so confidently projected in July was not being achieved. This was not our fault, and we knew whose fault it was.

Roosevelt's problems were not lessened by the criticism of Ickes' public-works performance. The federal projects had been started, although even these were delayed for replanning and for letting contracts; but the projects of states and municipalities were simply not getting under way. The delay was attributed to Ickes' elaborate processing, and he was currently defensive because of it. In his determination to have no scandals in his administration and no suspicion of favoritism he had caused his engineers to set up rigorous procedures. To comply with them, local works organizations had to be reorganized and only after convulsive reforms could their plans be prepared.

By September it was obvious that there must be a general quickening. A system was set up for making tentative allotments on a *prima facie* showing. This might have the effect, it was hoped, of making the states and cities hurry their plans. A thirty-day limit was fixed for presentation of complete estimates following tentative approval; but it always had to be extended. Also a technical board of review was set up to reconsider such projects as had been turned down on a first showing if Colonel Waite, Ickes' chief engineer, thought they might be satisfactorily reprocessed. Localities were forced to retain consultants, and this annoyed their officials. There was criticism also because federal projects had been more freely approved than local ones.

At a meeting of the Executive Council, I made a kind of report on what I had seen and concluded in the West; and it seemed to make an impression. Even Johnson, who had been getting more and more annoyed by our insistence that NRA was undoing other efforts, was subdued by the failure of his reemployment campaign. There was no denying that prices were rising faster than buying power and that agricultural income, although supplemented by AAA payments, was still falling. These were very serious sources of disequilibrium. The policy of inflation—or "reflation" as the easy-money people liked it to be called—was failing.

I returned to my old thesis that the control of prices ought to be selective—some ought to go up but others ought to come down, or at least to be held while others went up; but no means had been devised for turning any price downward. This could only be done by NRA; but any hope that this might happen had disappeared. That there were many reasons for this, we in Agriculture knew well enough. When the Reemployment Agreement had been decided on—the blue eagle campaign—it had been argued that the increased purchasing power resulting from it would more than compensate for rising prices. But as code after code was processed it had seemed expedient to Johnson—with Roosevelt's agreement—to make concessions that allowed freedom to fix prices at levels that would diminish purchasing power.

The results of not having had the toughness to tackle the real job of balancing or equalizing were inevitably being felt. The heavy industries were still paralyzed. Until they began to be active, recovery would not be impressive. What was needed was an expanding market for their products. We estimated that in each of the past several years there had been a deficit of three or four billions of capital needed to re-equip and modernize industrial facilities. Some thirty billions in all could well be spent in getting productivity to the point where it should have been by now. This capital was not being supplied, and projects for modernization and expansion were not being undertaken. None of this would happen until purchasing power was supplied to consumers.

It was still being said that Roosevelt was destroying business confidence and so preventing industry from recovering. It was true that the investment bankers were on the grill. Ferdinand Pecora's investigation for a Senate committee was giving financiers a bad time; and there was more to come. But the RFC was making more and more immense loans. It was complained that this, however, was to assist financial institutions rather than to help business. It was admitted that public works would create demand for steel and other materials; but they were slow, and in any case they were not voluminous enough.

If things went on this way it might, after a few years, be found that some people had been given a living; but it would be only the minimum produced by a run-down industrial plant, a restricted agriculture, and a lethargic and frightened working force. What ought to be done, the progressives argued, as the talk went round and round about our troubles, was to further increase farmers' incomes, persuade the president and Johnson to stop approving codes that allowed industries to raise prices, turn RFC toward the furnishing of large capital sums to industry for modernization, ease credits through the Federal Reserve Board, speed up works projects, and prepare to ask the Congress for even greater relief and works appropriations. Some of this was done as the weeks passed, but Roosevelt took all of us by surprise—that is, all except Morgenthau and Professors Warren and J. H. Rogers, who were to conduct the operations—by beginning immediately the manipulation of the price of gold, in order to raise all prices. This was the development Berle and I had feared all along. It was such an oversimplified remedy that we thought Roosevelt had long ago seen its fallacy. We should have suspected that Morgenthau, being close by as director of the Farm Credit Administration, would have gone on urging it. But we had not. Neither had Wallace nor Hopkins nor any of the others who might have seen what was coming.

What the currency manipulators set out to do was to raise prices by bidding up the price of gold and so day by day making dollars worth less and commodities worth more. No one knew, of course, just how fast or how far the operations would go, but the president made it clear in his fourth fireside chat what was intended.[1] This address was a masterpiece. As I read it through now, so many years afterward, and recall the troubled situation of that fall, I am still amazed at its confidence and its appeal. It did certainly put a better face on the situation

[1] October 22, *Public Papers*, 1932-33 Vol. pp. 420-23.

than was warranted; but it had almost the same calming effect as the Inaugural. It opened on a note of reasonableness. After all that had gone before it could hardly be expected, the president said, that results could have reached every locality and every person so soon. But there was some cause for satisfaction. Millions had been given employment, relief had been given to others, the Civilian Conservation Corps was in full operation, and farmers and homeowners had been saved from dispossession, the RFC was lending large sums to financial institutions, public works were being organized, and the AAA had to an extent relieved farmers. "But," said the president, "I do not hesitate to say in the simplest, clearest language of which I am capable, that although the prices of many products of the farm have gone up, and although many farm families are better off than they were last year, I am not satisfied either with the amount or the extent of the rise and that it is definitely part of our policy to increase the rise, and to extend it to those products which have as yet felt no benefit. If we cannot do this one way, we will do it another."

Then he spoke of NRA, claiming for it the abolition of child labor, the elimination of the sweat shop, and vast reemployment. But he came at last to what he had been aiming at:

The object has been the attainment of such a level as will enable industry and agriculture once more to give work to the unemployed. It has been to make possible the payment of public and private debts more nearly at the price level at which they were incurred. It has been gradually to restore a balance in the price structure so that farmers may exchange their products for the products of industry on a fairer exchange basis . . .

There were some, he said, who wanted a fixed value for the dollar; but it was his policy to restore price levels first, and then to adjust the dollar to this level. What the final level would have to be no one could say. That would be a matter for experiment. But when it was reached we should, he said, "seek to establish and maintain a dollar which will not change its purchasing and debt-paying power during the succeeding generation. I said it in my message to the American delegation in London last July and I say it again now."

He then explained that a government market for gold would be established by authorizing the RFC to buy gold newly minted in the United States at prices to be determined from time to time after consultation with the secretary of the treasury and the president.

"My aim," he said, "in taking this step is to establish and maintain continuous control. This is a policy and not an expedient. It is not to be used merely to offset a temporary fall in prices. We are thus continuing to move toward a managed currency."

In spite of the reassuring presidential voice, reaching again, as it had before, into homes throughout the land, there were skeptics. *Business Week* on October 28 suggested that the means chosen were inadequate for the purpose: "Neither economists nor international bankers believe that the degree of dollar rigidity suggested by the president's speech can be achieved by the manipulation of the gold market alone."

The hope that some management of the gold value of the dollar would be undertaken has been almost universal, but schemes put forward for its regulation have varied almost as widely as the motives of those who suggested them. Agriculture on the one hand has demanded inflation, even to the extent of printing fiat money, while the most orthodox banking groups have been content to recommend a stabilization fund to prevent extreme fluctuations until a decision is reached as to the ultimate gold content of the dollar. The need of control has been obvious. Since gold trading was abolished the dollar has drifted . . . it has been the pawn of the money game as played by international bankers and European exchequers . . . There has been little criticism from any quarter of the president's plan to trade in gold for the purpose of stabilizing . . . This is more or less what has been done by the British and the French. Experience seems to suggest that orderly inflation and revaluation cannot be accomplished without some such national control.

There was just a touch of complacency in the note appended to the fourth fireside chat in the *Public Papers* when they were later published. Roosevelt was never willing to admit that gold manipulation did not materially contribute to recovery. That it would not was plain to most of his helpers, and we were not surprised when he gave way in January and recommended passage of an act stopping manipulation and fixing the price of gold. But the moment's demands were met; and, together with other energetic measures, it would get him through the year with public approval unimpaired even if disaffection was spreading among businessmen.

☆ | CHAPTER 5 | ☆

Confrontation with Peek

W E WERE GETTING READY for the next Congress. Our own departmental budget, for instance, had been worked on for
weeks. This was my responsibility, although William Jump, our fiscal
officer, was actually putting it together. It was extraordinarily complicated because of the demands on us for reduction. We had succeeded
in finding our 25 percent cut after much anguish and complicated
negotiations with Douglas and his subordinates. This somewhat amused
Jump, as an experienced bureaucrat, because he was quite certain that
many of our bureau chiefs and project directors were already in touch
with friends on congressional committees who would see to it that not
much damage was done.

The Bureau of the Budget was a relatively recent institution. It had
been established in 1921 after something like a decade of agitation
among reformers; but congressmen had seen in it a threat to their traditional prerogatives, and had delayed it as long as they could. The old
system had been an inheritance running all the way back to the Continental Congress, before the adoption of the Constitution, when there
had been no chief executive. This had allowed the legislators to direct
the efforts of the administrative agencies. As long as there was no budget
to draw all expenditures together and present them as a whole, there
was no attempt at balancing spending with income. Congressmen traded
with each other for the support of provisions they used for patronage
or for local support.

Even in our time congressmen regarded the budget sent to them by the president as a starting point for the arrangements they preferred. They always called loudly for economy in general; but they were always maneuvering for the inclusion or expansion of their favorite projects. The continual struggle of the executive was to find support for activities of national rather than local importance and to balance outgo with income.

We might argue with the bureau, lose the argument, and see it prospectively reduce our funds, but there was no real despair. It was only necessary to do some trading. Indeed, even this was not necessary. Usually the congressmen were far ahead of us, having heard from protégés in the department how things were going. I had read about this kind of thing, but I was aghast at its extent when I was in a position to understand all that went on. I sometimes thought that a good quarter of the time and effort of Washington personnel was spent in these meaningless efforts; but I did not see what we could do about it. It was embedded in the system.

We were, after all, not anxious to be punished by annoyed congressmen; and any reform would require constitutional changes. At odd moments I speculated about reorganizations of the Congress, such as elections of all or some at large; about stricter party discipline; and about the possibility of self-denying ordinances by the legislators themselves. Such speculations by others would lead to the La Follette-Monroney Act much later (in 1946) requiring the Congress to accept a global budget figure; but even that would not be effective; and would be repeated in 1973 by an act setting up a budget bureau within the Congress itself. During all my time in federal service we had to operate with the system as it was. The work on this and other departmental matters had no attention from outsiders, accounting, I suppose, for its neglect by most of the upper administrative officers. Wallace, like the others, had only wanted assurance that plant and animal research would not be curtailed.

One struggle coming up at this time could not be escaped. It was inherent in the situation we had allowed to develop in the AAA. This seemed, when it was over, at the middle of December, to have been a clean victory. But if, at the moment, I regarded it as that, I was mistaken. Not much later the opposing forces would feel strong enough to challenge us again and this time would win. In the present case I made full use of all the avenues of publicity open to me; and it was this careful preparation that was responsible for success. When it was over,

George Peek was out; and I was being talked of as one of the really influential officials in Washington.

The past year had furnished some useful lessons. I had not only seen Ferdinand Pecora's investigation softening up the financiers but I had watched Roosevelt's manipulations. It occurred to me that my specious notoriety might be available for a tactical operation. It was becoming obvious that if we did not get rid of George Peek, he would get rid of us, and if a showdown was inevitable some preparation for it was in order.

My own most educational incident had occurred before we had come to Washington. Sometimes an experience of this kind has one effect and sometimes another. Its first effect on me was to make me overwithdrawing. It was a notable feature of the Brains Trust episode that its members, except for Moley, continued for a good while generally unknown. After inauguration, when we were dispersed into the administration, this continued for some months. Moley's flare of publicity amid the bizarre events of the London economic conference did not involve Berle or me. But I gradually emerged into notoriety as he faded from public sight; and that was mostly because of the manufactured publicity attending the proposed revision of the Food and Drug Act. But when the change began it came rapidly. By the fall of 1933, my every move was watched and recorded, and my opinions were matters of curiosity.

My harshest lesson had occurred in January 1933. One day a kind of minor Lincoln Steffens (I thought as I looked at him) had come into my office at Columbia wanting an interview. His name he said, was Forrest Davis. My reading about Steffens, I think, confused me. Somehow I conceived that Davis and I were talking confidentially as Steffens had done with his informants. I did take the precaution of saying that we were talking off the record. But I found afterward that this meant only that my actual words would not be quoted. The substance of what I said was repeated and only too clearly attributed to me. It was so nearly accurate that I could not repudiate it. It was good journalism; but it was not good faith.

A few days afterward I was in Washington on an errand for Roosevelt. Crossing Lafayette Square, I picked up a newspaper. It had headlines clearly referring to me. It said: *Roosevelt Adviser Outlines . . .* and in the text under a picture of me, looking very earnest and professorial, it was indicated that I was the "principal economic adviser" of the man who was about to become president, and that "while Dr. Tugwell's proposals may not be interpreted as literally foreshadowing Roosevelt policies, they may be considered as an authoritative outline of what the new administration plans . . . " And here, it said, is Dr. Tugwell's national plan, point by point:

1. Drastically higher income and inheritance taxes, particularly in the upper brackets; no sales tax.
2. A widespread public works program, possibly entailing $5,000,000,000 at the start; direct relief to the indigent unemployed; intense stimulation to semi-public works projects, such as slum clearance through RFC.
3. Reduction in interest and public utility rates.
4. Sound currency; no inflation.
5. A budget balanced as to current expenditures, with repeal of the eighteenth amendment a factor in raising revenues.
6. Restoring the balance between wholesale prices, especially for agricultural products, and retail prices to consumers; the Farm Allotment Bill, which already has passed the House is expected to accomplish this for the farmers.
7. Rationalizing the intergovernmental debt settlements—perhaps by remitting the interest items in the total sums due—and by basing the debtors' capacity to pay upon their ability to transfer goods or money in relation to gold reserves and value. Also rationalizing foreign trade arrangements, such as tariffs, and perhaps seeking a vast new outlet for American raw goods and manufactures in Russia.

There were several columns of expansion, tending to reinforce the claim that all this was authoritative.[1]

I was appalled. In the disturbed state of the economy, and with everyone waiting breathlessly for some pronouncement giving hope—or, in the case of bankers and businessmen, confirming fears—my forecast caused a minor furor. The reverberations went on for days. The columnist Rodney Dutcher, for instance, said:

Speculation [in Washington] has been rather furious as to the extent to which Tugwell's ideas may be those of Roosevelt. The professor is one of the closest and most trusted advisers of the President-elect, and is one member of the Roosevelt brains trust whose reputation has not been at all deflated. He says, of course, that he is speaking for himself. But there is a tendency to believe that he and Roosevelt see eye to eye.

[1] See the *New York World Telegram*, January 26, 1933.

I had found Moley as soon as I could and asked him to apologize for me. He telephoned at once. He did not deny, as he hung up, that Roosevelt, who was in Warm Springs, was annoyed. In fact, the journey I was to have made to see him next day was canceled; but, said Ray, these things happen and cannot be taken too seriously. Besides—and he twinkled a little—it wasn't a bad program. The trouble was that speculators could make a lot of money by having some firm preview of policy. Not only that, Roosevelt had not said what he intended, if, indeed, he had made up his mind, about several of the issues. Inflation was one of these; so was a large public-works program. The worst thing was that blurting out an intention might be a way of preventing it from happening.

I had thereafter considered myself to be more or less in disgrace; and I had been surprised that Roosevelt had not repudiated me. I knew something about the value of trial balloons, but I also knew that they had to be managed from the source of power, not by irresponsible subordinates. The affair blew over; but it caused me to retreat to a taciturnity which might have won me a good deal of ill will if I had not gradually emerged from it; but I took care not to be over-represented again as a spokesman, authorized or not.

It would not be true to say that I escaped notice as an official; but after this incident the notes about me—and others of the Brains Trust— were generally not headline material, even if we did figure a good deal in columnists' speculations. In June, for instance, we had been given a page in the *Literary Digest*, and I appeared now and again, along with Wallace, as shaping agricultural legislation. Once in a while it was said or hinted that I was more or less all over the place as a Roosevelt assistant. I gradually gained some confidence and began to lose my timidity. As the Peek showdown approached, I felt that I had the technique more or less in hand. I set out to use it.

Perhaps my early fears were partially relieved by an October article by that same Forrest Davis referring to his previous revelations and claiming for them that they had proved to be accurate. He even found reasons why I had not forecast NRA (the fact was that I had but that he had overlooked it). He crowed:

Few Americans anticipated before March 4 the swiftly evolving changes which were to transform the country from a land of despair into a land of renewed promise.

Yet on January 26—the *World Telegram*, in a published interview with Dr. Tugwell, gave a solid prophecy of the wonders to come which has proved surprisingly accurate as the New Deal has unfolded at home and abroad . . .

By now I was willing to admit that Forrest Davis had taught me something; but I had learned some lessons from others as well. Ickes regularly used not only his own remarkable gift for picturesque invective but the craving of Washington newsmen for inside stories. So did Hopkins, but with a good deal less finesse. Up to now I had merely explained the general issues over and over again to one after another of my acquaintances among the newsmen. I had thought it a point of rectitude never to reveal any information come by in conversation or to expose any family differences in the government—even with those of whom I was suspicious as to motive or whose connections I distrusted. And I did not depart far from those standards now, but we had reached an impasse; and it could not be overcome without forcing a favorable decision not likely to be taken behind the scenes without some outside disturbance.

Both in NRA and in AAA, issues of public policy were being fought over. To reveal what these issues were, and who were the protagonists, was possible without violating any principle of loyalty. Peek in AAA and Johnson in NRA were the fronts for conspiracies against what I regarded as the public interest. It would be unforgivable to sit by and allow them to succeed. I therefore told Ernest Lindley, who had moved to Washington from Albany for the *Herald Tribune*, all about it. I also told some others what I felt was necessary. There was quick response. The story was that a showdown was coming, that the president would have to choose, and that he could better afford to sacrifice the new administration than his old helpers. Besides, inquiry around town by the reporters, once they had caught the scent, convinced them that there was indeed a widespread progressive disaffection.

Wallace was more or less in the same difficulty as Roosevelt in making a choice, but with him there was the added weight that Peek was his rival for agricultural power. If things went much further, Peek would be Wallace's successor. There was no doubt that Peek's policies pleased the farm leaders, who had never been worried about his friendliness with the processors. This, to me, was the least understandable element in the whole situation, considering farmers' traditional suspicion of middlemen. I obviously underestimated the versatility of the organized politicians. Their tenderness with the processors was private. Publicly they represented themselves as farmers' friends. At any rate, when it came to conferring about policies, Peek's formula of not worrying about processors' profits as long as the farmers got higher prices was quite agreeable to them.

A few of us—Frank, Christgau, Howe, and myself—had succeeded in interposing the threat of exposure to various marketing agreements. They were all processed in various divisions of the AAA and approved by Peek's private counsel—he had refused to accept Frank's services, finally, and had hired his own attorneys. A group of agreements was awaiting Wallace's signature, and he was hesitating. He told the president what was up, but had not got much encouragement. The president, as a matter of fact, was approving similar industry codes from NRA because, as he said, there were "some good things about them"— labor provisions, mostly. But the progressives were indignant about his softness and were saying so publicly.

The particular occasion for the showdown in agriculture happened, however, when Wallace was away. I have never known whether Peek's group in AAA chose the occasion deliberately. At any rate the file came to me as acting secretary. I read it carefully, then wrote a rejection, saying exactly what I thought. I called in several newspapermen, explained the issue to them, said I was disapproving the agreements as a matter of principle and not waiting for the secretary's return. It would precipitate matters, I said, and would be of legitimate public interest. Peek would certainly carry the matter to the president after having it out with the secretary, and either he would go or I would.

It did not take long for Lindley to discover at the White House that the president might not like to choose, but that he would not let me go. In fact, I heard from Roosevelt almost at once. He gave me a chance, in a closely followed argument, to tell him again, but this time fully, where I thought the codes and marketing agreements were leading. I ended by venturing into strategy, saying that in my opinion he must in the end come to the course others of us had argued for. He had approved one code after another, knowing that we had studied and worked over them and had disapproved. Now, not because I had refused to approve several marketing agreements, but because the issue had become so public, he would have to make a choice. I knew much of what he had in mind; so I said plainly that Peek had to leave AAA or he would lose not only me but, I thought, Wallace. "Well," he said, smiling again after some thought, "there's the ambassadorship to Czechoslovakia."

I thought Peek would not accept that;[2] and so I suggested that he might be willing to work at opening the foreign markets he had talked about so much. This appealed to the president's sense of humor, always close to the surface. "Lordy, Lordy," he said, "how Cordell will love that!" Peek's and Hull's were completely antithetical approaches; Peek would bargain for markets and Hull wanted complete equality of treatment for all, which was why he clung so stubbornly to "most favored nation" clauses in our tariffs. Such controversies within his official family did not bother Roosevelt much unless they threatened public embarrassment. He had concluded that by now neither Hull's policy nor Peek's had much newspaper appeal.

This was the background for the happenings of the next few days. Wallace, on his return, listened to my side of it; I was by now apologetic for having acted in his absence. But he said, "No, no, it would have had to be this way anyway. What does the president say?" I told him of my conversation. I apologized for that too, since he was the secretary and it was really his affair. But although I had felt him to be a little restive lately, he was pleased that I had got the matter past the most difficult stage. And it was true that it was all in his interest.

I was disappointed a few days later when Wallace told me he had selected Chester Davis to succeed Peek. I thought I had earned consultation, and I was sure that Davis was not much improvement over Peek. But Davis belonged; he was part of the agricultural-political fraternity, and Wallace could not bring himself to offend this source of support. I warned him that he was asking for more trouble, that sometime he would have to break with them, and that he was meanwhile merely making them stronger. But he thought I exaggerated the difficulty. The selection of Davis inclined me to Hopkins' and

---

[2] Although Arthur Krock, in a column a few days later (the *New York Times*, December 10, 1933), said "they looked around for a high office to which he could be transferred with dignity and interest for himself. At this point Mr. Tugwell had an inspiration which suggests he is still a bit of an amateur in public affairs. Francis White is retiring as Minister to Czechoslovakia. Send George Peek there! But the President, who is not an amateur, knew that he could not tempt Mr. Peek with any place except one that permits him to pursue his hobbies of getting the farmer back on to parity, preferably through export trade." But Mr. Krock had rather infirm relationships with the White House. He had been refused a favor he very much wanted; and had lost some credit in the asking. He was wrong in this as in numerous other "inside" interpretations in New Deal days.

La Follette's view that Wallace was now being too much influenced by an ambition, as yet tentative, but likely to grow.

The tone of the comment on the Peek incident was set by the *Herald Tribune's* headline over Lindley's story—"Peek Due to Quit: Roosevelt Backs Brains Trust in Rift" (December 6, 1933). Arthur Krock in the *New York Times* (December 9) said:

In this week's encounter of men and theories at the Department of Agriculture the real 'winnah and new champion,' as Joe Humphreys would say, is Rexford Guy Tugwell . . . By a skillful mixture of discernment and tactics he finally maneuvered the blunt administrator of AAA, George N. Peek, into a position where the President had to choose between him and Secretary Wallace. The result was the obscuration of Mr. Peek . . . Friends of Professor Tugwell say that a slight twinge of alarm is now mixed with his natural pride in his achievement. This does credit to his intelligence and observations. . . . "Rex," say the friends, "doesn't want to stick his neck out too far."

This kind of speculation went on for two full columns.

Time put it somewhat differently. After an account (considerably garbled) of the events of the past two weeks, its story ended with the following paragraph:

There is friction in every administration. But friction in the Roosevelt Administration is apt to be peculiarly significant because most of it comes from basic differences between those who are quite definitely not Socialists and those who, for most practical purposes, are. The near-Socialists are led by handsome Rex Tugwell who wants honest labelling written into the food codes, and has for the same purpose drafted a food and drug bill. . . . Their strategy is to get as much done as possible under the guise of "liberalism," to avoid the honest label of "socialism."

This was an early intimation that the efforts of the advertisers and patent-medicine people to label me "Red" was really taking hold. Their alarm was quite evidently intensified by the success of the maneuver in Agriculture. The echoes of this alarm reverberated in the news and editorial columns all over the country. I was more than ever a marked character, to be taken more seriously now than before. If *Time* was willing to say that honest labeling was socialism, there was no telling how far less reserved publications would go.

Heywood Broun, clumsy and bearlike, but earnest, came to see me several times while our rumpus was going on. He was fascinated. He was not at home in Washington. It confused him, he said, to be so close to everybody who knew everything. But this was the kind of issue he understood. He wrote several columns of comment on our affairs; and, almost alone among commentators, deliberately defied his publishers. On December 14 he said:

It seems that Professor Tugwell is a Socialist. And why is Professor Tugwell a Socialist? I gather that he is a dangerous radical because he is sponsoring a bill which will cost the newspaper publishers some money . . .

And in two other columns of near dates he described visits to me. On one of them, he said, he startled me by saying that he hoped my personal life was all in order, because from now on I was to be investigated and, if possible, exposed without mercy. In another he described his first visit at some length:

Quite often I have read about Rexford Tugwell and in every case he was described as a youthful collegian filled with sophomoric inclinations to tear down all existing institutions. Today I met him and naturally my first question was, "Where are the bombs?" And immediately after that, "How old are you, Mr. Assistant Secretary?"

He said he was 42. I will admit that he could pass for less, but even if he heaped on a year or so this member of the Brains Trust is not by any accurate definition a fledgling. At 40 I was distinctly suspicious that perhaps I was not so young as I used to be. At 41 this vague foreboding became a certainty. The next year I bought myself a pair of slippers and a quilted dressing gown. Long before the age of 40 Napoleon had triumphed at Austerlitz. At a less advanced period Shelley was dead and Hannibal had crossed the Alps with elephants. Rexford Tugwell is not a young man. At any rate he knows his way about.

Again according to the placard I have seen in public places, the charge runs: "Wanted for Socialism" and so when I was ushered into the office of the Assistant Secretary of Agriculture, I extended my hand and exclaimed "Hello Comrade! Yours for the revolution." I then sang a few bars of the Internationale. Dr. Tugwell seemed puzzled, and inquired, "Have you got an appointment?" Even when I gave him a little of the secret ritual he failed to tumble. The newspapers have made a grave mistake about him.

Fiorello La Guardia, only recently chosen as our Mayor, is flaming red if set down beside the brigadier of the Brains Trust. I have no intention of insulting an extremely intelligent and personable young man, but if ever I saw a liberal, Rexford Tugwell is that specimen. I would describe him as Walter Lippmann with steel structure added.

Mr. Tugwell is sincere, earnest, and he isn't fooling, but he is not of the martyr mold. There isn't a trace of the fanatic about him. After all here is a middle-aged man who existed and prospered upon the faculty of Columbia University for several years without any jam whatever. I have no intention of imputing to him any lack of courage. For the thing which he believes he will fight hard. But the major part of his economic philosophy is by no means a swat in the eye for the world as it now stands. . . .

I quote Broun out of sheer vanity. There are perhaps not so many now who recall that shaggy knight. There were few people whose favorable opinion I would rather have had than his; but that he represented a minority of publicists, I had only too good cause too know. To be sure, Richard Wilson in the *Des Moines Register* (December 17) said that I "had emerged as the strong man of the Administration" and supported it with some three columns of comment which described me, my habits, and my family in that embarrassing detail spoken of by Broun. But others were not so honest or so kind. Paul Mallon and Carlisle Bergeron had me resigning all through the crisis, not as Lindley did, in protest, but in defeat—a kind of journalistic device I have never quite understood because it must after all be embarrassing to be proved wrong over and over.

It was Mark Sullivan and Frank Kent who carried the weightiest adversary burden. They did nobly, each in his own way. For former liberals they had made an inexplicable turnaround. Sullivan was aging, but his style was still effective. In the course of a long article on December 12 (in the *New York Herald Tribune*), he foreshadowed what was now to be the line of argument:

The conflict between Professor Tugwell and Mr. Peek as individuals is merely the conspicuous present outbreaking of a broad struggle within the whole of Mr. Roosevelt's administration between a group who envisage for America a profound social change in which private profit and private ownership of property as it now exists would be carried toward complete extinction, and, on the other hand, a group of old-fashioned Democrats and other conservatives who earnestly wish to keep the American form of government and social system what it has always been.

The struggle between these two groups is by far the most fundamental movement going on in America. Because it is deep, because it is like the early phase of a collision between tides, it comes to public attention only on the comparatively rare occasions when a disagreement between individuals becomes dramatic. The deeper struggle is far more fundamental than the controversy about inflation. To compare this basic struggle to the ordinary politics of Republican vs. Democratic would be both misleading and trivial.

There was more of this kind of thing from Sullivan. It was amazing how he could go on about it day after day, inventing variations on his central theme. But not once did he suggest that there was another difference, that between those of us who were centralizers and the defenders of individualism. That escaped him altogether. But then it was to be remembered what the purpose was: to alarm conservatives among the Democrats and to convince them that they ought to join forces with the Republicans. This was a natural alliance. It did come about soon and lasted throughout the rest of Roosevelt's time. At present the fright caused by the depression had not yet disappeared and the sins of business had not yet been forgotten. The conspiracy theme was effective for its purpose; but it was overdone.

Frank Kent's method was quite different. He believed in discredit; and he was ingenious in approaching it. His manner was light; he used irony, sarcasm, and belittlement. I quote a passage from one of his *Baltimore Sun* columns, just as the Peek affair was boiling up (December 6, 1933):

> The trouble with the "Young Liberals" of the Administration, as Mr. Lindley, close friend of the President, calls them, and whom he recently described as disturbed to the point of resigning, can be simply stated. They have been doing a lot of work but it hasn't been getting anywhere.
>
> In both the AAA and the NRA these bright young men, fresh from the Universities, and full of fire for the New Deal, have been drafting codes for practically every form of human endeavor. They put their whole souls into the job. They plan regulation on a grand scale and work everything out to the smallest detail. And then, when they think they have produced a masterpiece, they turn it in and those higher up pull it all to pieces. . . .
>
> Naturally this makes the "Young Liberal" resentful. He is crammed to his eyeballs with pride of authorship, and there is no species of pride which renders a man more sensitive. Inspired by almost religious fervor for the new experiments, his disposition is to regard those who maim the thing he has produced as sinister fellows, unsympathetic with the noble purposes embodied in the New Deal. Some of these Young Liberals have got themselves into a very inflamed state of mind indeed. . . .

This must be recognized as an excellent production of its kind. Much the same belittlement came from others, but none so accomplished as Kent's. His readers were assumed to be prejudiced against these fervid fellows. The old hands in Washington, politicians, ex-politicians, all the cynical leftovers of the Republican administration, and all the fixers gathered around the new agencies, regarded this as the proper attitude. They had no interest one way or the other in issues; they merely liked to accomplish things beneficial to the interests they represented quietly and in comfortable ways. They could sit down happily with Peek and his friends in a Carlton Hotel room and arrange matters. With me or even with Wallace, they never wanted to get into any room at all.

One of the members of the Kent coterie in Washington was a Roosevelt—Alice, the daughter of T.R. She was the widow of Nicholas Longworth, who had been a speaker of the House. She had been a White House darling in her youth; and she was completely unreconciled to the prominence of the Hyde Park branch of the family. She was full of ill-disposed stories illustrating the contemporary Roosevelt's incapacity for her father's former position; but most of all she delighted in belittling Eleanor, his wife. That lady's serious concern with her country's problems, her ubiquitous interest in good causes, and especially her naiveté and lack of humor, were endlessly lampooned in Alice Longworth's circle to the sound of high-pitched laughter. She invited me to lunch one day out of curiosity, as many of the Washington cavedwellers were doing. Usually I refused; but this time I went. My own curiosity about this rather raddled survivor from other days was as great as her own about a brash newcomer, so incongruous in the Washington scene. She had also invited a number of like-minded friends. I was alone in a lioness's cage.[3]

On this occasion jokes about the Hyde Park Roosevelts were somewhat muted, but since they were the current stuff of contemporary speculation, they squirted through cracks in the conversation like steam from a leaky boiler. We had a good time because in some exchanges I succeeded in putting my hostesses on the defensive. I had implied that they had had opportunities like Eleanor's but had not

---

[3] A passage in Nicholas Roosevelt's memoir *A Front Row Seat* (Norman, Okla.: University of Oklahoma Press, 1953, p. 36) puts very clearly the contrast between Alice and Eleanor, both so essentially Roosevelt and yet so very unlike: "As Eleanor grew in influence, the basic differences between her and Alice became more apparent. Alice was brilliant, picturesque, vitriolic—passionately absorbed in the day-to-day plays of the political game. Eleanor was sympathetic, fundamentally kind-hearted; believed in reform, and looked on politics as a means rather than an end. Where the steely quality in Alice made her an indifferent humanitarian, Eleanor, who had known more personal suffering than Alice, was quickly responsive to the troubles of others—so much so, in fact, that her sympathies frequently led her to support people and causes without stopping to look into their motives or to ascertain whether they were pushing her . . ."

used them. They must have been almost as unhappy, I said, in Hoover's time—he and his wife had been serious and humorless. Were the Hoovers immune from ridicule because they were Republicans?

My willingness to trade shafts pleased Alice, who was as smart as she was malicious. I won a certain tolerance by asking with a poker face when she remarked that Frank Kent, who was coming, was late: "Frank Kent? Frank Kent? Who is he?" Since one of the curiosities about town was my apparent indifference to Sullivan, Kent, and the others, this was recognizably in Alice's vein of discourse. My bland denial that anything was going on stopped the conversation for an appreciable moment.

When I met Dame Alice on occasions of a social sort after that, she was inclined to yield to me, so I fancied, somewhat more respect than she had for many of the other newcomers. Hopkins always treated her with ironic compassion too, and he was a real favorite with her set in a kind of half-accepting way. At least we would not be patronized. Wallace suffered visibly in such situations. He and his wife, Ilo, as members of a cabinet family, necessarily mixed often with the diplomatic set; and the diplomats mixed freely with the cavedwellers. The Wallaces often found themselves in the company of Alice and her friends. Ilo must have suffered a good deal from the wicked wit she had no means of meeting with returns in kind.

For the moment I shared what was taken for power; and everything that happens to an official in that position happened to me. The curiosity of the country—a reaction from all the publicity—was reflected in the corresponding curiosity of others than the capital's socialites. The politicians who had not before given me a thought, except perhaps to deplore the nearness to the president of such an amateur, now took a second look. I was being a good deal more carefully appraised, as I could see, after the successful maneuver in the Peek case. Arthur Krock was right; I was alarmed. My discomfort over personal notoriety had been acute enough before; I was now being deluged with it. All my defenses were not enough. My circumspectness, I had reason to think, would not be equal to all the opportunities for mistakes; but there it was—I had to live with it as best I could—unless, that is, I went back to Columbia, and this I quite often did think I had better do without more delay.

☆ | CHAPTER 6 | ☆

President and Cabinet

M UCH STUDY HAS been given the presidency, as is natural, considering the chief executive's dominance of the American political scene; but the offices of the cabinet have very little critical appraisal. What makes a good department head? What are his proper relations with the president, with the Congress, and with those who, if they can, will use his office for their own purposes? Aside from the few memoirs of cabinet members themselves, and some discussion of particular ones in contemporary comment, the literature is scanty. Before coming to Washington my notions about these offices were vague. Even after close observation for a considerable time I still had only a few reliable generalizations.

As to Wallace, I would not have administered the office in some ways as he did; I would not, many times, have made the choices he made. He was, for instance, a weak regulator; but that he was competent to direct the activities of our many scientists, and loyal to the president, there could be no doubt. Thinking about his office and of him, now, after many years, it still seems to me that he was a better secretary of agriculture than any of his predecessors, and the most useful of Roosevelt's department heads.

In 1933, even late in the year, he was still learning; but the early ineptness and fumbling, the overmodest attitude toward the president and members of the Congress, had disappeared. He was taking the leadership in agriculture, an enormous sector of the economy; but he was, more than that, becoming known as thoughtful and statesmanlike in wider circles. In his place I would have pressed harder and sharpened more issues; but I would undoubtedly have been defeated by the enemies I would have made. The truth is that I was often impatient with him.

Our relationship had to be close; but difficulties tended to multiply. I had begun as a temporary adjunct of the department with no thought of remaining long. Agricultural officials did not come from such places as Columbia University in New York City. They did not usually come from universities at all. On many counts I was ill placed. Circumstances, however, had settled me deeper and deeper into my position. As for Wallace, the social attention he got, the deference of his immense organization, the weight his opinions carried—all these had given him a certain confidence; but also he had found his intelligence to be of a higher order than that of most of those with whom he had to deal. This discovery gave this naturally shy and awkward man not quite a new personality but certainly new assurance.

The result may not have been altogether good, for he used his self-confidence in ways it was not suited for. He began, for instance, to use it in his political calculations. He began to see himself more clearly as a successor to Roosevelt; and others were quick to realize it. Those shrewd friends, Hopkins and La Follette, had already talked with me about it and what it was doing to him. I had to admit to having seen the signs. But what of it, I asked? Was there anyone better suited? But, they said, we would lose him for what had to be done now; he would not stick with us. There they had something.

He did soften toward those who could further his ambitions; and this included some sinister individuals. When Peek went, Wallace had the chance to gain the position at the head of the agricultural hierarchy that had been denied him while his leadership was threatened. Davis might have brought him the advice he needed; and he could have managed the political potential of AAA in a way to gain Wallace all the credit for such advances as were made. Davis, however, belonged to the old crowd. Wallace gradually became their prisoner. He began to overlook the attritions of the processors, neglect the poorer farmers and agricultural laborers, and allow it to be understood throughout the department that a hard policy in the enforcement of our many regulatory acts would not be supported. More and more the objective was narrowed. The incomes of farmer-owners—that is, the larger and more successful farmers—were to be increased; and this was not all. He began to reject complaints about his compromising.

Like other department heads in our government, he was in a most peculiar and anomalous position. Their establishments were under the direction of the president; but because of the size and complexity of their organizations, they tended to become autonomous. The president could not know much of what went on in any department or have much to do with its direction. Besides, secretaries were politicians, likely to be quite incapable of managing an organization. To make matters worse, many of the bureaus and operating divisions had congressional sponsors, and were filled with employees who owed more to some legislator as their patron than to their nominal superiors.

That the president had to "take care that the laws be faithfully executed" was the only definition of the "executive power" in the Constitution. The strange clause (in Section 2) saying that "he may require the opinion, in writing, of the principal officer in each of the executive departments, upon any subject relating to the duties of their respective offices" seemed to contemplate a rather distant relationship and had even given rise to some doubt that they were expected to be his subordinates. Legislators were inclined, on occasion, to interfere. There was some justification for this in another section saying that the Congress might "by law vest the appointment of such inferior officers, as they think proper, in the president alone, in the courts of law, or in the heads of departments." Since the heads of departments must be confirmed by a two-thirds vote of the "senators present" and since the Congress might permit these officers to designate their subordinates, the position of the president as head of the operating establishment was not altogether secure. There had often been secretaries who judged that their duty was more to the Congress than to the president. There were some in the Roosevelt cabinet.

The strong presidents—Jackson, Lincoln, Theodore Roosevelt, and now Franklin Roosevelt—had grandly assumed that their cabinet members were indeed subordinate. But these very presidents had been the ones most often embarrassed by department heads who possessed enough political strength to pursue independent policies. This had happened partly because they had been chosen more as representatives of strategic political groups than as administrators. Of these, in the Roosevelt cabinet, Cordell Hull was the most conspicuous. There were others, but he was the most notable southern senatorial Democrat. Wallace was certainly not chosen because he would be an effective departmental administrator. That was incidental to his representation of the progressive, largely Republican, farm constituency. He was now stretching out to represent all those with something to gain from agricultural revival, an impossible straddle. Roosevelt himself was holding together a loose coalition of southern Democrats, western progressives, and those who were disillusioned with Hoover. That this was impermanent was already obvious. The future Roosevelt coalition would have quite different components: the city machines, the labor unions, and those millions who benefited from the new concern for welfare.

Wallace would not see until after he became vice-president in 1940 that it was more important to conciliate the city politicians and union members than the southern and midwestern farmers. Then it would be too late. It would be the city bosses who would displace him for Truman in 1944. He would miss the presidency by only a few months; but he would miss it. This does not mean that a policy of appeasement did not further his career. He would, after all, become vice-president and would seem to be the heir apparent for four years. So he had a kind of success.

The question was whether, even if this policy was right for his own advancement, it was the proper way for a secretary to act. This I could not say. It seemed very bad administratively; but I was not one of those who, like Louis Brownlow and other administrative experts, thought of government as another great corporation. It was possible— and this was what they did—to construct a hierarchical system as a model, accepting the president as a literal chief administrator, with secretaries as his agents. But many secretaries had powers directly delegated by the Congress, and this was even true of some bureau chiefs. In fact, powers and duties throughout the government were frequently prescribed by law, sometimes in great detail, circumventing any presidential preferences. This made the Brownlow model so unreal as to be useless.

So far as operations were concerned, Roosevelt certainly spent very little of his time and effort on them; and Wallace spent very little more. But, of course, it was hard to separate administration from policy-making and from political maneuvering. It was, in fact, impossible to say where one activity began and others left off. It was all the more important that the next lower echelon, the bureau chiefs and the line organization —budget, personnel, physical services, and the like—should possess motivation, ability, and loyalty. The growth of the Civil Service and the improvement in organization had checked incompetence; but there was some smothering of initiative and a distinct lessening of willingness to accept presidential policy decisions.

Wallace had almost no interest in all this. He gave his time to departmental duties reluctantly and plainly felt that he ought to be doing something more important. He made no objection to my assuming managerial duties. On the other hand, the bureau chiefs very soon found that when my decisions were not to their liking they could appeal directly to him. And because it did not seem important, and because he thought bureau chiefs ought to know their work, he began to reverse me in an absent-minded way and without consultation. This got to be so frequent an occurrence that presently I demanded and got an understanding that department operations were my affair, except as to his special scientific interests. But he constantly forgot his commitment.

The real trouble was that Wallace, never having thought much about departmental administration, was willing to proceed in purely pragmatic fashion. We had a president who, more often than not, appeared to proceed in the same way—if he had any managerial formulas, they appeared only by inference as he acted. He wanted to enhance and strengthen the presidency for action. How far this ought to go, what its limits were, would be decided from time to time. This was true also of Wallace in the secretaryship. As to policy, the president expected to lay out the large design, and he had many ideas about detail; but there was a large area of discretion, and a cabinet member could be guided only by his own conception of what was required, or, as Ickes sometimes said—of others—"what he could get away with."

It was interesting to see how, under the influence of expanding demands, the traditional limits of federal responsibility were breaking down. An obvious contest among the branches was in process. We had to struggle every day with problems neither the separation of powers nor the sovereignty of the states any longer governed. The states, in depression, were vestigial; they seemed about to disappear or to become honorific relics as the national power grew and devised its own regional administrative areas. After the Hundred Days of the previous spring, the transfer of responsibility to the president and the consequent growth of administrative agencies seemed to have reversed the modern Republican effort to weaken the national center and the presidency. It could be seen, as soon as a firm leadership appeared, that this conception had been accepted only temporarily.

This last was interesting too. For a long time now, conservatives, reversing an earlier preference, had feared and distrusted strong presidents. The performances of Theodore Roosevelt and Wilson, especially, had convinced them that powerful executives were dangerous.

They had used all their influence to strengthen the Congress as a means of protecting their own interests. This strategy had broken down in the depression; and it seemed likely that all they had gained in twenty years might be lost almost at once. Indeed much of it had been lost already; consequently charges of presidential dictatorship were frequent, and editorialists were calling the Congress a "rubber stamp" institution.

It does not need to be said that the members of the Roosevelt cabinet and the later Executive Council had varying talents and loyalties. Any group of human beings would; but these, in origin and affiliation, were peculiarly various. Their notions of public service were warped by their political ties, and their competence was only such as they could develop. Few were even passable administrators. How some of them regarded the New Deal was later revealed in several memoirs. Farley, for instance, was devoted to the party but had no interest whatever in the social program—except that, when he did come to think about it, he was inclined to temper loyalty to reactionary friends with a natural warm-heartedness. Frances Perkins had a well-developed but narrow social philosophy; she was suspicious of the NRA and inclined to regard with Brandeis-like disapproval bigness of any sort and especially in government. Jesse Jones always intended to do exactly as he pleased; and what he pleased to do was to use the federal government's credit to assist the business system. He did have a vitriolic prejudice against Wall Street, but that was because he came from Houston and shared Texans' pretension to rivalry with the New York tycoons. Ickes was a tough customer who thought the president ought to be loyal to *him*. He was certain of his standards and allowed very little for any compromises except his own. So it went.

Among this company Wallace was unique. Aside from having, in a sense, inherited the secretaryship from his father, his superior intelligence made him different from most of the others. It operated avidly on facts and forecasts. He knew better than his colleagues what were likely to be the consequences of what it was proposed to do; and he used effectively the talents of a remarkably intelligent staff.

His kind of loyalty involved putting all this at the service of the president; and Roosevelt had quickly developed more respect for him than for any other member of his cabinet. His shy and inward-looking personality was poorly suited to the political arts, and he was not easy in their practice. He therefore stood rather in awe of a chief who used them so happily, almost carelessly, it seemed, for his purposes. This awe led him to accept, as I did, the decisions made for reasons we thought to be wrong or, at least, insufficient, but recognized to be beyond our ability to assist in determining. There might be involved matters quite hidden from us; and presidential timing might be adjusted to crises we knew nothing of. There was a good deal of questioning, but certainly none of that outright disloyalty latent, for instance, in the hearts of Farley, Jones, Garner, and Hull. None of these, except in the temporary and tactical sense, yielded any loyalty to the president as the shaper of national direction.

When these and many others in the executive establishment and in the Congress examined their inmost feelings they judged that what they stood for was being betrayed by Roosevelt. In their memoirs they have said, in effect, that they and not he were entitled to direct the activities they were responsible for. At the moment he had the power and they had to dissemble; but it was a grudging conformity. They looked for ways to check and hamper his program, covert and conspiratorial ways. They could cast doubt, try to amend or reduce, bring influence to bear, or plead for compromise in the name of a mythical opposition; and all of this they did. Roosevelt recognized and dealt with this amorphous opposition in his own way and time. He knew who were his loyal associates and genuine allies. He knew, also, who had to be used with circumspection.

The congressional progressives might carp and criticize too; but what he needed from them was only a grant of the right to shape the program and determine its timing. They yielded reluctantly. From Harry Hopkins, Henry Wallace, Frances Perkins, and Harold Ickes, as from me, he got a different kind of service. Hopkins was used without reserve, because his literal loyalty could be counted on. I made objections, but only in private. Wallace, because of his diffidence, sometimes turning to boldness under the stress of intellectual conviction, was just as loyal but not so much used because of his ineptness. Ickes wanted too much, right from the first, with a querulous insistence; and although the president held him to be a capable administrator, he was kept at arm's length.

Henry Morgenthau continued to be a puzzle. He was limited; but he unquestioningly carried out directions. Moreover, he gave the Treasury an efficient administration. He was almost pathologically jealous. This led him to dislike Hopkins and me, and our relations were always stand-offish. Roosevelt told me more than once that Henry had warned him about me. "He thinks you are compromising me with the conservatives," he said.

Thus Roosevelt's relations with his cabinet in some ways resembled those of the other Roosevelt. Various memoirs had described what those had been like. For instance, Oscar Straus[1] had written of the "kitchen cabinet" as a group of "unofficial advisers who met around the luncheon or dinner table and afterwards in the White House study, where the president spoke without reserve of his executive problems, and read for our criticism and counsel his rough drafts of congressional messages, speeches, and notes to foreign governments." But on the whole, T.R. had treated his official cabinet with reserve and even with a kind of disdain. Both the Northern Securities suit and the taking of the Panama strip—two momentous decisions in their day—were undertaken without cabinet consultation.

The "kitchen cabinet" was an old institution; it went back to Jackson's group—William B. Lewis, Amos Kendall, Duff Green, and Isaac Hill. Jackson was the first of the presidents, apparently, who had discontinued cabinet meetings altogether. No later president had gone quite that far; but Wilson had obviously regarded his secretaries as administrators of their departments rather than as advisers on high policy. When the *Lusitania* was torpedoed it was dwelt on by the Washington correspondents that Wilson did not call together his cabinet or consult with any members of it, but, just as Lincoln had done, awfully communed with himself.

The authority for Roosevelt on cabinet problems ought to have been Woodrow Wilson, considering his years of service in that president's administration. But evidently not much had been learned from Wilson, who had begun, as a student at Princeton, with that exaggerated admiration for British institutions so many young political scientists have, and had proposed that the members of the cabinet be given seats in the Congress. He would have allowed them to take the initiative in legislation and given them some responsibilities of the present standing committees.[2] But this, it should be noted, was an early opinion.

[1] In *Under Four Administrations: From Cleveland to Taft*, Boston, Houghton Mifflin and Co., 1922.

[2] This article was called "Cabinet Government in the United States," and was published in the *International Review*. It was reissued by the Woodrow Wilson Foundation in 1939 with an introductory note by T. K. Finletter, who, himself, made a somewhat different suggestion in his *Can Representative Government Do the Job?* (New York: Reynal and Hitchcock, 1945). Senator R. M. La Follette, apparently without knowing of Professor Corwin's proposal, made a similar one in 1943. Senator Kefauver carried on the campaign. (See the *American Political Science Review*, April 1944, pp. 317-25). There will be others. The overwhelming burdens

Wilson, as president, was satisfied with the system that had borne him to the top.

The easy solution for the crisis of representative government on the American model might well seem to be the one adopted by the British. There could be no executive-legislative conflict in that system because all the cabinet members and the prime minister himself had been elected to Parliament and were chosen from the majority. Thus there existed no clear separation of powers, and no checks and balances. There was no written constitution for judicial reference. Whatever policy was devised was carried through into legislation and became final. No court could reverse it.

The adoption of this system in the United States would require drastic structural changes. Proposals for modification involving no constitutional change—such as that of allowing cabinet members congressional seats—were small concessions. The British system rested on the membership in the Parliament of the executive officers. That we could not have. If cabinet members were given seats, their whole character and orientation would be changed. The president would lose such control of their operations as he had.

What we had in Roosevelt's first months was the best situation, almost, in American history with respect to movement and change. The president was allowed to lead and the Congress closed in behind, granting the necessary authority. Nevertheless, even in the frightening days of spring there had been uneasiness and muttering; as the new session in 1934 was approached, the indications were that there would be much less willingness to accept presidential leadership. But it was hard to see what he could do about this.

imposed on representative government by the enlarged responsibilities makes some change inevitable. So much time and energy are spent in legislative-executive struggle that the larger questions of policy are neglected, sometimes submerged in the incidents of that conflict.

Codes and
Marketing Agreements

I F THERE WERE no clear criteria for measuring the duties and successes of cabinet members, there were even fewer for those of such lesser officials as myself. We were presidential appointees. Some had been recommended in the first instance by immediate superiors, but that was not always true. Charles West and Oscar Chapman in Interior were Farley's suggestions to Ickes. Sumner Welles, who, when his special assignment in Cuba had been carried out, would become undersecretary of state, was an old Roosevelt acquaintance and was regarded with reserve by Hull. Turner Battle in Labor was ignored by Frances Perkins. An assistant secretary (at that time only State had an under-secretary) was never chosen because he was a promising administrator or even because he had established a competence for the work of his department; and this, I should have to confess, included myself.

The consequence of this, as would be expected, was that we were likely to be supernumeraries. In the worst cases—such as that of Charles West and Sumner Welles—the secretaries did not trust them, gave them nothing to do, and bottled them up in offices where they were free to find some occupation of their own, as long as it did not interfere with the secretary's activities. Even in the best cases the situation was difficult. The secretary developed his own staff, and the operations of the department naturally centered there. To utilize assistant secretaries in any serious way it would have been necessary to do what the president had suggested to Wallace and me—consider the assistant secretary as an alter ego, give him charge of operations, and reserve the secretary for those matters laid before him by the assistant secretary. I never knew this to be done.

The best departmental administrations in the New Deal were those of Ickes and Henry Morgenthau, but I seldom heard them praised for it. This was probably the reason more efficiency did not develop; there was no credit in it. A secretary was a more or less significant figure because of his "standing." That was an almost indefinable quality; but it had more to do with his contribution to policy and his relations with the public and the Congress than with the more obvious reasons for his being: his administrative support of the president and his counsel on large matters.

A secretary's presidentially appointed subordinates could not have separate thoughts about policy, or if they did, these could not be expressed publicly. They could not even make final decisions about administration—as I was finding out. Mine was a special case. When I understood that I ought not to have been a departmental official at all, as I soon did, I made repeated suggestions that I should leave, but I was overborne by Wallace and the president. They merely smiled at structural arguments; but, as I said, they were not the sufferers—I was. I was being allowed wide leeway in writing and speaking. I even had permission of a kind to write and say things my superiors would have said if they had been free to say what they liked. I was never recognized as a spokesman; I could not be; but since it appeared that I was a continuing intimate of Wallace as well as a White House familiar, what I had to say was paid attention to.

As to administration, I simply did the best I could. Wallace, I think, might have recognized me as the administrator if he had been able to, although his strong interest in scientific matters would have made it hard. But he soon found that our operations were of interest to lobbyists, to the farm leaders with whom he had to maintain relations, and to numerous congressmen. None of these was willing to be fobbed off with an assistant. Whether he wanted to or not, he had to discuss the enforcement of the Packers and Stockyards Act, the regulation of the commodity exchanges, and meat and seed inspection; these were legal requirements. And he had to know why it was proposed to close down a research project in Missouri or to locate one in Georgia rather than North Carolina. He was also asked embarrassing questions about food and drug legislation that he really knew little about and was not interested in. He soon found that he was being held answerable for whatever I did; and sometimes he did not approve.

We tried to find ways out of this, for instance, by the dividing up of duties. From time to time Wallace would simply say that in questions having to do with sugar, or experiment stations, or regulatory acts, or conservation—for illustration—the responsibility would be mine; but it never worked well. For one thing, the questions had a way of getting tangled together, or they developed minor crises and got newspaper attention, or congressional questioning intruded, and before he knew it he was involved and had to catch up on all that had been done, and perhaps defend actions he had not known about.

Wallace never criticized; he appreciated my careful subordination; but whenever we tried delegation and compartmentalization we found it breaking down. I regard it now as remarkable that our cooperation went on as long as it did. The strain of my special relationship with the White House was considerable. But we never had any break, and none but friendly discussions about policy or administration. I should have taken more seriously our differences about the injustice being done in the operations of the AAA. It was natural for an Iowan to assume that the more prosperous farmers would take care of their subordinates in the pattern of traditional rural life. Since there were as many farm workers, sharecroppers, and poorer tenants as there were farmer-proprietors and since their condition was even more desperate, something ought to have been done about it; but there was no interest among any of the agricultural hierarchy and so Wallace could not be moved. I was late in concluding this; but it finally undermined my relations with him and outlawed me with the farm organizations.

The old department did take on new spirit. Even the most traditional bureaucrats were energized. In spite of the restrictions and contractions imposed by the economy drive, new projects were being undertaken with emergency funds. The bureau chiefs finally realized that this was a unique opportunity for improvements they had hoped for but never really expected to get. The Bureau of Public Roads and the Forest Service were the first to realize this and almost immediately undertook expansions. The highway planners began to visualize a genuine national system with standards they hitherto argued for hopelessly (there were then no separated, two-way, four-lane intercity highways; and none were landscaped). The foresters began to think of eastern areas to match those in the West, of the adaptation of trees to climatic conditions they had not before been able to endure, and of recreation areas made accessible to an increasingly motorized people.

The entomologists began to think in larger ecological terms. The bureaus of plant and animal industry, prodded by Wallace, were shaken out of their orthodoxies. They began to develop surprising and novel ideas about biological improvement.

The AAA drew public attention as an attempt to adjust the agricultural industry to its economic situation; for some of us it was not enough merely to reduce the acreage devoted to the staple crops. Those acres ought not to be wasted. The first drive had been against the surpluses without any plans for the released land. From the first there were guilty feelings about this. More of some foods was needed for nutrition. More meat, milk, eggs, fruits, and vegetables were the obvious ones; people would buy them when they could; meanwhile all those acres taken out of production ought somehow to supply the need.

Our revulsion against simple reduction was expressed in a really ingenious invention, evolved in discussions among us during the summer while acreage reduction was going on. This was the Federal Surplus Relief Corporation, formally organized early in October. It was conceived as a partial resolution of the intolerable dilemma we felt ourselves caught in as production was restricted. The idea grew on us as we thought of it. Such an agency could assist in disposing of the existing surplus and could make restriction less necessary in years to come. Also it represented the acceptance of responsibility for feeding and clothing the nation. Combining funds belonging to AAA and those assigned under the National Recovery Act for relief, incredible amounts of agricultural products were bought and distributed to the needy by the corporation we established. It was the first of several to be chartered in Delaware, as a private corporation would have been, and was thus able to carry out its vast activities with relative freedom. Hopkins was made president; the other members of the board were Wallace and Ickes. It was Frank, again, who supplied the legal ingenuity. The organization was to go on being useful for years, being absorbed in 1935 by the AAA when relief was largely liquidated and works were adopted for the continuing reduction of unemployment.

Roosevelt and Wallace, neither of whom had any part in the inventing process in this case, accepted our proposal with obvious relief. The president said in his statement about it that it resolved a paradox "which had choked farms with an abundance of farm products while many unemployed had gone hungry." It was one in the eye for Hearst and for Coloned McCormick of the *Chicago Tribune*. There was literally nothing Roosevelt liked better than a refutation of reactionary propaganda.

I had hoped, in spite of misgivings, that the situation would be better after Davis was substituted for Peek. It was a chance to start over if Davis would have it that way. I especially hoped that he would prove more liberal. The cotton-reduction program had been unforgivably hard on the sharecroppers. They were simply expelled from their homes. So were the tenants of farms elsewhere. These outrages were the direct result of AAA regulations. The farm lobby had managed to keep all the new advances being made by labor from reaching their own hired workers. There was no collective bargaining for them. It was galling to see this going on and not be able to do anything about it. I protested, and Frank offered alternatives in the legal discussions, but we were simply ignored. Since Wallace was convinced by Davis that owner-farmers would be alienated if any such conditions for compliance were made, he approved what was being done.

I have spoken of the interesting fact that there were roughly six million farmers but also six million other rural workers. They ought, of course, to have had equal attention, but they had no way of getting it. They worked for others but not in large groups as factory workers did; and so they could not bargain collectively. They had little part in the social or political life of their communities; and in the South, of course, they were segregated and isolated. Especially, they were of no interest to politicians, since they were prevented from voting by various devices (the literacy test, for instance). They accepted their fate with resignation, and began the sad migration to the cities that would go on for generations.

Certain northerners took an interest in the sharecroppers' condition. Norman Thomas, for instance, the perennial Socialist candidate for the presidency, espoused their cause; and there arose a kind of protest movement among liberals. The attention this attracted only annoyed the proprietors, however, without having any real influence in Washington.

I was gradually excluded from AAA proceedings, but it ought to be noted that two developments of importance resulted from the protests. These were the transfer to NRA of all the marketing agreements, except those of the first processors; and the setting up in AAA of a land-use planning division. Getting rid of the marketing agreements was a relief. We had been struggling with them for months and had reached something of an impasse. I thought the views I had represented were as mild as could possibly be reconciled with the public interest. We had, on October 24, over Peek's protest but with Wallace's concurrence, issued a model agreement for the guidance of industries preparing agreements for submission. There was violent objection to three provisions. One required access to books and records; one gave the secretary power to remove members of industry committees; and one incorporated a number of provisions having to do with grades and standards. These last were similar to ones in the proposed Food and Drug Act and came at a time when the furor over that bill—as I shall recount —was at its most intense.

The president agreed with us that these were necessary provisions. He said so. Yet the implication was plain that similar ones ought to be included in the NRA codes; and every day he was signing these without any such provisions. This was an inconsistency to be explained only by his anxiety to complete the code-making process. He promised that the protections we asked for would be incorporated when revision and enforcement began. It was more probable that the revisions would loosen rather than tighten the restrictions; but he would not agree that this need be so.

It was therefore a real relief to have most of the decisions removed from our jurisdiction; yet it was a defeat for our principles, as far as the processing industry was concerned. We had not been able to persuade Johnson—we had some time ago given up any hope of persuading him—but neither had we been able to convince Roosevelt that he had only to present a stiffened front to get all that was asked. He was afraid it would delay or interrupt the code-making now going on at such a satisfactory pace. I argued that even if it was, our ultimate credibility was being jeopardized. Sometime he—and the rest of us—were going to have to defend our use of the powers delegated to AAA and NRA. We were fatally weakening any defense we might make.

But again, this had got beyond the point where it was our decision to make. We—Frank and I, joined less emphatically by Wallace—had every chance to argue the matter; but we simply did not prevail. And now we were to be relieved of responsibility. We would still have first processors—meat packers, millers, milk distributors, etc.—to deal with; but with this reverse in the record, we should be reduced to making protests with the expectation of being overridden. It was a substantial victory for the protesting industries. Almost certainly it would result in the abolition of this approach to government-industry stabilization efforts. If it did not, time might cure the defects—time and public pressure—but we thought not, having sampled the opinion of all our progressive friends. They were by now thoroughly disillusioned. They said what we did not yet admit, that the whole attempt at stabilizing had gone wrong and ought to be stopped. We must go back to trust-busting as Brandeis wanted us to do.

There was appropriate jubilation among the industry representatives. *Business Week* on December 17 stated the issues fairly:

> The sizzling effect of the President's decision to turn these codes back to NRA, from which he took them on 21 June, still has Washington somewhat uncomfortable. . . . The "liberal" crowd, headed by Assistant Secretary of Agriculture Tugwell and Jerome N. Frank, counsel for AAA, have certainly taken a set-back, for the transfer of the food industry codes to NRA was not to their liking and is considered in their group as a distinct disavowal of their views as to how codes ought to be handled. Dr. Tugwell had stated his views freely in print, holding that codes should be prepared in the best form possible by the government and then submitted to the industries concerned, while General Johnson at NRA has held that industry should draw them up and then government should take a hand in revision.

But *Business Week* was mistaken in emphasizing this last point. What we were really concerned about was the establishment of code-making principles. And it was on this point that we had been defeated. From this time on, there were no principles; but it would not be our responsibility.

☆ | C H A P T E R 8 | ☆

Toward a Permanent Policy

THE OTHER OCCURRENCE I have referred to—the setting up of a land-planning division in the Bureau of Agricultural Economics —was a cause for satisfaction. AAA, if it simply paid farmers for reducing planted acres, would do nothing to reclaim the natural grass and forest land that had been broken to the plow. There was, besides, the serious soil erosion deplored by the conservationists. It might be possible, we thought, to use benefit payments for checking destructive practices.

There was also something else we might do. We might purchase submarginal land and retire it permanently from cultivation. This would contribute something to reducing surpluses and would furnish areas for reforestation, for recreation, and for grazing. One indefensible feature of our operations had been that payment was being made for the disuse of land for one year only. Unless there should be annual payments these acres would come into production again. We could not go on indefinitely paying a rental to farmers all over the country simply for not using their land.

At the moment these suggestions were regarded by most of my colleagues, and by practically all legislators, as fanciful. They were intent on pleasing "the farm folks," as Wallace called them. But it was not farmers but lobbyists we dealt with. They were politicians who were bound to try to get what the farmer, in his most selfish moments, wanted. We had been bold enough to insist on the control of production after a whole generation of resistance to that discipline, and of attempts to use every other futile scheme. The lobbyists had been determined to avoid any control; but it had been accepted as they had assured us it never would be. Perhaps other conditions would be accepted too, reluctantly at first, but with good spirit when understood.

This would be congenial to Roosevelt's desire for enlargement of the public domain and for checking rural rot everywhere. Wallace saw the point; but, after consulting with Davis, he decided that such a program would not be acceptable. There was no disposition in AAA to make any move not approved by the processors and the lobbyists. That, obviously, was where the opposition came from, not from the farmers themselves; but nothing, for the moment, was done. There was, however, one concession: a planning committee.

For a long time, joining immediate farm relief with the shaping of a permanent agriculture had been seen as a possibility. In 1929 I had written an article for *The Annals of the American Academy of Political and Social Science* called "Farm Relief and a Permanent Agriculture." As I read it over now, I realize that I had pretty well anticipated the nature of the difficulties we were having. The final paragraph, in fact, was a fair appraisal of our present dilemma:

> Few public authorities in the world have dared to enforce expert opinion in opposition to rule-of-thumb practices; and the United States is not one of them. It may be set down, in fact, as the most reluctant of all. It is, however, true that our greatest solicitude has characteristically been for the rights of individuals and enterprises outside of agriculture; we might interfere there perhaps more readily than elsewhere. Then, too, the farmers are forever at the doors of Congress asking for relief. This conjuncture of attitudes may just possibly give the expert his chance. We may offer the farmer assistance on condition of good behavior—the good behavior consisting in growing those crops which seem wise in such amounts as seem desirable and by such methods as social prudence dictates . . .

This indicates what one who was quite outside the circle of agricultural professionals was thinking several years before our efforts began. Much more important were the really informed approaches. E. C. Banfield has summarized these in convenient form in the following paragraphs from a paper of his called "Organization for Policy Planning in the U.S. Department of Agriculture."[1]

The Program Planning Division was not without antecedents in the Department. For one thing, the idea of production planning and control

[1] This paper was published in *The Journal of Farm Economics* for February 1952. Footnotes have been omitted.

had a history. The Department had been issuing "outlook" reports since 1923 in the hope that it might thus guide the production of several million farms somewhat in harmony with demand. Howard B. Tolley, who became chief of the Program Planning Division and had been an assistant administrator of AAA, was a pioneer in this outlook work. When it was clear that the outlooks could not do what was needed, Tolley suggested the creation of state, regional, and national planning councils with authority to zone land and map types-of-farming areas. His idea was to have the Extension Service persuade farmers to make the adjustments called for in the plans. Earlier, W. J. Spillman, the Department's authority on farm management, had made recommendations along the same lines.

Formally, of course, the Program Planning Division was the staff agency of a single bureau—one bureau among many, and Tolley reported not to the Secretary of Agriculture but to the bureau head. But in practice, the case was quite different. While the old Department went about its pre-New Deal routines, the multitudinous authorities of the AAA Act were being used to create what was in effect a new Department of "action programs." The Program Planning Division was the central planning agency of this Department, and since it was with this new Department that Secretary Wallace and his top assistants were almost entirely concerned, the division was really a staff aid to them.

For the first time, this planning effort would concentrate on the future of agriculture in the national economy. Howard Tolley, who was a competent if conservative economist from California, having become head of the division, would be able to give the work of the Bureau of Agricultural Economics a focus it had hitherto lacked. Tolley was one of those in AAA who had been very suspicious of Frank and me. We had opposed some of the marketing agreements he had worked out for his California friends, some of the worst, measured by the public interest. But we hoped that in this new work his irritation over these incidents would be forgotten. In the first few months of the new regime we could see many reasons for hoping that all of us would be able to work together for the good of agriculture and of the country.

It was encouraging too that Wallace had allowed an article to appear under his name for our first *Yearbook* (December 1933), discussing the possibility of retiring submarginal land from production. The number of acres involved was about forty million—about the extent of New England. It could be bought at no more cost than the rentals by AAA during the next eighteen months.

If the aim was to reduce the farm plant as a whole, in order to deal with a continuing tendency to produce surpluses of staple crops, it would be more economical to acquire entire farms rather than rent parts of them. There were places where to reduce acreage 15 percent the government was paying a rental large enough to buy a quarter of the land involved. Besides, in these risky agricultural areas there might in the long run be a larger return from forestry or grazing.

This might indeed be the official beginning of something important. We should have to think too of the people living on these unproductive farms. The long depression had already reduced them to poverty; many were going to the cities, but there were no opportunities for them there. At the moment it was not possible to forward these ideas; but during the next year drought would settle over the plains and the dust storms would begin. Then the trek of the "Okies" to the Pacific Coast, out of the short-grass counrty from Montana to Texas, would become a national disaster. Because of the combination of poor lands and poor people, the land retirement and resettlement scheme would have more appeal. The first step was to spread the idea of submarginal-land retirement. The funds needed would be large; and for funds congressional approval was needed. The idea was exciting; but hope that it might become actual was deferred. What would be done would be with the use of funds disposable by the president. The Congress was completely unmoved.

☆ | CHAPTER 9 | ☆

The Tugwell Bill
Becomes Copeland's Bill

T HE LEGISLATION we had put together for the regulation of food and drugs was becoming an acute disappointment. There had been innumerable conferences with representatives of the affected industries, and we had carried on our publicity as best we could. There had been support from many diverse sources; but the continued opposition from the press had become more unscrupulous as the weeks passed. It was now clear that hopes for passage during the emergency session were futile. Of all our friends, Heywood Broun had been the most loyal. A quotation from one of his columns (that of December 14) will show how forthright his attitude was:

The knives are being sharpened for Professor Tugwell's hide. The charge is being made that he wants to upset American institutions. I'm afraid that there may be some truth in this. The Pure Food and Drugs Act which has been prepared under his direction would be certain to interfere seriously with the sale of certain patent medicines. He had the audacity to suggest that advertisers should not be allowed to make false claims. He thinks that it is inexpedient to offer rosewater under the assertion that it is a very Verdun against the invasion of all germs.

It is the inalienable right of every American citizen to take whatever blame fool nostrum he pleases into his system. Only a paternal and bureaucratic government would attempt to deny the free-born the inalienable right to pay for the privilege of assimilating impurities.

Our forefathers were mowed down at Bunker Hill in order that their descendants should continue to enjoy the privilege of being mowed down.

225

In a recent and forgotten magazine editorial Al Smith declared that young college professors allied with the administration were intent upon turning us all into guinea pigs for experimental purposes. He overlooked the fact that one hundred million of us are already guinea pigs living in the pens of quacks and fakers.

Depend upon it—high sounding names will be found for the fight against the Tugwell bill. Nobody will confess that he hates to see easy money drift away. It will be an argument playing to the tune of an anthem.

And a week before (on December 7) Drew Pearson's column had outlined the situation as follows:

The drive against liberal forces within the New Deal now looks like a death battle. One side or the other—the Left or the Right—is going to have to get out.

The fight at present is centering on two things. One is the securities bill, branded by bankers and brokers as stifling the money market. The other is the Agricultural Adjustment Administration.

In the latter are two distinct groups. One—the liberals—is headed by Secretary of Agriculture Wallace. The other—the conservative—is headed by George Peek, co-administrator of the AAA.

Wallace has gathered round him a group of progressives, some of the hardest fighers in the New Deal. They include Professor Tugwell, Legal Counsel Jerome Frank, Economic Adviser Ezekiel, Consumers Counsel Howe, Paul Appleby and Gardner Jackson.

The drive against them is being led by groups of meat packers, tobacco companies and milk dealers, whose codes they have opposed.

The strategy of the attack is to brand the Wallace group as "Reds." The plan is to pick off one man at a time. The attack is now centering on Tugwell. Various interests want him out of the picture. They have two big things against him. He is the author of the Pure Food and Drugs Act and of the liquor control code.

What few people know is that in both of these, Tugwell is the goat. He was merely carrying out instructions. Roosevelt himself ordered him to draw up the Food and Drug Act. The President is its chief supporter. The liquor control plan was ordered by Wallace—but Tugwell got the blame.

So Tugwell is branded a dangerous "Red." Confidential business letters are broadcasting this. Several business concerns are putting out press releases with the same implication.

Both Wallace and Roosevelt, however, are backing him 100 percent.

Although these supporters were as courageous as they were inaccurate, they were a good way from being typical. By far the greater part of the publicity, in the thousands of smaller newspapers and in the magazines, offered direct and indirect detraction without any pretense of fairness. An article from *Business Week* (for October 28) furnished authentic information but used the adjectives expected by its clientele:

In the dying spasms of the last Congress, the Department of Agriculture's cocksure brain-truster, Professor Rexford G. Tugwell, suddenly introduced his revamp of the 27 year-old Food and Drugs Act. It was trampled in the stampede of more urgent legislation. The professor picked up the bill, dusted it off, and is determined to put it through the coming session. Already the air is full of attacking and defending superlatives, of sentimental tear gas.

The bill is designed to modernize food and drug supervision, to extend to advertising the provisions that now restrict labeling, to bring into the federal harness the hitherto footloose cosmetics industry, to provide a curb bit and reins by which the Secretary of Agriculture may exercise almost absolute discipline. This bill is frankly an advance on a new front in the struggle to bring business more firmly under government "guidance."

Business Week also mentioned our most effective propaganda exhibit, called by the sympathetic reporters the "Chamber of Horrors." It had been in the department patio for some time, and Eleanor Roosevelt had paid it a much noticed visit; also it had been exhibited at the Chicago Century of Progress Exposition and at such other places in the country as would attract attention. In spite of all the efforts, however, our bill had been buried in committee. Worst of all, Senator Copeland, who had introduced it as a routine matter, was now making it his own. He was hardly a trustworthy custodian for the document we had produced but he was the legislator through whom it had to pass. We heard of various ways it was likely to be modified; and all of them were emasculations. Any bill pushed by Copeland would have only the provisions approved by industries to be regulated. We had hoped they might admit that the disciplining of the worst offenders would make the honest ones more respectable; but even this was more and more doubtful. Campbell, the administrator, and his colleagues, in the best phlegmatic tradition of the Civil Service, took it all as part of the day's work. They carried on endless, mostly fruitless, conferences; they exploited every opportunity to make allies; they were more than reasonable about concessions; and they never admitted that defeat was inevitable. If it came they would simply start over.

Before the middle of December there were hearings. By now I had concluded that it would be better to get myself out of this particular effort if I could. The opposition had invested too heavily in my authorship of the "Tugwell bill" to allow this to happen if they could help it; but my participation did neither the bill nor myself any good. I told the president frankly that if any more was done he would have to manage it. He called in Copeland and the three of us had a talk.

The senator was a product of Tammany politics, with the flushed well-fed look of a prosperous professional. His shoes were fine and shiny; in the lapel of his well-tailored coat there was a fresh carnation, renewed every morning. In the Hearst press and on the radio, sponsored by one of the products our law might affect, he had made a good thing of medical advice. He and I sat for a few moments beside McIntyre's desk while we waited. As we exchanged pleasantries, I knew that we could find no way of touching him. By introducing it, without consulting us, just at the end of the last session—in June—he had seized control of the situation. The food, drug, cosmetic, and advertising trades were suppliants for favorable amendments. He was enjoying his role and would not be anxious to see its end. Roosevelt had nothing to trade with beyond the ordinary patronage, and that would not protect the provisions our lawyers, David Cavers and Milton Handler, had carefully framed. Our moment had passed. The suggestion that the consumer protection begun by T.R. in 1906 could be renewed had excited Roosevelt at first; but he had given up and now there was no effective support. As winter came on many other issues had higher priority. There was snow on the lawn outside the south windows; and it had powdered the trees and shrubs.

When we were seated beside his desk, Roosevelt began. "Royal," he said, "we've got to pass a law. These fellows who have made so much noise about it have fixed things now so that we have to do something. I know about the opposition, but it sounds worse than it is. Do you think you can have some hearings and get them over before Congress meets?"

"Well, Mr. President," the senator said, "a lot of manufacturers want to be heard, but I've got it pretty well lined up now. We'll get through it next week."

The president pressed. "How many changes will have to be made?"

"A good many," the senator answered, "but we will have a bill."

"Well," the president said, "can't you convince the better manufacturers that they will be better off with the chiselers out of the way?"

"The trouble is," said the senator, "that a lot of the worst stuff we are aiming at is made in back rooms in small towns or in little scattered factories. You know the big drug houses don't sell snake oil and alcoholic tonics, and they don't offer diabetes or cancer cures. We could persuade them by going easier on advertising. Our trouble is going to be with senators and congressmen who have friends among the little fellows and who like the support of the country papers where the snake-oil people advertise. You'll have to take care of the lot of them."

"I'll have Jim Farley work on it," the president said. "You get the hearings over and the drafting done. We ought to get it out of the way."

Copeland was going to have to run again presently, and he was at least respectful. I thought I had never seen Roosevelt so withdrawing and cool. Usually the charm showed itself very early and business became a part of a pleasant conversation. This was different. They were both New Yorkers but with different—and competing—affiliations. Neither liked or trusted the other.

We went out with hardly any break in the chill. I told Campbell, who was waiting in my office when I got back, that I liked the situation less than ever. We could count on nominal support from the White House. Maybe the president really did feel that he was committed; but he had other interests, and consumer protection was interfering with some of them. He shook his head. "Don't take it too hard," he said. "If you had been here as long as I have, being ignored by all the policy people, you'd think this was real progress. I never expected to hear of a president and a senator discussing a new food and drug bill."

I was touched; I knew Campbell would never quit and would never give any ground. He could not, in the end, be beaten; but the end seemed awfully far in the future. I jumped up. "Let's go see the secretary," I said. And we did. I broke in between two appointments. "Look at this man," I said, "he's breaking my heart. He works and schemes and gets licked; then he starts all over again. He's absorbed more punishment than we will ever be able to take. And what happens when he does get a break? Is this legislation called the Campbell bill? No, it's called the Tugwell bill. And now it is to be the Copeland bill. But all the time the strength and intelligence going into it has been Campbell's. He's your bureau chief as well as mine. You simply must go up to the hearings and be his front next week. I can't do him any more good. I know you don't like it much. But how can you bear to see such dedication wasted?"

Campbell blushed; and Wallace simply said, "You're right, of course. I'll have to do it." And he did. He made a good job of it; and he worked on all the friends he had on the hill. I was happy to fall in behind.

The hearings I shall not describe. For those with an interest, the *Congressional Record* can be read; and I must say that David Lawrence's *United States News* presented an account[1] that will satisfy anyone but a historian. No bill would be passed while I was in Washington; but, in my pantheon at least, Walter Campbell was a hero. Nothing that he could do was left undone, ever. The long ongoing fight wore him out, but it never touched the source of his serenity.[2]

It had been a notable feature of the talk between Roosevelt and Senator Copeland that there had been no mention of public interest in the bill. Sometimes this had seemed considerable, and we had made sure that Roosevelt was informed. There were also supporters at the hearings. In this, however, as in so much else in American life, the real power was highly concentrated. A senator did not care very much if a middle-class League of Women Voters approved, or even if the

---

[1] December 11, 1933, pp. 2 and 12. Cf. also *Business Week*, December 16, 1933, p. 8, for another kind of account.

[2] Perhaps I may summarize, for the sake of completeness, what the reforms we were proposing amounted to. These items are from the memorandum we prepared for Wallace to present at the hearings:

1. Cosmetics were, for the first time, to be brought within the statute;
2. Mechanical devices and preparations claiming to bring about changes in the structure of the body were included;
3. False and misleading advertising was to be prohibited;
4. Informative labeling was to be required;
5. A drug which was or might be dangerous to health under the conditions of use prescribed in its labeling was to be prohibited;
6. There was to be a promulgation of definitions and standards for foods which would have the force of law;
7. The prohibition of added poisons in food or the safe tolerances therefor were to be included;
8. The operation of factories under federal permit was to be prescribed where the public health required it;
9. New and more effective procedures for the control of false labeling and false advertising were to be provided;
10. There were more severe penalties in cases of repeated offenses.
11. It was stated that the first intention was consumer protection; but it was also made clear that it would be expected to operate in the interest of all honest manufacturers.

American Federation of Labor sent a minor official to testify; and Roosevelt knew well enough how weak we were.

The supporters included professors of public health, like Haven Emerson; together with representatives of consumers' organizations. The real attention, however, was commanded by such opponents as Charles Wesley Dunn of the Associated Grocery Manufacturers, A. R. Whitemarsh of the Wholesale Grocers' Association, J. H. Beal of the National Drug Trade Conference, and J. A. Benson of the Association of Advertising Agents. Then there was my special self-appointed caretaker, W. L. Dailey, Washington lobbyist for the National Editorial Association. He represented, he said, 12,000 daily and weekly publications. It was he who had promised to make me a "Red" and had fairly well succeeded. His testimony, it may be believed, was listened to most carefully.

I was pleased that E. R. Squibb and Co. appeared to approve and that the H. J. Heinz Co. was represented and said that the bill was neither unreasonable nor impracticable as most of the others had been saying. We began to keep a private roll of honor. These two firms headed the list.

By this time the lesson in government furnished by the food and drug experience was hardly needed. It was no more than reinforcement for the more consequential lessons from NRA and AAA. But there was always something special about this. There was something degrading about the abasement of elected representatives before those among their constituents who made no pretense of decency. It was by now a matter of common talk among newspapermen that one senator was "the magic rub senator," another the "crazy crystals senator," and another the "gargle congressman" and so on, except that the firm name, so closely associated with the representative, was used. Such tie-ups were a familiar phenomenon; but those who would have been brought under control in this instance were more flagrantly open. Their products were injurious or worthless; they were preying on a human desire for health, beauty, and social approval. It was a thoroughly nasty business; that it should have reached and dominated the deliberations of the Congress was a sickening fact, but a fact it was and it emphasized, for all to see, one of the worst weaknesses of representative democracy.

Where was the unity we needed for the great issues looming on the horizon? Or indeed for the struggle we were in for recovery and stabilization? Even in so clear and admitted an issue as the exploitation of the helpless in mean and cynical ways, the getting of private profit at public expense was paramount. If we could not subdue patent-medicine and cosmetic manufacturers, establish the minimum of honest labeling for food products, eliminate poisoning and deceit, how should we establish the much less clear and critical standards of fairness in other industries? There was, I afterward thought, more alienation of trust in government, more suspicion of democratic institutions, generated in this fight than in all the other more important but less spectacular issues put together.

CHAPTER 10

NRA Goes Wrong

I T IS NOTED in Roosevelt's *Public Papers* that on November 17 the National Emergency Council was established by executive order, and that on December 19 the Special Industrial Recovery Board was absorbed into the new organization. This simple statement concealed a decision to abolish the board and allow Johnson to deal directly with him. This must have appeared to the public, and might appear to historians, as a rather logical simplification. Everyone, in fact, conspired to create that appearance. Frank Walker, who was to be the executive director of the new board, and Secretary Roper, who was chairman of the Recovery Board (as secretary of commerce), produced the necessary formula. As for those of us who dissented, we would not surrender our consciences to Johnson's keeping; and he would no longer ask us for approval of his codes. The new Council would not supervise NRA, even nominally; but we had done what we could.

The last meeting of the board was held on December 12. It was the twenty-sixth meeting. We had, until then, been assembling weekly since June 19 in Roper's conference room in that large Department of Commerce building referred to by Roosevelt as "Hoover's monument." The room was furnished in the best big-business style. I recall mostly wood, leather, and the hum of air-conditioning machinery, not so efficient then as it was to become later. Like the "temporary" Navy building maneuvered into being during the war when Roosevelt was assistant secretary, it was situated in what was called "foggy bottom," the depression that caught and held relentlessly the muggy heat and winter damp of the Potomac basin.

Roper was a conciliator. He always sought to soften acrimonies. The colloquy with General Johnson ran as follows:

Chairman Roper: General, do you wish to say anything?

General Johnson: It doesn't seem to me as though we have done much the past two weeks except fight. Of course, the trouble now is that we are down to the clinkers in the bottom of the grate in the construction of codes. . . .

Mr. Brown (assistant administrator): I might say that the secretary has inquired at past meetings as to the number of codes. The number of national codes we have before us now has been reduced to 900 by consolidation, of which 150 have been approved so far.

Chairman Roper: Are they in such a state of progress that you think probably the code era might be concluded within two or three months?

General Johnson: Yes, I think undoubtedly so. There is an enormous accumulation of codes to be presented to the president that are depending on other codes before they can be put though. I think that about 90 percent of all the employment in the country will be covered by the first of January, or at the latest, the 15th. I do believe that the making of codes is drawing to its close, but then comes administration, which is quite a different thing.

Chairman Roper: It occurred to me that in view of that situation it might be well to have this board meet on call in the future rather than at a definite hour and day as heretofore. While you are considering that point, I just had a talk here with Mr. Walker. . . . I suggested the other day to the president that in view of the scope that was given to his coordinating committee, as I recall it, under Mr. Walker if you please, it might be well for this board now just to be absorbed in that, since the personnel is practically the same, rather than having the same personnel meeting on two days and maybe getting so weary with meetings that you would not come at all.

General Johnson: Another aspect of it is that the functions of the boards are so near alike that you might get all kinds of crossed wires.

Chairman Roper: That is what I am afraid of. I think it is always dangerous to have these overlapping boards . . . So, if it is agreeable to the board, we will await word from Mr. Walker. I think the president is friendly to it . . .

Commissioner March:[1] That is the coordinating board you speak of?
Chairman Roper: I think they call it the Council.
General Johnson: It is the Emergency Council, head of the emergency
    organizations.

Since the Emergency Council had been established by executive
order on November 17 and this was December 19, it seems strange that
Roper should not have been aware of its functions or even of its name.
Actually it had not yet met. It would, in fact, have its first meeting
that afternoon. But that it was mere pretense to credit it in advance
with the assumption of the Special Industrial Recovery Board's responsibilities everyone in the room, including Roper, knew very well. What
had happened was that Johnson had complained bitterly to the president that the board was making itself a nuisance by insisting that the
codes should be reviewed with some standards for reference.

The truth was that if there were any standards they existed in
Roosevelt's mind, and he did not intend to make them explicit. He
wanted room to maneuver, to give a little here and take a little there;
in other words, to bargain. But most of all he wanted the code-making
to be completed in a hurry. This was partly because he felt that with
their codes finished and in operation businessmen would settle down to
producing. It was also partly because he meant standardization to
follow putting the codes into effect. Revision could then take place
in an atmosphere less contentious and strained than that prevailing at
the moment. Also there would be experience available and a code
authority to bring the proper kinds of pressure to bear. Actually, there
was another motive. He had to move quickly because Johnson's blue
eagle campaign had reached the fiasco stage. After so much ballyhoo
its failure was embarrassing.

Some of us had repeatedly argued, or attempted to argue, that common standards for all the codes were essential. It was our belief that
the larger industries were finding themselves able to get a strangle-
hold on the economy. They intended, we suspected, to raise prices,
restrict production, and allocate capital and materials among themselves. This was not only against the public interest, generally conceived,
but it would hinder rather than encourage recovery.

The argument had gone on and on. Roosevelt had tired of it, and
this was his way of bringing it to an end. Considering that we could

[1] Chairman at that time of the Federal Trade Commission.

point to certain standards spoken of by himself and quoted in a guiding pamphlet circulated by the National Recovery Administration[2] itself, we felt that we had a compelling argument. The most important of these principles, apart from the procedural instructions, were in sections 7 and 8. There, a quote from the presidential statement on the setting up of the administration was taken as a guide. It said:

I am fully aware that wage increases will eventually raise costs, but I ask that managements give first consideration to the improvement of operating figures by greatly increased sales to be expected from the rising purchasing power of the public. That is good economics and good business. The aim of this whole effort is to restore our rich domestic market by raising its vast consuming capacity. If we now inflate prices as fast and as far as we increase wages, the whole project will be set at naught. *We cannot hope for the full effect of this plan unless, in the first critical months, and, even at the expense of full initial profits, we defer price increases as long as possible.*[3]

There followed this statement:

In the drafting of codes, attention is especially directed to this suggestion by the President that the Recovery Administration cannot be effective unless the consumer's buying power is protected. There will be full protection for the consumer. The codes should recognize the interest of the public in the matter of prices.

There were also these other important directions:

At the hearings described in paragraph 2 every trade association or group proposing a code should be prepared to establish by evidence the requirements of section 3(a), clause 1, of the act which provides: that such associations or groups impose no inequitable restrictions on admission to membership therein and are truly representative of such trades or industries or subdivisions thereof.

And of section 3(a), clause 2, of the act which provides: that such code or codes are not designed to promote monopolies or to eliminate or oppress small enterprises and will not operate to discriminate against them and will tend to effectuate the policy of this title.

We in Agriculture—including, on this issue, even Peek—had had trouble with Johnson almost from the first. The controversy became

---

[2] This was *Bulletin No. 2*, National Recovery Administration. It was signed by Johnson, but countersigned also by the members of the National Industrial Recovery Board; and so it was binding, as we thought, on all of us.

[3] Italics appear in the original *Bulletin.*

heated when the reemployment agreement was proposed. It not only threatened to raise farmers' costs and so aroused Wallace and Peek, but excited John Dickinson, and Harold Stephens as well.[4] Getting together, we prepared a memorandum stating our objections; and they were made plainer in board meetings, held at our request on three successive days, July 17, 18, and 19.[5]

Our protest was futile. We did not succeed in preventing NRA from entering on a course we believed to be fatal. We would have had Johnson go on preparing one code after another for the large industries, gradually imposing the standards and criteria we thought necessary, as well as building up an enforcement organization. He was determined to have freedom in conceding whatever was necessary to get codes into operation.

Both Wallace and Peek were disturbed. Peek had tried to get exemption from the blanket agreement of the industries under our control, but he was either ignored or put off. Of course, we knew that such treatment could only be ventured by Johnson if he had Roosevelt's support; but our argument with Roosevelt—one we pursued persistently—was lost too. What went on in the recovery board is reflected in the transcripts; but they can only be understood by realizing that attitudes were being influenced by knowing or sensing what Roosevelt wanted. The Reemployment Agreement was failing and he was falling back on an industrial expansion that he trusted would follow completion of the code-making process. The main purpose of NRA—self-government for industry within carefully administered standards—had been sacrificed. We did not have to wait long for justification. Even before the end of August the board's discussions were pretty much centered on "chiseling" and on complaints concerning concerted price increases. The indignation of farmers made a special problem for us in Agriculture; but similar protests were coming from many other sources.

The reemployment campaign was just coming to its unhappy end. Stephens was doubtful of its legality and had sent out instructions not to proceed in any cases of violation. News of that sort gets around very fast. While Johnson was making lyric speeches and leading parades,

---

[4] Dickinson was assistant secretary of commerce and Stephens was assistant attorney general.

[5] The transcripts referred to here were mimeographed and circulated to those present. One survived in my files and it is from that copy that my quotations are taken.

businessmen were violating the agreement freely. The campaign seemed likely to become even more ridiculous than some of us had feared at the outset.

Our attack on Johnson in the National Recovery Board had been returned to again. Wallace, at my request, made a rare appearance at a meeting late in August; until then I had represented him and the department. We had furnished him with data from the lumber code to illustrate the way prices were being fixed. We had evidence in that instance for what we suspected was a general condition—the outlawing of sales "below the cost of production." This was a phrase we had had our troubles with in agriculture. We had had to defeat a strongly supported amendment to our act proposed by John Simpson, the demagogue who was then head of the Farmers' Union. This would have required price-fixing above the cost of production. The catch was that costs depended on how the figuring was done; moreover, they would not be the same for any two farmers. Simpson's intention was to press for prices covering the highest costs anyone could think of. His idea of the cost of raising wheat, $2.25 per bushel, may have been true for inefficient farmers; but most of the crop could hardly have cost more than one-third his estmate. Since wheat then ranged around fifty cents, he would have put us in the position of raising its price arbitrarily by several times.

We could now show that at least one industry—lumber—was being allowed to write permissive provisions into its code. Turner Battle, speaking for the Department of Labor, supported us, saying it had been reported to his department that the larger manufacturers were "making a statement to the effect that their code would force out small competition." Johnson was evasive and spoke of "experiments." NRA, he said, was learning every day. His annoyance was obvious. At a later meeting, we resolved that a committee should be set up to study price-fixing. Hopkins had voiced a protest about the effect of rising prices on his relief organization. "We find ourselves," he said, "able to give the same amount of relief only by very marked increases in dollars." And he had many examples to cite.[6]

---

[6] Transcript of September 6. *The United States News* for December 18, 1933 published almost a full-page summary of reemployment efforts:

April-May:	Agitation in Congress for 30 hour week; 13,000,000 unemployed persons.
June:	NRA comes into being.

It will be remembered that one of the reasons why NRA was sponsored by Roosevelt, and why the act was passed in the special session of spring, was the threat of a thirty-hour law being pushed by Senator Hugo Black. It was organized labor's conception of the way to relieve unemployment. From the very first, under Section 7(a), dealing with the issues of hours, wages and working conditions, labor leaders had intervened in the shaping of codes. Roosevelt, Frances Perkins, and others were very pleased with these provisions. They were obviously willing to neglect consumers' interests for labor's gains. This was like the difficulty we had in AAA when farmers' prices were raised. Consumers were nowhere when it came to bargaining for privileges.

But neither farmers nor organized workers, nor both together, made up the whole economy. It was important that general buying power should not decline; and by late autumn we were beginning to suffer the inevitable consequences of a rising cost of living. If Hopkins was indignant about this for his millions of families on relief, there were millions of other families scarcely better off who were also caught without increased incomes to meet rapidly rising costs. The problem could not continue to be ignored.

There was the complication also that farmers were becoming convinced that industry was gaining at the expense of agriculture. There were outbreaks of renewed agitation and even some violence in the West. Especially John Simpson and Milo Reno were rousing their followers; and Father Coughlin was less and less restrained as discontent furnished approving listeners. Also there was always Huey Long to proclaim loudly that his alternatives were simpler and surer than all the New Deal folderol.

As far as labor was concerned, not all was well in spite of apparent gains under the codes. Not all workers were treated alike; and many

---

July:	Code hearings begin; blanket code issued; textile industry goes under first code.
August:	Strikes break out: National Labor Board begins to function.
September:	Other big industries go under codes, including oil, lumber, steel.
October:	Farmer and industrialist attachés on NRA start in Middle West.
November:	Industry brings out Swope plan for self-regulation: Supreme Court test of NRA looms; consumers and labor demand more voice in industry.
December:	15 million persons working under 143 approved codes; unemployed reduced to 9 millions; payrolls up $50,000,000 a week over March.

employers were unfaithful to the codes or to the reemployment agreements. To meet a pressing need—which ought, as could soon be seen, to have been met by special legislation—the president had set up early in August a National Labor Board.[7] Senator Wagner, who had assumed the chairmanship, had labored faithfully for a long time to conciliate the many disputes among the contestants for advantage. But he and his board had found themselves swamped by protests arising from violations or from self-interested interpretations of labor provisions in the codes. These had become an unmanageable flood by December.

A good deal of attention was paid in the press and elsewhere to the goings-on arising from these various controversies and protests. Almost no attention was paid to what some of us believed were the central issues. We had very little support for our efforts to bring about the industrial stabilization that we had conceived to be the mission of NRA. There was much more recrimination than genuine attempt to find fairness and stability of countervailing forces.

A consumer "section" had been set up in NRA to match the one in AAA. If there was to be a struggle for advantage, and if organized support would be important, consumers ought to have every possible chance to make themselves felt; but that opposition to the prevailing way of making codes was ineffective could by now be seen all too clearly. Some of us had anticipated it all along and had therefore pressed for more regulatory pressure at appropriate points. But that too had failed to materialize, being sabotaged without check, as I have explained, at every point, and being bargained away in Roosevelt's anxiety for haste. This was the reason for our repeated attempts, both in NRA and AAA, to get reconsideration and changes in policy.

The background of our final attempt to change the course of NRA was quite adequately described in the six-month review article printed by the *United States News* (on December 18, 1933, p. 14). It explains—what seems to puzzle historians—why NRA was failing:

Under the pressure of the blanket code and the drive of public opinion, industries rushed to get approval for individual codes of fair competition, many of which had requirements on hours and wages less severe.

In late July and early August there was a heavy period of hearings or

---

[7] By executive order, *Public Papers*, Vol. 2, pp. 318-19. The members, beside Senator Wagner as chairman, were William Green, Leo Wolman, John L. Lewis, Walter C. Teagle, Gerard Swope, and Louis E. Kirstein.

codes for many of the country's largest industries, including steel, oil, and lumber.

At about the same time there began to be a wave of strikes over the country. Labor was waking up to the rights it was guaranteed under the Recovery Act. The American Federation of Labor was quick to take advantage of the situation and dispatched organizers into the field to line up workers in the mass production industries.

It was during this period that the National Labor Board came into being. This agency was created to adjust disputes by invoking powers of the National Recovery Act. Out of the experience gained in the field, the Labor Board evolved a formula for dealing with disputes. This formula called for hearings of the interested parties, then an agreement to return to work pending a vote of employees on the type of organization they favored.

This scheme worked in many disputes, often without recourse to the election, as representatives of employers and employees agreed on the terms that would be accepted for organizing workers. But the activities of the Labor Board grew so rapidly that regional boards were created in the industrial centers of the country to gain quicker action when strikes threatened.

Labor came through the period of strife without any weakening of its rights under the National Recovery Act. However, on October 19, President Roosevelt clarified the language of Section 7(a) in a letter to General Johnson. In it he said:

"There is nothing in the provisions of Section 7(a) to interfere with the bona fide exercise of the right of an employer to select, retain, or advance employees on the basis of individual merit." But he added, "In view of many cases of notorious abuse Section 7(a) does clearly prohibit the pretended exercise of the right as a device for preventing employees from exercising the right of self-organization, designation of representatives, etc." General Johnson said in amplifying the President's language:

"It means that—pretending an open shop—you cannot hire a man and then, discovering that he has a union card in his pocket, fire him for dropping a monkey wrench."

At about the time that labor disturbances began to quiet down, a new outburst occurred over price advances. Farming districts, where income had not increased appreciably owing to low prices paid for agricultural products, struck out at the Blue Eagle as the cause of their difficulties. It represented to them the emblem of a higher living cost.

This opposition was the signal for a rallying of all of the groups disapproving of the effort to impose a form of government supervision over industry. Soon the country was resounding with criticism of NRA and General Johnson started on a swing into the farm country to make his answer.

Soon, too, Gerard Swope came forward with a scheme of industrial self-rule to replace the NRA. Under his plan there would be created a super-chamber of commerce in which industrial groups would function with a minimum of governmental concern and with few restrictions protecting labor. A cry went up over the threat of government control of industry through the codes as imposed now.

The attack on the NRA program coincided with the progressive slump in business and manufacturing activity during the fall months. By December it had pretty much died out again as government bounties flowed into the farm districts to revive hope among the rural population, and as business began to pick up in the cities.

It was also tempered by an outline of policy made by General Johnson concerning the part the government is to play in enforcing the provisions of codes. This statement showed that the General was inclined to let industry run its own affairs, free from government interference, just so long as it actually conducted the administration efficiently and effectively. In case a code authority fails or is unable to administer its code, or abuses its authority, then the federal government plans to step in.

After this statement of policy, both the Consumers Advisory Board, representing the public and the Labor Advisory Board, representing labor, sought to gain membership on code authorities. This would have given the consumers and labor a voice in the management policies of industry.

Industry objected strenuously to this grant of power and General Johnson decided that the request could not be granted. Instead, new boards are planned to include representatives of the buying public and of labor, to watch the operation of individual codes and to report on their functioning.

On December 13, General Johnson named government representatives on 90 code authorities created under the Recovery Act. In his instructions to these observers, who serve without vote, the General said that they are "to avoid the fact or appearance of dictation or coercion, and function as co-workers in an undertaking of public interest, concerned only in faithful administration of the code."

The government agents, however, are to warn and guard against threatened deviations from codes, to watch operations so that they do not promote monopolies nor tend to eliminate small enterprises, to recommend such "other matters as in his judgment are important to the welfare of the industry, or to the public interest, or to the consumers or employees affected by the provisions of the code . . ."

As for the future, General Johnson has told industry that it now is presented with an opportunity it long has sought to build the machinery

for industrial self-government. He has promised that the supervision of
the national government will only be such as is necessary in case industry either fails or is unwilling to run its own affairs.

Concerning the direction NRA was taking, we made one final effort
in December. The relevant colloquy ran as follows:

Tugwell: I have a matter in connection with the model code. I do not
know whether Mr. Wallace has commented to this board about the
model code as yet, but we have talked it over between ourselves
and we have rather violent objections to one particular point.

Chairman Roper: Can you refer to the item?

Tugwell: Yes, it is the item about cost of production . . . we go back
to the general background of this act: a long history of dependence
upon competition. Prices were theoretically determined by competition and were therefore fair to all parties to a bargain—consumers,
because sellers competed, and so on. But industries for a long time
have had areas of rigidity intruding on a general system of flexibility and there were areas where industries could fix and sustain
prices either by monopolies, or by some other method, either legal
or extra-legal. The theory of the NRA was that we had gone so far
in establishing areas of rigidity and there had been found so many
ways of escape from the standards and limitations imposed by the
anti-trust laws, that it was better to take industries out from under
the anti-trust acts and set up new ways of protecting the public
interest in such matters as price increases.

If that were done, and carried out in a conscientious manner,
it would mean that the industries would logically be forced to
accept full public control of their prices. That would be the limit
of supervision. Any place in the range between complete freedom for
industry and complete control by the public through a governmental
agency, there could be limitation imposed.

It is our feeling that as the model code is set up, and as a good
many of the codes now in operation are constituted, there has been
a complete neglect of protection for the public from price increases
either by competition or by public authority. So that, to all intents
and purposes, industries are being freed to establish whatever prices
they please. And we think the results are beginning to be apparent.
Industries are being abandoned to "enlightened self-interest."

Chairman Roper: Always enlightened?

Tugwell: Not always enlightened, sir; and I think we are making a great
mistake in not reserving to the public further rights in the codes to
control prices. All else, from the point of view of the public, is
minor compared with the injury that may be done to consumers,

243

and through them to society, by unrestrained increases. And when it is suggested—as in this particular section of the model code—that selling below cost is forbidden, the door is opened to suggestion from industry as to what cost of production is. Nobody has ever defined cost. The Federal Trade Commission has labored for years over definition, and they are thoroughly disillusioned. And because of inability to define we get to something finally such as is illustrated in a number of the codes already signed. . . . In the lumber code the kind of thing I refer to is illustrated. First, it states the cost-of-production principles, then it says, to all intents and purposes, that, in accordance with the principle, the code authority may fix prices.

It mentions also fair value and indicates that fairness is abused on the valuation of standing timber and that it will be taken into account in fixing prices. But then, a little further along it will be found that fair valuation is to be determined on the basis of market prices. This is circular reasoning; and it is what always results. This is the same dilemma into which public utility control falls.

We think these codes are going through with a very serious lack of attention to the problem of price control. What is likely to happen when industries attempt to fix their prices without considering the probable buying capacity available for the goods they produce is that there will be no power available in the government for correction. The model code contains no provisions enabling government to bring industrial prices into such relation with each other that each can buy what the other makes.

This is further explained in a memorandum we have drafted.
Chairman Roper: Would you like to suggest an amendment?
Tugwell: I would rather submit a memorandum at this time including a suggested amendment.

There was support from Commissioner March (chairman of the Federal Trade Commission) and objection from Mr. Brown (General Johnson's assistant).

Tugwell: I will also say this. Secretary Wallace and I have submitted other memoranda to this board and to General Johnson—we have copies of all of them in our files and we will get them out for you to see if you like—but still the situation remains exactly as it was. I shall submit my memorandum without feeling that anything is likely to be done. But we should like to have our own record clear.

The result of my pressing the matter was that the board requested "all codes to be submitted in advance of submission to the president."

Then there were doubts; and the doubters thought it better to ask the president whether this was not, in his view, the board's responsibility. I was asked to frame the question. I did it as follows:

The question whether all the codes should be considered by the Recovery Board in advance of their submission to the president has been raised. The regular procedure, as indicated by the terms of reference of the board, would seem to hold it responsible for approval or rejection. This procedure is not being complied with, and the board would like to have a definition of its responsibilities in the matter.

What followed was that the board's request for direction was taken to the president. Johnson argued that the board was interfering and that the interference would cause delays. The president agreed; and our hopes for setting NRA right were extinguished.

CHAPTER 11

Winning Some, Losing Some

I N SPITE OF THE disappointments about AAA, NRA, and the food
and drugs legislation, two occurrences during 1933 provided a
certain satisfaction. One was the establishment of the Soil Conservation
Service with H. H. Bennett at its head; the other was the rejuvenation
of the Forest Service. Others were not so satisfactory.

The Subsistence Homesteads Administration was a project that
could not succeed. It was persistently credited to me; but this was
a mistake. It was a Roosevelt scheme. There did seem at first to be an
extremely respectable support for it as part of a back-to-the-land movement; and M. L. Wilson, who became its administrator, did what he
could with it. The trouble was that it ran contrary to the drift of the
economy and actually was suitable to no more than a few of the many
families who had been so badly hurt by the depression. As I have said
in another place (*The Brains Trust*, 1968) I had often discussed this
with both Roosevelts during our pre-campaign days in Albany. I
thought the project an impractical and even condescending scheme
for ordering people's lives. A man who had lost out in urban competition
was not likely to succeed in the complicated business of farming; and
establishing small industries as part-time employment was a philan-
thropic enterprise only a few businesses would attempt. So I argued;
but I had no effect at all on the substantial number of back-to-landers
—including the Roosevelts.

Concerning soil erosion, Bennett had for a long time been trying
to impress the public with the vast, tragic, and unnecessary losses of

our topsoil. He had at least succeeded with me, and I had corresponded with him about it as far back as 1924, when I had been writing the section for *American Economic Life*[1] dealing with the means for improving agriculture. He was now an employee of our Bureau of Chemistry and Soils. He thought that lingering over "experimentation" had been too protracted and that the time had come for action. He argued that there had been undue emphasis on expensive mechanical means for preventing soil depletion and that farmers themselves must be encouraged to undertake simple means for saving their own land. He had no objection to "demonstration projects"; indeed, he wanted to see some of them undertaken. They would show, he said, that for all soil types, climatic conditions, and land-surface circumstances, there were inexpensive ways to stop the losses.

When, during the summer, we had been encouraging the various government bureaus to make proposals, several of our own bureaus had submitted plans for the expansion of erosion control. Elaborate ones for terracing and dam building came from the Bureau of Agricultural Engineering. Others coming from the Bureau of Chemistry and Soils relied on soil improvement. The Bureau of Plant Industry urged special plantings, rotations, and the use of cover crops. Then, of course, there was the special problem of the overgrazed rangelands where no more than restriction of grazing was needed.

One day when I happened to have these projects assembled on my desk Bennett asked to see me. He had heard of the various submissions and had become so indignant that he could make an unorthodox approach to higher authority without asking leave of his own bureau chief. He was somewhat surprised to be asked in without ceremony; but he was set to explode and meant to do it anyway. I said that I had been going to ask his advice shortly and that he had come just at the time I needed some help. He was inclined to splutter but did catch himself enough to ask, "What in the world for?"

"Well," I said, "I have all these proposals here; and it seems to me that none of them is adequate. I was going to ask whether we haven't had enough experimentation, and inquire why we didn't get to work with what we know." I paused. "You look kind of annoyed," I said.

[1] A text written for use in the Contemporary Civilization course at Columbia, and published in 1925 by Harcourt, Brace and Co., New York, but adopted in other colleges during the next few years. One of the curious results of my connection with the New Deal was that practically all of these adoptions were canceled. I could only suppose that the reputation given me by the press was responsible.

"I am," he replied; "if you mean by annoyed that I am damned good and mad, then I am annoyed. I can't believe you really mean it."

This kind of evangelism was all too rare. I had learned to look for signs of it and put it to use when it seemed appropriate. We proceeded then and there to elaborate a scheme for an entirely new attack, outside the old bureaus, using all the techniques now so well known, that farmers themselves could handle. It would include demonstrations, but most of them would be on private land. I thought this would require subsidy. "What?" he said. "Pay farmers to improve their own land? This is something I have dreamed of for years. But I've always been told that federal money could only be spent on public property—federal property at that."

My view of that, I said, was that land was a kind of public trust. Private soil was washing into public streams, and a national resource was being lost. I thought we might find a way to do it. He left in a glow. Subsequently I talked not only to the president but to Ickes about it. Why not, I said, set up a special section in the Public Works Administration? After it had got well under way, it could come back to Agriculture as a new bureau. Ickes fell in with my scheme. But that enterprising empire-builder, as I might have suspected, was thinking of laying claim to all the land agencies, and this would be another. I did not penetrate the source of Ickes' cordiality in this instance. Before long I had cause to regret my carelessness.

During my western trip, when I was well out of the way, Ickes established the Soil Conservation Service as an agency not of the Public Works Administration but of the Interior Department. When I returned it was to meet indignation among the bureau chiefs in Agriculture and unprecedented reproaches from Wallace. They, and even he, were convinced, in spite of my protests, that I had engineered the whole affair. Ickes was as bland as the traditional cat after swallowing the canary. "I'm going to get the Forest Service too," he said. "Why don't you come over here and run the whole thing?" This was the first, but not the last, such proposition. This one I did not take seriously. I only remonstrated and said to myself that I would wait my chance, and if I could, correct this particular mistake.

By December the Service was prospering under Ickes' protection. He was seeing that it was supported with Public Works funds. Moreover, he was clearing away legal obstacles and encouraging Bennett to assemble a formidable corps of experts. The operation was very popular—almost as much so as the Civilian Conservation Corps. Since he was being criticized for slowness in getting started on a puiblic-works program, he had use for that popularity. His intention now was to show everyone who was the true conservationist, he or Wallace.

I ought just to say that when I found occasion to relate this whole story to Roosevelt I got from him one of the heartiest laughs I had ever been responsible for—and I had brought him a good many others. He sympathized, I discovered then, with Ickes' desire to amalgamate the land services, but, as with so much else, he felt it necessary to avoid quarrels irrelevant to the main business of that year. Concerning soil conservation, I protested that it was clearly an agricultural enterprise and that Ickes had taken it over with the intention of being provocative. He refused to worry about the Wallace-Ickes feud—he always refused to worry about such differences. They kept things stirred up in ways he considered harmless. He even seemed to regard them as diversions of some use in troubled times. This might be why he had allowed Johnson so much leeway, tolerated the presumption of Jones in running RFC, and watched as Peek continued on his collision course with Wallace. On this occasion he signed the executive order I had prepared taking Soil Conservation away from Interior and placing it in Agriculture. Because I had seized a moment when Ickes was away, he came back to accuse me of treachery, and for some time his annoyance with me dampened our relations.

My second contribution to the conservation complex was the appointment of Ferdinand Silcox as chief forester. I had become acquainted with Silcox during the First World War and learned then what an extraordinary talent he had for managing complex situations. He had subsequently left the Forest Service to become a professional mediator; and I had met him on a few occasions in New York. His work for the Employing Printers' Association had been a good test of his talents. The New York printing trades had had almost no labor trouble during his regime. His sympathy with the workers and his willingness to advocate their just claims had transformed the industry into a model of cooperative effort. He had talked extremely difficult employers out of their hard positions time after time and brought the whole industry into stabilized internal relationships.[2]

[2] Silcox died prematurely and I wrote an appreciation of his work for the *New Republic*: "Forester's Heart," May 13, 1940.

When Major Stewart, the chief forester who was heavily burdened with all the departures from traditional procedure involved in the expansion of the Service to utilize Public Works funds and to adapt itself to the complicated problems of the Civilian Conservation Corps, committed suicide, we were left with a vacancy best filled as quickly as possible. What was needed was a chief who could adapt himself to the new circumstances and could enlarge and improve the existing forests, expanding them especially into the East—one of Roosevelt's ambitions. He also hoped to set up new small forests in many places, and to plan for the shelter-belt program out on the prairies. There were the larger hopes, too, of a consolidated land service, and, working through NRA, of securing a new approach to lumbering on the private lands being so ruthlessly decimated.

Such a leader was not to be found among the old-time foresters. They were traditionally inclined to concentrate on guardianship and to have defensive attitudes concerning their responsibilities. Both Wallace and I thought that forest research ought to be emphasized— not the utilization of forest products so much as the study of forest ecology, of genetics, and of all the subsidiary ways of improving the trees and grasses on the millions of acres now in our charge and on the others to be acquired.

We had the advantage of dealing with a president who had special knowledge and interest, going all the way back to his service in the New York state legislature when his first committee assignment had had to do with forests and waters. I moved quickly as soon as Silcox's special qualifications occurred to me. The president had never heard of him; and he was not on any of the lists of suggested candidates coming from the forestry schools at Yale and Syracuse. I could count on one thing: even if Silcox had left the Service some years before, he was still well known in the profession. He had, after all, been a regional forester, and so was one of the elect. This might have been offset by the claims of those who were at present close to the top of the hierarchy, except that they too recognized the demanding nature of the emergency. I put it to them that it was a situation calling for a kind of skill Silcox had demonstrated. It was lucky, I said, that there was available a professional who could assist a president who might at times have difficulties with the lumber men as their codes were formulated and administered, and with the Congress. We would have need for funds to carry on permanently after the emergency funds were withdrawn. My point was conceded.

I did not do so well with the officials of the forestry schools. They had their own candidates. Also they had ticketed Silcox as a maverick. The president listened to them. But I persisted and was even passionate, making the argument over and over that we had to have someone who was unorthodox and flexible. I finally persuaded him to see and talk with Silcox. Then I had to win over my candidate. He had a permanent and very highly paid job. What I had to suggest was that he undertake a risky and novel venture of a very doubtful sort at low pay. He made some difficulty about it, but he did come to Washington, and, after introducing him to Wallace, I hustled him over to the White House. That, I hoped, would be all that was needed. I was confident that he was Roosevelt's sort of man.

It turned out to be so. From the first five minutes of that interview, I had no doubt that I had won. The president's doubts were dissipated and Silcox was amazed by Roosevelt's grasp of the problems. They formed a firm friendship; and we had one more able and trustworthy ally for the work to come. Within a few weeks the professionals had accepted his leadership as loyally as I could possibly have hoped. Moreover, he became at once a member of our small group of progressives available for all kinds of duties. He was understanding and inventive; he had a national view; his breadth and depth made him much more than merely a Forest Service chief. He became the leader of the whole conservation movement, trusted by all who were in so many ways involved in it, and tireless in the Service.

Roosevelt's selection of M. L. Wilson for Subsistence Homesteads was a less happy choice, although it has to be said that the difficulties there would have been too much for anyone. "M.L." was the philosopher of the agricultural group. Subsistence Homesteads appealed to his ready humanitarianism; and the channeling of the Rooseveltian goodwill into better homeplaces for disadvantaged people appealed to his sympathies. He would turn out to have no talent for administration or for meeting the criticisms so soon to descend on all the New Deal agencies. Presently he would find more suitable activities; but for the moment he was happy and hopeful. It looked just at first as though this might be—along with TVA, the Civilian Conservation Corps, and the Soil Conservation Service—a minor but useful and popular undertaking. In spite of my old skepticism I was persuaded that it might become a creditable effort. How could it fail to be with such enthusiastic backing from both Roosevelts, Louis Howe, and the considerable number of back-to-the-land enthusiasts generated by the depression?

I was wrong. When it went to pieces Roosevelt would transfer it to my keeping, and its failure would add measurably to my later woes.

All this was less important than the contests in AAA and NRA. During the fall, I made several addresses, mostly on the same theme. I was trying to do my part in stemming the formidable reaction now clearly impending. In a Chicago speech late in October, I attacked my enemies:

> Those people who would have us crawl back to the old ideas, like wounded animals to an abandoned den, misread the temper of the people as well as the intelligence of the present government. We are trying to show that heaped-up corporate surpluses and the overconcentration of wealth are not the life of trade but the death of trade. Incomes must be transformed into higher wages and higher incomes to farmers, not simply stacked up in sterile hoards of capital, if wealth in any large and gratifying sense is to breed again.

Commenting on this and other efforts somewhat later, Louis Hacker, the historian, had this to say:[3]

> It did not avail Mr. Tugwell, who was rgearded as the leader of the Brains Trust, to protest that he did not believe in national planning, the transplanting of Russian methods here, or the adoption of governmental controls in violation of the Constitution; despite his insistence that he was a conservative (which, economically speaking, he really was), the Assistant Secretary of Agriculture was made the victim of a good deal of open misrepresentation and covert abuse . . .

And going on to speak of the general New Deal situation he observed:

> Other agencies were also at work. On October 15, 1933, Alfred E. Smtih, who by now had openly identified himself with the forces of big business, laid down the first barrage for what turned out to be a concerted attack on the New Deal from the right, when he referred to it as the "heavy, cold, clammy hand of bureaucracy." He was immediately followed by the newspaper publishers Paul Block and William Randolph Hearst. Mr. Block, in a signed editorial in his own newspapers, which was reprinted widely as a paid advertisement, told Washington that it had not yet proved its capacity for running its own business; how then did it dare run the business of everyone else? What industry needs from the administration is encouragement and not hindrance, for nearly everyone can sense

[3] Louis M. Hacker, *A Short History of the New Deal* (New York: F. S. Crofts and Co., 1935), 109-110.

that business is right on the edge of an upward move, but too many "cooks" or "experts" are at present blocking the road.

Mr. Hearst was even blunter. The New Deal was a "socialist dictatorship"; and it was imposing upon industry, struggling toward recovery, shorter hours and higher pay and greater employment and heavier burdens in every direction than industry, weakened by depression and only newly recovering, was able to bear. On November first, Mr. Gerard Swope, president of the General Electric Company and at the time head of the Industrial Advisory Board of NRA, launched industry's heavy drive when he proposed that the control of business be turned back to its own leaders and the functions of NRA be vested in a privately conducted National Chamber of Commerce and Industry—under a shadowy government supervision. When H. I. Harriman, president of the United States Chamber of Commerce, and General Hugh S. Johnson, the National Recovery Administrator, gave the Swope plan their immediate blessing, it was no longer a secret that the New Deal was meeting with organized opposition from without and disaffection from within.

Hacker's book was being written about this time, and neither he nor the other contemporary commentators anticipated Roosevelt's amazing majorities in 1934 and 1936. He assessed disaffection as much more important than he might have later on; but so did many others. I must say I was not worried about this nearly so much as about the reaction of my colleagues. They listened fearfully to the few noisy reactionaries, both left and right, who dominated contemporary comment. Resolutions weakened. Trimming and appeasement spread and began to influence policy. The reactionary argument should have been refuted, but all around there was head-shaking and cautionary advice.

I judged that the tide of approval was still rising and that we ought to carry our appeal to the public. But others, especially in NRA and AAA, had long faces. They were already defeated and looking for an easy retreat. Roosevelt was not confused about this; but nearly everyone else was in a shivery mood. Roosevelt told me he was deluged with warnings; but he was not yet convinced that Al Smith, Paul Block, and Hearst, who were getting so much publicity, spoke for many others. He could not convey his conviction to Swope, Harriman, and other businessmen who were on our side; but neither could he seem to convey it to the politicians and to the members of the Congress who were supposed to be allies. So he too, in the interest of keeping control, seemed inclined to be cautious and withdrawing. He did not discourage my efforts, such as they were; but he was not persuaded that the policies of NRA and AAA were feeding the reaction. I was sure that to do what the businessmen demanded would not only hinder recovery but seat them firmly in control of the policy-making machinery. They would use it to prevent the stabilizing effect we sought. We were failing to set up such a management of the economy that the "concert of interests" he had spoken of so often might be achieved.

The Christmas holiday was no very cheerful season. The trees on the mall were bare; only the boxwoods and hollies had kept their green. Several times ice had filmed the reflecting pool where in other seasons the Lincoln Memorial was mirrored. Mostly now wind-blown leaves, swimming in melancholy disorder, served as a reminder of fading hopes. The Potomac was yellow with Shenandoah topsoil and its banks were littered with dirty patches of snow.

My days still began early and ended late; and they were still divided between my department office, the White House, and various errands around and about the rest of Washington. I had been assigned to a new committee on foreign trade policy whose chairman was the entertaining and worldly-wise Robert Lincoln O'Brien.[4] I was often in the old State, War and Navy building, but I was often in the Treasury, too, and in Interior or Commerce. As I went, whenever I could, I undertook to discuss with colleagues of my own progressive bent what seemed to me the central issue of that time and our failure to prevail in its solution. I do not see, in the many accounts of those days, much recognition that this issue was just then being fought over and the campaign lost. Our difficulty was that winning would be proclaimed as a horrifying departure from traditional Americanism. This, I was sure, was what worried Roosevelt.

People like Swope and Harriman, for instance, modified their proposals for the reform of NRA to include an industrial board for self-regulation with no government intervention at all. They had convinced themselves that such a scheme would be adequate and, naturally, would please the business community. This, I suppose, could be called a positive suggestion, but most other businessmen wanted either to go all the way back to what they called freedom, or simply wanted their trade associations relieved of anti-trust threats so that they could limit production and fix prices.

The businessmen had not got all they wanted; but they had pre-

---

[4] Once Cleveland's secretary. I became very fond of him.

vented the establishment of stabilizing institutions. We talked among ourselves, Frank and I and our progressive friends, in curiously reminiscent terms of chances missed, of mistakes made, and of failures. Our lost opportunity would not be retrieved now short of another severe crisis. And that crisis we did not expect to arrive while we were still on the scene.

IV

1933 Ends; 1934 Begins

☆ | CHAPTER 1 | ☆

Appraisal

WHEN THE SPECIAL SESSION of the Congress had adjourned in mid-June it had provided most of the legislation necessary for relieving the worst distresses and for starting the processes of recovery. By now, too, most of the administering agencies had been set up and their regulations written. Presently, it could be claimed that the promised financial reforms had been undertaken and that the Warren plan to raise prices by buying gold was in operation. Private possession of the metal had been made illegal and all payments in it, even those provided for in bond contracts, had been made invalid. In addition, all shipments abroad had been prohibited. It was, however, becoming evident that money was a more complicated subject than Roosevelt had understood. But neither Wallace nor I had expected that monetary measures would solve our agricultural problems. So we were not disappointed.

Depression, for farmers, was not recent; it had gone on for more than a decade; and during that time some measures for relief had been tried and had failed, others had been rejected. As I have explained, the law we had finally been given—the Agricultural Adjustment Act— had allowed us to adopt several alternative policies. About the one Wallace and I favored, there was still serious disagreement. I have described how our internal quarrels came to a climax late in the fall, with George Peek resigning in a flurry of public recrimination and with Chester Davis becoming his successor. This had been the result of avoiding policy decisions when the act was passed. Peek meant to use marketing agreements. Wallace and I meant to use the domestic allotment plan. We had won.

On a day in December immediately after this disturbance those of us most concerned met to consider what we should do next. Wallace was worried by repercussions among the farm leaders; and, of course, Davis had been a lobbyist for several farm organizations and represented their point of view. Davis had assured us that he was willing to try the allotment device; but I doubted his good faith and had said so to Wallace and to Roosevelt.

I was still concerned also about those people who were deliberately being left out of the benefits now being distributed; but since I had been protesting about this for some time without effect, I had no expectation that there would be any change. Wallace had continued to argue that if the larger farmers improved their own situation they would take care of their tenants and laborers. It had always been that way. But this was the trickle-down theory so familiar in business. I had thought it thoroughly discredited.

Reducing production was still an approach politicians disliked—the requiring of a discipline farmers were certain to resent and certain to evade if they could. There were already appeals to "freedom" and "individual rights." Wallace hoped that he had quieted conservative critics, but I was skeptical. The demagogues who were demanding instant results would be silenced only by increasing incomes for farmers.

The trouble in the farming country had gone on so long because no leaders had had the courage to say that adding to the enormous surpluses year by year would have to be stopped and that production would have to be adjusted to domestic demand. It could be hoped that as prosperity returned, production could again be increased; but more wheat and cotton, at least, would not be needed in the foreseeable future.

The farmers' own committees were now allocating acreages and accepting responsibility for enforcement. Allotments were being made locally, and the program would indeed be domestic. We hoped our scheme would quickly prove its usefulness. Those opposed were most importantly the processors. Their profits from a large volume would be more than from a smaller one; and they were reluctant to see farmers established in a firmer bargaining position. They were inclined at the moment to be less aggressive than was their habit in dealing with agricultural officials because it was so obvious that something drastic must be done. At the same time they had not given up the struggle for the kind of program they preferred. This was the selling in foreign markets so long advocated by the powerful farm bloc. But failing that, there were the "marketing agreements" I have described. The processors were still saying that if they were exempted from the anti-trust acts and allowed a free hand, they would pay the farmers enough more to lift them out of their depression. Whether consumers would—or could—pay the higher prices was something they ignored. Also there was no suggestion in this scheme of a way to reduce embarrassing surpluses. This had been said to them in innumerable conferences, but they had not given up. They had been influential so long in successive administrations that they simply could not believe their demands would be rejected. Why should agricultural officials have any concern for consumers? Their duty was to make farmers more prosperous.

Peek was gone now; but Wallace's policy of placating lobbyists for the farm organization had landed Davis in a position not very different from that of his predecessor. A battle had been won, but the war would be lost if our allotment scheme did not succeed.

The news commentators had given me credit for unseating Peek. It was true that I had done nothing to avoid a conflict so embarrassing that an end to it had to be found. Before that I had tried to be conciliatory enough; and actually I had had a kind of respect for his bluff shrewdness. There was never any doubt about his opinions; and there was never any chance that they might be modified. These qualities, however, were consistent with a finally intolerable opposition.

Roosevelt always disliked such choices; and when Peek refused the ambassadorship he was offered and was made a special adviser on foreign trade, Hull was as annoyed as Roosevelt had anticipated. There was practically open conflict from the start, and it would end as it had to after an embarrassing interlude. Peek had no luck in Roosevelt's administration; but actually no one was paying attention to him any more.

I quote here, as representative of the comment on Peek's resignation, the last paragraph of a long article by Arthur Krock in the *New York Times* (December 8, 1933):

During the campaign, by some chance or other, most of the spot-light directed on the "brains trust" struck Professor Moley. Professor Tugwell was prominent on the set also. But somehow he didn't stand out often, and that continued throughout the first part of Mr. Roosevelt's administration. Lately, through no wish of his own, perhaps, the spot-light has followed him about. It is not likely to leave him soon, even though, as he says, he wants to get away from it all.

Wallace and I, being newcomers to Washington, were meanwhile learning together about our departmental colleagues and their problems. Most of them we respected for their dedication to the improvement of the land, its crops, and its livestock. They had developed methods of holding together a nationwide system of small enterprises. Once I had identified myself with this purpose my determination to return soon to Columbia began to weaken. This was simple avoidance, excused because I was so continuously involved in so many causes and enterprises. Anyway, I should have known by then that I was unusually susceptible to affection for institutions when I became involved with them. This was happening now; but I kept on pretending that soon I would find a suitable time and situation for withdrawing.

I never got to the point of considering myself indispensable, and if I had, a sharp correction was supplied by an elderly bureau chief one day when he was objecting to one of my suggestions for change. What he said was that appointed officials come and go but civil servants go on until they are retired for age. He was not being offensive; he was merely stating a fact. He was somewhat surprised when his remark seemed to have struck me as humorous, and more so when I asked how many *he* had outlasted. He wasn't sure, he said, but it must have been half a dozen. I had a certain revenge in that instance. His bureau was combined with another and he was returned to his laboratory, where he served out his time. He was right, nevertheless. The permanent people had only to be patient and front-office disturbers would presently have disappeared.

By year's end it was quite apparent that departmental reorganization would not come to much. Budget procedures were improved, and this gave us somewhat more control over the activities of the bureaus; but Wallace confessed, after several rejections of proposals made by me, that he thought the department might as well remain essentially as it was.

I must say once more, what so many other newcomers have had to learn, that congressional procedures for assigning functions to federal departments were strange and wonderful. They had resulted, as I have noted, in Agriculture having, in addition to the bureaus recognizably related to farming, others put there because of convenience to influential congressmen or because it was feared they might be bothersome unless controlled by an amenable secretary of agriculture. So we had not only the Food and Drug Administration, the Bureau of Public Roads, the Weather Service, and the Forestry Service but many regulatory acts to be administered, such, for instance, as the Packers and Stockyards, the Pure Seed Law, and the inspection and grading of meat. The day might come when activities would be distributed to more logical places; but that day had obviously not yet come.

If, however, what I had been expected to do was simply not to be done, why should I stay? The answer was that most of those I worked with felt—or said—that I supplied something they had not had before. This was an understanding of what they were doing together with some influence that made the doing more effective. Besides, I was regarded with suspicion by some important elders at Columbia. I might not be welcome if I returned. Roosevelt's experiences with the manipulation of gold had had little effect; but injections of purchasing power—relief and public-works expenditures and payments to farmers for compliance with AAA reductions in acreage—had begun to register. Increases in the price level—inflation—were changing the relations between creditors and debtors, favoring, of course, the debtors. The Columbia School of Business had close relations with the New York financial establishment. That establishment was made up of creditors. They were glad to see business improve but not to receive payments for debts owed to them in cheapened dollars. They were furious with Roosevelt, and, since I had been given a factitious importance as one of his counselors, I was blamed.

There was more. The notoriety accompanying the "Tugwell bill" had successfully tagged me as generally anti-business and from this position it was a short jump, in simplistic journalistic prose, to anti-American. Taking it all together I was no longer respectable, and to some members of the Columbia faculty—not my old friends in the college—I was an active liability. There were visible shudders whenever I was referred to as a Columbia professor.

Actually, I was more to blame than I was willing to admit. I made no particular effort to explain myself and my friends must have had to defend me over and over from convinced detractors. The Federal Reserve system had failed during the depression and needed repair. Particularly, it had not prevented all those bank failures; but Roosevelt's emergency attempts to reestablish liquidity by inflation seemed to Columbia conservatives to be horrifying departures from sanity. Willis and like-minded others attached much of the blame to me. I could have been more conciliatory; but I refused explanations I thought I ought not to be called on to make.

So I began to think of something else. I have not mentioned my association with the faculty members of the Yale Law School. This had come through Frank, who had called on several of them for temporary assistance in setting up the early regulations for AAA and especially for several of the more difficult industries. The reviving liquor trade as prohibition ended was one of these. Another was sugar. It was produced in the Philippines, in Puerto Rico, and in Louisiana, and by beet growers in the West. Like most other products it was in surplus, and there was vicious infighting among the various producers to get the largest possible part of the domestic market, where quota arrangements kept the price higher than elsewhere. This would make a really representative account, if it could be told in full, of unrestrained struggle all over Washington—in the Congress, in the department, in the White House, and even in the courts—for advantage. It was an unequal contest, since Philippine, Puerto Rican, and other producers had no legislative representatives. Only those of us in the department were likely to defend the outsiders from the sugar-beet lobby. When, in an excess of zeal, I offered to take over the sugar problem, Wallace was only too glad to agree.

It was in this—and in other similar matters—that we found the law professors so useful. I recall that Thurman Arnold, for instance, went all the way out to the Philippines and stayed for weeks. Abe Fortas and a dozen others, including Wesley Sturges, who later became dean of the law school, were engaged in the writing of regulations and negotiations concerning them. It was tedious and unrewarding work.

In October I was asked to take part in several law-school seminars. This resulted in an invitation to become an "associate." This involved only visiting duties; but there were suggestions that I might join the faculty permanently, and the prospect was inviting.[1] It was the most adventurous of all American schools of law, one of its innovations being the giving of professorships to a few scholars who had studied public law but not private law. Apart from my Columbia circle it

---

[1] The appointment by the Yale Corporation's Prudential Committee was dated November 11, 1933.

was the most congenial academic group I had ever known, and for a while such a possibility seemed a good deal more attractive than going on in my present welter of notoriety.[2]

By this time I was being continually harassed by reporters. Crossing the country, during the fall, I was met at every plane stop by a clamoring group of interviewers who demanded responses to questions only Roosevelt himself could have answered. Since the planes of those days had to refuel frequently, this meant that every few hours I was called on to think of something to say. There was a lot going on in Washington, and it was affecting every individual and every economic interest. Much of it was not understood, and there were fears that the results would be good for the unemployed, perhaps, but not for their former employers. The press associated me with attempts to discipline businesses and to injure creditors much more than with agricultural problems.

I could not speak for Roosevelt or for Hopkins, Ickes, or Jones; but my refusals to answer questions about their responsibilities were taken as evasions. I was rapidly acquiring a reputation for secretive conspiring; and the conspiring was dangerous to everyone of substance. There was something to all this. I was an unusual assistant secretary of agriculture, obviously not confined to departmental affairs. Also I was writing and making speeches calculated to explain the New Deal as I saw it and I would like it to be. If I was harassed, it was partly my own fault. I could have kept quiet.

---

[2] It was this desire for attention to wider issues than the technical ones usually taught in law schools that led to the appointment later of W. H. Hamilton, who went there from years as head of the Brookings Institution, where, during his regime, I had also been an occasional visitor.

CHAPTER 2

Uneasy Adjustment

HOPKINS, IT MUST BE admitted, later became difficult to work with; but in this first year he had not yet acquired his later sense of importance. He was doing what he could to ease the damage of the depression, to see that the basic wants of people—food and shelter first—were met. This was what he had been brought from New York to do, and he intended, very simply, to do it. He always wanted more funds than were allotted to him, but he always stretched those he had as far as they would go and refused to malinger because of disappointments. He was always annoyed because Roosevelt insisted that direct relief should be kept at a minimum. The differing motives were obvious. Hopkins wanted to stretch his funds, and Roosevelt insisted that the unemployed should work for any benefits they might get from government.

In a few months after his arrival Hopkins had become one of the White House circle. He and I had met at the Congress Hotel in Chicago during the convention; but he had stayed only briefly and had taken no part in the proceedings. He had stopped by as a matter of courtesy to his then principal, Jesse I. Straus, who was administrator of unemployment relief in New York state. Hopkins was his deputy. Straus had formed a businessmen-for-Roosevelt organization, and its headquarters was in the hotel. It was by this accident that we had discovered common interests.

We did not meet again until he came to Washington in May. He had had no part in the campaign; and he was, in fact, only Roosevelt's second or third choice for administrator of relief. He knew that, and he knew why others had refused to undertake the job. Its potential for trouble was all too obvious. This did not give him the least concern. It was, indeed, a stimulant. It amused him to upset conservatives; and the criticism that came his way he regarded as evidence that he was being effective. He was determined to go on as long as he could. This was no more than recognition of extreme hazard, for what he was undertaking to do would very rapidly become unpopular with all those good people who still thought that direct aid undermined character. Hopkins represented the New Deal in one of its most vulnerable phases; and his careless courage was much appreciated by those of us who recognized his contribution to recovery.

It was my opinion then and later that Hopkins' casually conducted operations were the most immediately useful of all the emergency efforts. Roosevelt began by recognizing help for the unemployed to be the duty of a decent government; but it was far more than helpful to individuals—it was an economic starter. It created a demand for goods. Supplying them furnished employment. This, more than anything else, gave the economy such lift as it had in the first months.

It was only natural that Hopkins and I should be drawn to each other. At any rate, we did become personal friends as well as close collaborators. As he proceeded to his first task of enlarging relief rolls and then to the improvising of his first works organization, he was in training, so to speak, for the later close relationship with the president, but neither of us knew then that this was so. When I could not persuade the officials of AAA to take an interest in the neglected rural population, Hopkins readily agreed that they were just poor people who needed help, and extended his reach beyond the cities into the countryside. This mitigated to an extent my disappointment about the neglect of tenants and laborers by AAA.

In those days, Hopkins offered no advice outside his own area. He was not, as I then was, a member of numerous committees, or engaged in negotiations with visitors about international economic problems. He single-mindedly devoted himself to rallying social workers all over the nation. The miseries and distresses of those days would have been far more than they were if it had not been for him—and the economy would not have stirred into life as it soon did.

He was as careless about what he said as he was about his personal appearance. He was already tormented by the ulcers that would finally end his life prematurely. Because of his extravagances he was always short of funds and often deep in debt, but if this worried him he did not let it be known. Several times I had spoken to Roosevelt about his situation, explaining that, what with alimony to pay, and his way of living, he really did need more money. Roosevelt was not one to give personal counsel; at least not very often. When one of his associates got into trouble, he simply picked someone else. He gave no counsel to Hopkins either; but he did see that he got more income and, finding him more and more useful, accepted him into the small circle of helpers he felt he could trust.

Hopkins' assistants, Aubrey Williams, Corrington Gill, Jacob Baker, Robert Hunter, and Leon Henderson, were curiously like Hopkins in their approach to their work. They had no hesitation about improvisation on an enormous scale. Their operations frightened and sometimes scandalized more orderly officials. I often told them I was glad not to have their responsibilities. If that came strangely from one who was already being pictured as a destroyer of institutions precious to the orthodox, it was nevertheless true. I spent a good deal of cautionary energy on them—without much effect. In fact, however, there were never any serious scandals in the distribution of all those millions of relief dollars. This is one of the most remarkable observations to be made about those chaotic times. Social workers are often criticized; but their dedication and earnestness cannot be faulted. This was in spite of Hopkins' frank attempts to conciliate local politicians, who might have been expected to use the free flow of money into their constituencies for their own purposes. They were checked in this by Hopkins' state directors, who tried to see that all in need were treated alike. The politicians were able to claim credit—and were encouraged in doing it—for the relief given and the works undertaken. That no one was shut out because of being a Republican or favored because of having voted for Roosevelt was used everywhere as evidence of impartial care for the unfortunate. Somehow Hopkins' people were able to persuade state and local officials that this was a virtue they could point to with pride.

This, of course, infuriated conservative congressmen in both parties who felt that men ought to work and support their families and had no patience with his argument that their troubles came from causes beyond their control. Roosevelt kept announcing that relief was only temporary and that public work was no substitute for private employment. Meanwhile, however reluctantly, he allowed Hopkins' operations to continue.

As a result of these efforts, the winter of 1933-34 was markedly different from the previous two. The long dreary soup and bread lines gradually shortened. If nobody had much, nearly everyone had something; and, best of all, there was a recurrence of belief that things were now changing for the better rather than continuing to become worse. It was not only the people who habitually lived on the margin of destitution who were relieved. The depression had reached into the middle-income group, those with skills, even professionals, and deprived them of goods and services they had been accustomed to. Such people had debts. They had engaged themselves to pay, over long periods, for their homes, for their business properties, for automobiles and the other appurtenances of living. When they could no longer meet those debts, the recognized arrangement was that the properties or goods should be foreclosed and repossessed.

There had been a certain relief from these hazards. Not only were homeowners able to borrow and meet their mortgage payments; the banks, being made less demanding by the liquidation of their assets (through the enormously expanded RFC), were able to modify or stop their foreclosing and extend their debtors' credits. Even those who grumbled about government interference were quite willing to accept such assistance. This was most ironically true of those financial institutions—banks, insurance companies, and even big business concerns—whose officials were loudest in deploring the unbalanced budget.

There was a discernible surge of renewed assurance, not really justified by any changes so far made in the institutions that had failed so miserably. The causes of depression had not been touched. There could be another; or the one not yet ended could worsen instead of improve. About this there had been a frightening lesson. After an upward turn just after the emergency actions during the spring, there had been a sinking spell during the fall when everything seemed to go to pieces again. It was this that had caused the quick transfer of funds from Ickes' slow public-works organization to Hopkins for the very different kind of works he hastily organized. His neglect of every caution and his single-minded care for the unemployed worked a miracle. In weeks, not months or years, local officials under his loose arrangement gathered together simple tools and materials and put men to work in great numbers; they were able also to reinstate many public workers who had been let go as the financial crisis tightened. The others were the shiftless leaf-rakers so persistently denounced by acidulous critics; but it was they, with their wages, who furnished the demand for goods necessary to begin the general recovery.

Presently, too, farmers' benefit checks were helping. The country agents had been able to get organized about as rapidly as the social workers. Between them, Hopkins and Wallace were Roosevelt's main support. He had still not been entirely convinced—although it later seemed incredible—that the creation of purchasing power was the first necessity. He was happy about the emergency works program, although, as Hopkins kept telling him, the appropriated funds went only about half as far as when used for direct relief. He still preferred to have people's characters protected at the expense of less assistance than they might otherwise have had.

Years later, when the note concerning an executive order (on means to prevent monopolistic practices under NRA codes) was written for his *Public Papers* (1934 Vol., 55), the lesson was finally acknowledged. What he said there was this:

The rebuilding of the purchasing power of all classes of the population was the cornerstone of our program of recovery from the very beginning. . . .

This was an afterthought. It simply was not true of this first year, although it was the policy some of us had labored to convince him was necessary. He had tried other expedients; for instance, the raising of prices by the buying of gold, and the expanded operations of the RFC. He was searching for something more agreeable than the reconstructing of purchasing power. He acknowledged only reluctantly that the failure of demand was the root cause of our paralysis.

This should not be misunderstood. He had said—and meant it—that government had a responsibility for people's welfare, and, having allowed a depression to occur, with all its attendant miseries, must do whatever it could to make those miseries less; but he had not admitted that the first necessity was enlargement of purchasing power. He was still very much attached to annually balanced budgets. He had spoken of paying for unemployment relief from the savings gained by reducing ordinary government expenditures. As I have noted, he had even ventured a figure of 25 percent—an estimate he had felt must be made good. Hence the Economy Act; hence his orders to all of us about finding ways to economize.

He was discovering now—but not yet admitting publicly—that neither the reduction of governmental costs nor experiments with gold purchases were enough. What was really effective was increased demand, a consequent rise in prices, and renewed liquidity throughout the system as debts were discharged.

Beneath the surface as the new year began, there were certain indications of more trouble. Inflation, however necessary after a long period of deflation, unsettled many arrangements and relationships. The processing tax had made food and clothing more costly. Hopkins had to increase his relief benefits and the wages paid for public work. If government had more income through the tax, still more was being spent.

Roosevelt's hope had been that private industrial activity would be enlarged, and to an extent it was; but the massive unemployment had not been reduced to manageable proportions. It would seem incredible to a later generation, horrified by an unemployment rate of 6 or 7 percent, that there was once one of 25 or 30 percent and that the economy had somehow survived. Before inauguration the numbers of the unemployed had been put at about thirteen millions. It was now about ten millions, an appreciable reduction; but that the problem had not been solved by the reemployment agreement, or, as yet, by Hopkins' and Ickes' efforts, was all too obvious.

More would have to be done. It was confidently predicted that there would be dramatic improvement in the agricultural sector during the next crop season. Farmers were already paying some debts, buying some machinery, and living a little better. There was gradual unfreezing of assets pledged to bankers, mostly as yet because the RFC was astoundingly liberal with multi-million-dollar loans or even outright buying of frozen collateral held by the banks. There was, however, the question whether government could continue to give employment to ten, or even eight, millions of people or support so many families through direct relief. It would require something like a third—perhaps more—of all public expenditures. Where would the funds come from? The only present source was printed money, and printed money would be depreciated money. Inflation was a tax on everyone, especially on consumers.

The intention had been to raise prices in order to establish something like the levels prevailing before the onset of the depression. This would enable farmers as well as others to pay their debts. But this would happen only if they could sell their products, and this they were prevented from doing by the higher prices enforced by the processing tax. It was a dilemma and as yet Roosevelt had found no way of escaping it.

☆ | C H A P T E R 3 | ☆

The Trials of Notoriety

MY SITUATION AT this time was described in the following excerpt from *Kiplinger's Letter* for January 27, 1934. This was a "dope sheet" subscribed to by businessmen for "inside" information on official activities. Most of the information was imaginary, but their capacity for self-delusion was apparently limitless, and it was widely read.

Tugwell. We get scores of inquiries about Tugwell from agricultural trades and industries, most of whom fear, distrust and dislike him, because of his reputation for radicalism.

Here's Tugwell: He is frankly a theorist, without practical experience either in business or in politics. He thinks there are times, such as these, when the forced application of theories will result in more practical good than the application of practical ideas, which he thinks don't go deep enough to help. He doesn't always recognize a FACT when he sees one. He is radical, or ultra-liberal, but he isn't essentially a revolutionist, and he isn't a sentimentalist. His current writings do not seem as radical as his past writings. He wants POSITIVE government action, rather than drifting. He has very little understanding of human relations in the concrete, and an utter indifference to the impression which he personally makes; he just doesn't care a damn. He is not a good politician; he would make a better adviser than a public official. His sincerity and honesty of intention are beyond question.

This kind of appraisal was spreading in late 1933 and early 1934. I was still able to foregather with legislators, to discuss matters of policy with fellow economists, and generally to get a fair enough hearing for whatever suggestions I had to make concerning policy. I was then thought, I believe, to be the most reliable expositor of administration intentions; and this was not only because of my supposed association with the president, but because what I said made sense in the circumstances. So, at least, I like to think.

Roosevelt did or said nothing to discourage me. Once in a while he even spoke of a speech or an article. Gradually, however, as my deliberate detractors began to bring their weight to bear, and as my avenues of expression closed, a change began. I had fewer opportunities to speak, and when I did speak what I said was tortured in printed reports into the meanings agreeable to the manufacturers of my stereotyped personality.

Roosevelt could not defend me publicly or denounce lies and misrepresentations, although he did write an indignant letter to the publisher of the *New York Times* about a particularly outrageous report of my doings. The account, he told Ochs, was completely untrue. I do not recall that this resulted in a correction; but perhaps it did make the Washington bureau of the *Times* somewhat more cautious. He could and did continue to make use of my services. Later on he would no longer be able to do that freely; and I too should be in a withdrawing temper from the continuous pounding. But that stage had not yet arrived. By September I had been so visibly exhausted that he suggested the working trip I have spoken of. It was a welcome break with the kind of work I had been doing for months.

I traveled to Glacier Park by railway, stopping at Chicago for a day at the fair. At the park I was met by Bureau of Public Roads administrators for the western division, and various relays of them took me all the way to Santa Fe. From Montana we went through Idaho and Washington and south through western Oregon to San Francisco. There I was picked up by the then deputy chief engineer of the bureau, who piloted me during the rest of our trip. From San Francisco we took the coast road to Los Angeles, where we turned inland through southern Nevada and Utah, across northeastern Arizona into southern Colorado and then down to Santa Fe.

In the company of state and regional representatives of the various departmental bureaus—Forest Service, Agricultural Engineering, Chemistry and Soils, Animal and Plant Husbandry—who joined us at intervals and went as far as their interests reached, I worked through the national forests and the experiment stations. I saw the new CCC camps, the great dams being built—Grand Coulee, Boulder, and Beaver—and was initiated into the exciting field of agricultural experiments—apple, citrus, date, vineyard, rubber, erosion control, road construction, dry farming, rice, and livestock. I would thereafter be a more useful administrator. I learned more in our thirty-odd days of travel than I would ever have been able to learn by studying reports and reading correspondence. Communication from the field where I had seen what was being done would have a reality it could not otherwise have had.

It was while I was in the Northwest that I heard of Moley's resignation. This was the virtual ending of a working friendship, and it would leave me much more on my own in Washington than I had been before. Until then we had been an unusual team, at least as concerned our mutual confidence. We had never quarreled, we had been helpful to each other, and we had never wavered in loyalty to a common cause. We did not always see things the same way. I did not like his close association with the financial people who had restored the banks to their former situation; and he no doubt thought me too adventurous in suggestions for reform. Curiously, I do not recall discussing such differences at any length. We seem to have agreed not to agree but to award each other the confidence that each was honestly pursuing a common ultimate purpose.

We had been useful to Roosevelt in matters outside each other's interests; and it was no longer necessary for us to meet frequently. I had made the transition from pre- to post-inauguration tasks more easily than he. He had resented the inevitable decline in his intimacy with Roosevelt, or rather, the sharing of that intimacy with many new people. For some of these, like Henry Morgenthau, he had always had a certain dislike; others of them he regarded almost as intruders—Ickes, for instance. They had never been heard of before, he seemed to think, and ought to be heard a good deal less of now. But his real trouble was with his own colleagues in State. He had less respect for Cordell Hull now than he had had at the beginning, and, if possible, he had less respect for William Phillips, Herbert Feis, and others with whom he had to associate. He made no attempt to conceal this; and after the fiasco of the London economic conference, it was inevitable that he should be pushed out. Everyone could see that it must be so. After all, Hull was an entrenched southern Democrat; and Moley had no political foundation whatever.

Roosevelt handled Moley's transition badly. It was the kind of rearrangement in which he used, as he admitted, "cowardly tactics." This particular weakness was one he would never overcome.[1]

After a few years, Moley's critical appraisals of Roosevelt would become immoderate. Fortunately by that time he and I would have few contacts; but when we did meet some matters would be avoided by tacit consent. I was much more inclined to take Roosevelt as he was, to expect nothing myself, and therefore not to be disappointed. I was able to argue with him, because I thought it useless merely to please him. Moley did not do this. What he demanded, Roosevelt told me, was to "have his hand held." This a president cannot do for any individual. Those who are his helpers cannot expect affection or consideration, only an appraisal of their usefulness in existing circumstances. As Moley began to engage himself elsewhere, I was given additional duties.

I found it hard to get used to my curious reputation. The attacks were mounting in number and in intensity. I continued to make an effort to turn the notoriety to some use. I tried to keep in touch with our progressive friends, and to keep them informed. I often got them hearings with Roosevelt. He needed them; but he could not, now that he was president, be their leader. He had to head the Democratic party, and that was a coalition whose most powerful elements were conservative and southern.

The progressives were weak because they were scattered and few, and because they differed among themselves. Olson in Minnesota, the La Follettes in Wisconsin, Norris in Nebraska, Wheeler in Montana, Johnson in California, Wagner and La Guardia in New York (although he had lost his seat in the last election), and Cutting in New Mexico. They and what they represented were a potential force, even if a limited one; and Roosevelt did see, if he could not acknowledge, their essential rightness. If their assistance had been stronger he might have made his way into new country without constant awareness of latent opposition. He was, indeed, giving most of his effort now to futile battles, gaining small victories when he should have had large ones, giving up important objectives to attain essential ones; and much of this was because progressivism was not becoming a political move-

---

[1] This was the only notable fault that faithful collaborator Sam Rosenman would admit when he came to write *Working with Roosevelt* (New York: Harper and Co., 1952).

ment. It was made up of individuals none of whom acknowledged the leadership of any of the others. What I could do in the next few years was not much. But what I did was all that anyone did to consolidate their support.

I could see afterward how little chance I had had to accomplish what Roosevelt wanted; but, of course, I could not see it then. I was badly placed, for one thing. I was a subordinate appointed official rather than an elected one. But also I made the mistake of attempting too much at once—of undertaking battles on more fronts than were necessary or could be successfully fought; and once engaged, I could not or would not withdraw. So I would become not so much a symbol of progressivism as a kind of crackpot radical. Most of this transition happened in 1933 and 1934. By the end of my first year I was confirmed as a notorious character.

☆ | CHAPTER 4 | ☆

No More Surprises for Now

I F ROOSEVELT WAS DISCOURAGED or even worried, it did not show.
His message to the regular session of the Congress in January can
only be described as bland and cheerful. We were, he said, "definitely
in the process of recovery." Lines were being drawn between those
who understood this to mean a "return to old methods," and those for
whom it meant a "permanent readjustment." He was prideful about
the fortifying of the government's credit—the Economy Act, he said,
had done that. Then he claimed for it also a "strengthening of the
financial structure." Eventually there would also be a "medium of
exchange" with less variable purchasing power. He regretted that our
"sister nations" had found themselves so handicapped by internal conditions that they felt themselves unable to discuss stabilization with
worldwide objectives.

He went on to say that AAA had made good progress in restoring
farm prices to parity and the Tennessee Valley Authority had begun
planned land-use policies and flood control, a beginning that must be
extended to other watersheds.

Unfortunately, he said, he could not regard the world situation with
optimism. At the recent conference in Montevideo it had been made
clear to the other American republics that interference in their affairs
would be avoided; but in other parts of the world, progress toward
peace or even trade agreements was prevented by preparations for
aggression.

Concerning unemployment, the efforts of state, local, and private agencies would continue to be supplemented; but there were dangers in direct relief and the effort would be "to move as rapidly as possible to publicly supported work and from that to the rapid restoration of private employment." What was being done now was temporary; there was in view "an integrated program, national in scope." It was intended to go beyond recovery. Self-help and self-control were the essence of the American tradition. These values would dominate all planning for the future.

He ended with a conspectus. It was necessary to have mechanical invention, machine production, industrial efficiency, modern communications, and broad education; but "the unnecessary expansion of industrial plants, the waste of resources, the exploitation of consumers, the accumulation of stagnant surpluses, child labor . . . speculation with other people's money"—these had been consumed in the fires the exploiters had kindled, and it must be made sure that as American life was reconstructed "there should be no soil in which such weeds" could grow again.

The message was meant to be reassuring, and action was emphasized. It is quite apparent to the backward view, and it was apparent to many then, that his optimistic appraisal of the situation was sophistical. Nearly every statement needed considerable modification; and some came close to being deceptive. It was true that there had been some reemployment, but there were still all those millions remaining to be absorbed into industry. Businessmen had found that they could get credit for cooperation without in fact giving any. The six hundred or more codes, most of them hastily thrown together, granted the long-sought privileges of immunity from penalties for price-fixing and permission to allocate markets; but there were no exacting rules for fair competition or any protection for consumers. Self-government for industry had already become self-indulgence for each business without relation to the economy as a whole or to other industries. The government had not been made a senior partner; it had not been made a partner at all.

What could be claimed, and what had excused Roosevelt's approval of the defective codes, was the progress made in gains for organized labor. The original purpose of establishing a system of countervailing powers under government supervision had been submerged in these peripheral activities.

This would have been difficult to understand without some knowledge of his long interest in social reform, kept active by Eleanor and

those others in New York who had been so indignant about sweatshops
and child labor in factories. The state had taken the lead in legislating
such conditions out of existence when Smith had been governor; and
Roosevelt had kept Frances Perkins, the ablest of the reformers, in his
official family there. Now she was secretary of labor, to the annoyance
of the labor hierarchs who were making such trouble for her as they
could. Roosevelt was elated by the opportunity to expand the protections
of the New York welfare statutes to the nation and to add collective
bargaining. If he rather than his secretary of labor got credit, that
was what was due the responsible political leader. The difficulty
with all this was that the original purposes were lost in the bargaining
between workers and employers. It was the beginning of an alliance
that held enormous dangers for the future.

John L. Lewis, leading the union forces, had taken center stage at
NRA and had nearly robbed General Johnson of his eminence in
flamboyancy. There had been times during the summer and fall when
Lewis and Johnson were more prominent than Roosevelt. Both had
remarkable oratorical talents. The contest between them for attention
was a theatrical attraction. Johnson, however, was an official charged
with an important duty; Lewis was merely pushing for the recognition,
in all the agreements, first of miners' rights and then of those all
union members were demanding.

Roosevelt knew by now that he would somehow have to get rid of
Johnson. He had fortunately been relieved of Peek and must now find
some better way of managing NRA. The accounts of turmoil wherever
Johnson was involved and of the exaggerated claims that concealed the
deals offered businessmen for quick agreement to the codes were quite
true. Roosevelt's detachment had become fictional. He would not recognize publicly that NRA was out of control; but its chaotic condition
could no longer be concealed. Johnson had been the inventor of the
blue eagle campaign, and Roosevelt had supported him. If Johnson's
conduct was outrageous and if the reemployment scheme had not
worked, Roosevelt could not escape involvement. The reporters and
commentators saw to that. What was equally important was that both
Peek and Johnson had been Baruch men. The denial of a cabinet
post for him had been partially compensated for by the jobs given
Peek and Johnson. With both of them gone, Baruch had no reason for
continuing his support. Evidently, however, Roosevelt felt that by now
his own strength was such that he would soon be able to ignore the
disappointed statesman. There were, of course, those legislators who

owed so much to Baruch, and this might at some point be embarrassing; but Johnson was behaving more and more erratically. He would have to go.

He would not quiet down. He turned up everywhere; he was at once reactionary and seemingly radical. He told his audiences he meant to save the business system from itself. It had only to follow his directions. He blustered; he threatened; he denounced chiselers; he called on a remarkable vocabulary traceable to his experience in the cavalry. Meanwhile NRA was an uncontrolled riot. For a while it served to show that the administration was concerned; but the truth was that unemployment was not notably reduced and that the codes were open to criticism from both extremes—the conservatives and the progressives.

A winter with ten millions unemployed could only be tolerable by contrast with others when there had been thirteen millions. There was, however, first FERA, then CWA. Through them Hopkins made government the employer of last resort. The work done was not very useful, sometimes; but it furnished workers a certain income. Hopkins, however, had the imagination to do more than employ those who could only rake leaves, shovel snow, or dig ditches; he would soon see that skilled workers were employed at their old trades, and would even have theater and artists' and writers' projects. He made a simple but sufficient answer to his critics about this: "They need to eat too," he said. So one of the liveliest programs of the New Deal was taking shape by midwinter.

The number of those whose lives were made tolerable by Hopkins' efforts might from public accounts seem to be few and his projects ridiculous. Many laborers did, in fact, spend much of their time leaning on their rakes or shovels. Hungry and exhausted men could not make dirt fly; but, however unfairly, they were expected to. It was evident that Roosevelt would not be sustained in the policies that had produced the debacle in NRA and that provided income by giving vast gangs of laborers hand tools and putting them to work. He was expected to produce recovery, to get industrial activity going again, with factories running and trade lively. He had said he would do that, and he could not excuse himself from the responsibility. It looked now, even though it did not appear from anything he admitted, that present tactics had had about all the effect to be expected of them.

Still, the situation was better in some respects. Those who had been anxious about losing their homes were by now relieved—or many were—of that anxiety. The Home Owners Loan Corporation was being helpful; and in early March an expansion would be recommended that would guarantee principal as well as the interest on a new issue of bonds. That would already have been done (in January) for refinancing farmers' debts. These measures and the flow of checks for compliance with the AAA reduction campaign had relieved some of the worst anxieties.

It could not be denied, however, that there were many who had implacable objections to what was being done. What they wanted was an immediate return to what they regarded as normality. Even farmers, whose depression had been deepening for a decade, had strong reservations about unemployment relief, unbalanced budgets, and even the assistance they themselves were getting. They wanted to raise crops and livestock and be well paid for them in a free market. That these conditions had been responsible for their troubles in the first place did not in the least alter their belief that they ought to get profitable prices for all the crops they could produce; AAA had not satisfied them. It was hard to measure the various kinds of dissent and alienation. Farmers were normally Republicans anyway. They had always believed, against all reason, in high tariffs and had refused to accept the fact of closed foreign markets. All that could be done to satisfy them would probably not be enough. The more conservative members of the Congress, many of them Democrats, were grumbling audibly. Roosevelt had pushed them hard against their deepest inclinations. He could not expect much more of them.

My own anxieties were shared by my progressive friends. I say *my* progressive friends because the sharpness of division between those with whom I had close relations and those others who were followers of Brandeis was becoming much more visible and more significant. There was no doubt now that self-regulation under government supervision was a lost cause.

Bob La Follette, like his father, whom he had succeeded in the Senate, was an indignant individual anyway, and he was especially unhappy. He had worked for the kind of NRA we had wanted and seen it weakened and altered as lobbyists had prevailed on the committees to excise the necessary disciplines. It was now so thoroughly discredited that only a complete overhaul could salvage it. For this Roosevelt might well wait too long and then not have the influence to get the needed amendments.

Much more likely, it would succumb to the combined forces of self-serving businessmen and resentful Brandeis followers, unlikely cooperators but ones who together would be effective. The orthodox progressives were able to say that what they had known all along would happen had happened. The less enlightened businesses, given a chance, were simply taking over the economy, free for the first time from the anti-trust laws and contemptuous of consumers' interests. They had been bitterly opposed to increasing the power of the unions, but had begun to see that the cost of labor's gains could simply be passed on to the buying public. Lewis had won collective bargaining, but he had helped effectively to ruin NRA.

No, our hopes for a rationalized system of industry, each of its units dealing with those it sold to or bought from, and under rules of fairness established and enforced by public authority, were rapidly vanishing. If we wasted a good deal of time lamenting and planning futile tactics, it was because we thought the future of the economy so dependent on escape from the planless chaos that had brought on the depression.

Roosevelt listened but remained evasive. He would finally call a conference, early in spring, to "review" NRA; but by then the situation had already become hopeless. He was by now making defensive concessions to the believers in simplistic *laissez faire*, attempting one of those impossible maneuvers Moley would later speak of—the "weaving together" of absolute opposites. In Moley's illustration it was free trade and protection. In this case it was regulated industrial self-government and free competition.

When Roosevelt spoke (on March 5) to a meeting of some six hundred code authorities, he began by saying that the law had been meant "to promote organization in industry for the purpose of co-operative action in trade groups and to induce and maintain united action of labor and management under adequate government sanction and supervision." This was an adequate statement of what had been intended. Its recitation, however, betrayed how far the reality was from the intention. He seemed to acknowledge this by going on to say that now the code-making had virtually come to an end it was time for reassessment. In less haste it would be possible to correct mistakes. This would be the task of the coming months.

It was all too apparent that NRA pleased no one. Making a note on this speech for his *Papers*, Roosevelt said that the time had come by then for stock-taking. The great problem ahead was not the expansion of NRA but rather "the concentration of its efforts in those directions most promising of permanent gain, the elimination of many policies and practices shown to be of dubious value and the imperative need for defining fundamental principles and policies for improving the machinery of code compliance." He had allowed things to get out of hand.

In May a policy board would be established. It would be "charged with working out acceptable, desirable policies as to code provisions." Still later (in September 1934) a National Recovery Board would be established to take over Johnson's duties, and quite possibly it might have worked out that rationalization some of us had hoped for; but the Supreme Court would intervene and Roosevelt would not push for the simple amendments the court must have accepted. By that time he would be so annoyed by the indiscipline and so torn by the controversies—whipped up continually by the growing corps of Brandeis-Frankfurter recruits to government—that he would simply give up and consign industrial policy to a considerably enlarged anti-trust division of the Department of Justice headed by Thurman Arnold, who, I may say, disappointed me by his acceptance of so futile a task.

There were other disappointments in this first year; and if NRA was the worst, it did not seem beyond rescue then. The forces gathering to destroy it could still be overcome. The suggestion for a board to take Johnson's place was already being discussed. Ickes and I already had a candidate for its chairmanship—Robert M. Hutchins, president of the University of Chicago. To this Roosevelt agreed, and when the time came would get Hutchins' consent. Then for some reasons unknown to us he would change his mind. The board would finally consist of S. Clay Williams, A. D. Whiteside, Sidney Hillman, Leon C. Marshall, and Walton Hamilton. I would always think that Hutchins' abilities and energy might have made the difference that would have saved the experiment.

CHAPTER 5

Roosevelt's Methods

I COULD SEE NO WAY of softening the animosities gathered about my unwilling person. I discovered gradually that I was even at odds with those with whom I should have been allied. This was the rapidly increasing number of young men contributed to the government by Felix Frankfurter, whose influence came from having courted Roosevelt for years. He had some sort of need to serve a prince—as he himself put it. He was also a Brandeis satellite, and Brandeis was certain that I represented the collectivism he recognized in NRA.[1]

The first of this group no sooner got themselves settled in than they sent for others; these, being placed, were able to place still more. So it went until there were hundreds. The first lot wrote the banking laws, the Securities and Exchange Act, and similar promised "reforms." The others, in multiplying numbers, drafted the regulations making the new legislation effective. They were competent and their intentions were definite. They meant to rescue the American people from monopolists, and they meant to do it by making existence for them so difficult that smaller competitors would have opportunities they had long since lost.

The orthodox progressives regarded all bigness as inherently bad.

[1] This antagonism to collectivists as well as Frankfurter's wooing of Roosevelt can be followed further in the collection of Roosevelt-Frankfurter letters annotated by Max Freedman (Boston: Little, Brown and Co., 1968). Also in my essay following publication of those letters in *The Political Science Quarterly*, March 1970.

Large organizations must be broken up and returned to the sizes and relationships of a hundred years earlier. This condition was past any chance of being recreated by legal prosecutions; but manifest unreality was ignored in the name of individualism with amazing ease and unanimity. This conviction that bigness was evil came easily to young lawyers wanting to serve the public rather than enter the offices of large firms devoted to representing corporations. It put them on the side of those who were having a hard time in the cruel economic world. Legal training taught them to be adversaries, not to think seriously about economic organization. The devising of ways to make technical advances advantageous to the whole community was quite outside their area of consideration. Corporate entities were to be attacked, not civilized and made useful.

That some of us—a few—should insist that free competition was hopelessly anachronistic, a denial of the obvious technological future, was infuriating to them. As they increased in numbers they gained more influence in administration circles. They had Frances Perkins on their side. She was a reformer of the old school. More important, they had the justice himself, who received every Sunday in his consciously unpretentious old-fashioned apartment. The disciples gathered round; they heard the word and went forth thereafter to battle not only the legions of big business, but those of us who thought their theory empty and their dream of an America made up of little people carrying on little businesses long past possibility.

Roosevelt was torn between the view often expressed by La Follette and myself and that urged on him by Brandeis and Frankfurter. For many years he had regarded Brandeis as the model of a reforming liberal. As an eager young man Roosevelt had regarded Brandeis as the main source of progressive ideas. That these were no longer tenable in a high-energy economy he seemed to be well aware; but the challenge of identifying and protecting the public interest in that economy was not an easy one. The NRA was intended to do that; but it was opposed by the old justice with the fervor of one whose most precious hopes were in question.

Actually we did not know—no one knew—whether Roosevelt really saw the world as it was or whether he saw it as Frankfurter's young men, swarming into Washington, saw it. The Brandeis thesis was clear and simple: a struggle was going on between forces of good and evil; the good ones were the little ones and the bad ones were the big ones. If the big ones got control or threatened to, they would have to be matched by regulators, but preferably they ought to be broken up. The advantage of the breaking-up policy was that it reduced the government's functions to those of seeing that bigness was made impossible. If combination and increased scale were allowed, an ever-growing army of bureaucrats would have to labor endlessly at making the corporate giants behave. Competition, actualized, would make fairness automatic.

Berle and I had argued for recognition that large-scale production had not only been made possible by new technologies but had been made necessary by the needs of a continental nation with a growing population. Family farms would not produce enough food and fiber; small concerns would not produce enough steel, automobiles, machinery, power, and all the other goods demanded by an urbanized society. Collectivization was here to stay; the only question was whether it could be made to work in the public interest without actually being publicly owned. We contended that it could. Most of the abuses charged to it could be eliminated by mutual agreement, all conforming to established standards; but these standards must be set, or at least approved, by representatives of the public, and restraint must be applied to those who might seek to profit from others' compliance. This had been the argument we had gone over and over with Roosevelt in Albany. It had seemed at the time to be accepted. What we had not realized was that other voices were being heard, and that our arguments were far from conclusive. Roosevelt, we saw now, had been speculating about using something from each and finding compromises.

To proclaim, as the traditional progressives were now doing, that NRA had failed and should forthwith be abandoned was to ignore the emasculation of its disciplines as it had been amended and the softness of subsequent administration. Roosevelt was forced to admit by January 1934 that his avoidance of choice between enforced littleness and the recognition of technological enlargement was no longer possible. Johnson's codes were falling rapidly into the disrepute they deserved. Should NRA be reconstituted; should the codes be rewritten, public members admitted to code authorities and enforcement provided for? Or should the clamor of the orthodox progressives for abandonment prevail?

Roosevelt could no longer expect to have it both ways. The powerful business interests, whose lobbyists inundated Washington in immense and increasing numbers, were sending voluminous reports to their principals. Could Roosevelt possibly appease the Brandeis disciples, who never stopped whispering that a state like Mussolini's and Hitler's would surely follow code-making? It could already be seen what it would be like. So they said.

When Johnson could hold on no longer, Roosevelt would find others to take over; but meanwhile he was still temporizing. The meeting with the code authorities on March 5 was some sort of response to the growing criticism. In speaking to them he was defensive. He rejected the claim that NRA was a borrowing from communism or national socialism:

The objective was, as you know, to apply remedies [to the chaos of unrestricted competition] in the American way and not to copy those being tried in other countries . . . I am always a little amused and perhaps at the same time a little saddened—and think the American people feel the same way—by those few writers and speakers who proclaim tearfully either that we are committed to communism and collectivism or that we have adopted fascism and dictatorship. The real truth is that for some years in our country the machinery of democracy had failed to work.

He went on to defend self-regulation as an essentially American method. He also apologized for having approved codes that were being criticized by saying that in a period so short it had not been possible to perfect many hundreds of such complicated agreements. Now the time had arrived "for taking stock and for correcting manifest errors." This was a promise of change with some concession to his progressive critics; but he still seemed to think that free competition and corporate concentration could be "weaved together."

There was certainly more to come. I must confess to having hoped that, with Johnson gone, as now was inevitable, and a competent board installed in his place, NRA could still be saved. I wrote and spoke about it. I also began to be asked again by Roosevelt to confer with various people looking to a coming reorganization. Frank and I spent a good deal of time gathering suggestions wherever they could be found.

As will be imagined, we hoped as well that AAA would be reconsidered and amended, one change being the sharing by laborers and sharecroppers of the benefits flowing so generously to those who needed them least. Considering the lobby's strength, it might only be possible to make some other kind of provision for the relief of these millions. It was this problem that the resettlement effort I shall outline presently was intended to meet. Meanwhile my outspoken criticism of AAA in full functioning was annoying Chester Davis and the agricultural hierarchy. Things were going well for them. Farmers were getting benefit checks and reconstituting their capital. They were paying off old debts, too, and were once again in good standing with local bankers. What Davis wanted from me was silence while progress toward recovery for his clients proceeded. This he was getting from Wallace, and even Wallace was now regarding me as a disturbance.

Douglas was still giving trouble of another sort. He was persistently resisting any and all spending, especially spending for the research and experimentation that made up much of our department's work. But he was finding, as Jump had said he would, that the influence of our bureau chiefs among congressmen was preventing the drastic reductions he had hoped to make. It was still a time when the appropriation committees scrutinized proposed budgets line by line. Much as I deplored this as a governmental practice, it was now convenient. It served to protect our essential operations from the budget slashers.

My open clashes with Douglas in meetings of the Special Board for Public Works were the cause of further polarization between those who now assumed that government must provide employment and those who were outraged by such extravagance. Hopkins was better protected, since he had no board, and, indeed, had no dealings with Douglas at all. He simply got his allocation from Roosevelt and used it as he pleased.

But all these enemies—Davis in AAA, Johnson in NRA, and Douglas in the budget—had minor effects compared with those resulting from the engagement with the purveyors of doubtful nostrums and unlabeled foods. My intention to destroy these virtuous industries could be unknown only to those who never saw a newspaper or listened to a radio broadcast. My position as a convinced enemy of American institutions was rapidly being consolidated. I seemed always to be turning up as a critic of advertising and the other sales endeavors of business.

Sometime during the height of the food and drug disturbance, Mrs. Roosevelt called me and suggested that I come to a luncheon she was arranging. When I arrived she barely suppressed a wicked smile as she introduced me to the principal guest, a lady who turned out to be one of the editors of *Good Housekeeping*, a magazine that offered to approved products something known as the Good Housekeeping Seal of Approval. This was supposed to guarantee the quality of any product carrying it. Consumer advocates said any purveyor could acquire it if they bought a satisfactory amount of advertising space in the magazine, a charge infuriating to the magazine's sensitive proprietors. The lady in question was very high-and-mighty. She was accompanied by her court; but there were others present—all women—who regarded her with reformist suspicion. The antagonisms among the guests were palpable.

Mrs. Roosevelt placed me next to the visiting editor, and waited for the acerbities to develop. They were not much delayed. I was asked what I had against advertising. I was frank. I said that as it was being used, it persuaded people to buy indiscriminately. Sometimes they got their money's worth; but often they were cheated. Worse, sometimes they were harmed. She interrupted to say that advertising was indispensable to business. Besides, advertisers—especially such as were allowed to appear in *Good Housekeeping*—were restricted to products of known quality. I asked her whether she had examined the chamber of horrors assembled by the food and drug people. She shuddered. It was a shame, she said, that such an unfair exhibition should be displayed as representative. I was ready for this. I was specific about several products she was not prepared to defend.

She had lost her temper by now, and Mrs. Roosevelt showed concern. Her practical joke had gone too far. The situation was saved, however, in a most unexpected way: an awkward waiter spilled a bowl of tomato soup into my lap and I was able to withdraw without dishonor even if with some damage to the striped trousers I had been told were appropriate to the occasion.

Confrontations with opponents in the open were not frequent and were not profitable. I avoided them whenever I could. There were several reasons for circumspection. The most important was the conclusion I had reached, without being told, that consumers were not a constituency Roosevelt cared to placate. This, deplorable as it might be, was merely political realism. I had no right to insist on policies beyond offering whatever arguments I could muster; and obviously advice about voters was not something to offer Roosevelt. If he refused the suggestion that a cause could be made of an issue his predecessor Roosevelt had found profitable, he must have his own reasons for it.

He apparently was not going to tell me, however, that I might not proceed on my own and get as far as I could. I understood that I must not involve him beyond the limits he recognized. These I had to find on my own. A personal crusade was out of the question. So the food and drug revision was turned over to Copeland. The same was true of other issues I had been interested in—except that in some of these the position had quickly proved to be right. Two of these were now coming clearly into sight. NRA must be taken from Johnson and a defensible self-government system must be devised; also, gold purchasing had so obviously failed that other means of "reflation"—a suddenly popular word—would have to be given more play.

Roosevelt did recall to me on one occasion, changing the subject we had been discussing, a phrase I had repeated to him the spring before from a speech I had made at Columbia. Speaking of recovery, I had said that what Hoover was doing was like trying to encourage a tree to grow by applying fertilizer to the branches rather than to the soil around the roots. This was the contrast of relief for business with relief for consumers. The phrase had stuck in his mind. We do have to create demand, he said, don't we? I had no need to answer, but I did venture a conclusion from this.

Benefits for farmers had indeed increased their purchasing power, but the processing tax used to pay these benefits had raised prices for consumers, so limiting their ability to buy. It was, in effect, a sales tax. Benefits might better come from less regressive taxes. Hopkins was so clearly saving the situation that he ought to have more funds to use where they would do the most good—among those who would spend every cent they got for clothing, food, fuel, and rent. Together with the postponement of mortgage foreclosures and the prevention of wholesale bankruptcies, these were the most powerful engines of recovery. The rest was desirable enough, but none of it was immediately essential.

It was easier to be happy about what could be seen coming than what had been going on during the last six months. I was quite sure that Roosevelt was edging around to operations more genuinely remedial than the ones he had undertaken until now; but any lingering hope for self-governing business under government auspices was fading fast. Those who should have been our allies had sabotaged our efforts. AAA too had been turned over to the old hierarchy. In sum, we might recover; but it would take new initiatives; and we were not likely to reconstruct the business system so that activity might again begin within new guiding principles.

CHAPTER 6

Roosevelt's Grand Maneuver

S INCE WE WERE coming to the end of the monetary experiments and since Roosevelt now realized how NRA had been damaged, the next six months would be a time for revisions and for getting them accepted in spite of disillusions. It may be recalled how, during the approach to his candidacy, and then during the campaign, he had allowed his performance to be dictated by the senior Democrats. A small coterie of these—mostly senators—had conspired with Howe and Farley to deliver a majority of the delegates at the convention. They had preferred him to other contenders such as Smith, Ritchie, Baker, or Byrd. Then, as he pursued votes in the campaign, he had trimmed his themes to their advice, or, at least, had allowed them to say what issues he should avoid. Since the professionals were convinced that Hoover was defeating himself, the preferred strategy was clearly indicated. No considerable interest should be offended. This excluded a very small number of the affluent, mostly financiers, who could be charged with various unethical, if not criminal, practices. They were fair game; and nothing was to be lost by pillorying them.

In this way Roosevelt attracted southern support, many of the farm and progressive votes, and those of all who were sufficiently disillusioned with Hoover. The success of the strategy was measured by the victory, and during his first months in office he had been disposed to go on in the same way.

It should be noted that the seniors had no objection to the severe treatment of Wall Street. Most of them were from other parts of the country and were traditionally resentful of the financial overlordship exercised by the New York establishment. When the Pecora investigations, continuing in the Senate, turned up sensational instances of misbehavior, they were inclined to applaud. Even Jesse Jones, now operating so freely with the enormous funds allocated to the RFC, was from Houston, where a new plutocracy was being established. Jones stood, as someone remarked, slightly to the right of Hoover—who, indeed, had first appointed him to the board of the RFC. Jones was in no doubt about his mission. It was to salvage as many as possible of the concerns in charge of American enterprise. He was prepared to take such risks as were necessary for this, knowing that his was an effort fully supported by the conservative congressional Democrats. His liaison with them was intimate, and they refused him nothing. By now his commitments had reached incredible size. They frightened some people, but expressions of that fright were surprisingly muted.

The whole country was amused when an imaginative reporter, for no reason at all placed a dwarf on J. P. Morgan's lap as he was testifying before Pecora's committee. The front-page photographs quite successfully deflated that haughty financier. This seemed to be just what was needed to complete the conviction in people's minds of a new vulnerability among the barons in the canyons of lower New York. It ensured a central place in New Deal operations of punishment for those defilers of the "temple" Roosevelt had spoken of in the Inaugural.

No one knew better than he that this was a sideshow. It satisfied an appetite for revenge—not a very nice sentiment, but a convenient one. Someone must be punished for the fears and sufferings, the disappointments and frustrations of the past few years. The nation had suddenly plunged into panic and lingering paralysis just at a time when it had seemed to be moving forward on an irresistible tide of prosperity. Nothing could be more irrelevant than a dwarf sitting on the knee of one who typified and symbolized Wall Street; but Morgan was the perfect representation of arrogant power, all broadcloth, stiff linen, jowls, and supercilious expression. He was brought low. In fact, the central ganglions of the tight eastern financial empire were irreparably damaged by Pecora's revelations. Jones saved some New York institutions, along with others, from bankruptcy, but the most spectacular rescues were in such places as Chicago, Detroit, Cleveland—and Houston.

It was already evident that Jones had as little respect for the president as he had for other easterners. His deals must have furnished some moments of concern; but Roosevelt was already showing the remarkable ability to make use of incongruous collaborators that would characterize all his years in the White House. As long as Jones was doing what it was convenient to have him do, it made no difference whether any respect went with it. In fact, if the rescue of some great concerns turned out to be colossal mistakes, it would be convenient to have it known that it had been done without the president's specific consent.

It was about this time, although it was disclosed only gradually, and seemed to be forced by events, that the grand maneuver began that by the next national election would change entirely the constituency Roosevelt would rely on for support. The voters he had counted on in 1932 were no longer reliable; but a new—and far larger—coalition was forming. If it was true, as was being said, that the results in 1932 had been less a victory for Roosevelt than a defeat for Hoover, clearly what was building up for 1934 and 1936 was a personal following such as had not been known since Theodore Roosevelt had carried the country in 1904. If he had to let some voters go, he would rely on others who had either been indifferent or opposed in 1932; and there would be many more of them.

The blandness of the 1932 campaign had at first been disappointing, but when the plan was understood, its development had had its own fascination. It did, of course, make all the efforts of the so-called Brains Trust seem to have been wasted. None of the analyses or syntheses worked out so carefully were of much use in the campaign's appeals. They had, however, remained in Roosevelt's mind, If he seemed to ignore such basics as the need for reconstituting purchasing power and adopted the useless tactic of restoring business confidence, he must have had his own reasons. But we had been justified. By year's end he knew that AAA and the Hopkins relief efforts were the most effective of all the New Deal initiatives.

Reviewing what had happened, it was easy to generalize that the castigation of the financiers had been a wholly unsuccessful substitute for the plans he had discussed with Berle and myself during the spring. Recovery, in our view, was going to be an unpleasant ordeal for a good many people who deserved whatever happened to them. There would have to be massive assistance for the lowliest citizens; correspondingly, those who had been successful would have to pay for it. Many of the lowly ones did not vote; that characteristic of the electorate was well known to the professionals. Most of the moderately well-off—or formerly well-off—did vote, and many contributed to campaign funds. The professionals regarded it as foolish beyond calculation to advocate any radical schemes while seeking their votes. It was realistic in the sense of realism that defeats itself when the consequences begin to appear.

Roosevelt had said that government could not be indifferent to suffering; but the impression had been that things were going to be put back the way they had been except for punishing a few miscreants and changing a few rules to make their machinations impossible in the future. If he had said he was going to demand any such sum as $3.3 billion simply to be spent for relief, the elders might have abandoned him even before the campaign. However, he *had* asked for $3.3 billion, and by now, at the beginning of the new year, he was about to ask for more. Those who would eventually have to pay for this generosity were not too worried as yet, although there were plenty of conservative Jeremiahs who were predicting disaster. The tolerance, of course, was because the payment was being deferred and was, indeed, almost out of sight in the future. Inflation would sometime be seen as a devouring monster. Now it seemed an easy recourse.

There was another thing. A contest always goes on between debtors and creditors. The economy runs on credit; and credit is created in the back rooms of banks. Those who borrow promise to pay and hope to do so. They even give collateral as pledges of good faith. Their collateral is foreclosed if they cannot pay. The entire system depends on this arrangement. If large numbers of borrowers default, and if bankers discover that foreclosed collateral cannot be disposed of, a liquidity crisis results. No more loans can be made because there are no funds. The collateral remains in storage, so to speak; and both debtor and creditor are paralyzed. In these circumstances each blames the other, and the activated enmities are quickly and inevitably transferred to political forums.

There are many more debtors than creditors, however, and this is taken account of by professionals. A politician with any sense of reality will appeal to debtors, not to creditors. He may, at the same time, try to please the creditors, for whom he has another kind of consideration. They pay his bills. Jones was unfreezing the creditors' collateral—taking it out of storage—so that their operations could resume. Roosevelt's scheme also included the release of farmers and homeowners from imminent foreclosure to satisfy mortgage holders. If this in effect took over their debts with government funds, that too could be done without pain to creditors.

It was true that the enormous—for that time—expenditures for relief caused cries of outrage. There were no objections—or very few—to the rescue of the banks even while some bankers were being indicted for malpractice. This was because the validity of the system was not questioned; only the few who had plundered it were being punished.

It was too obvious to be missed, however, that the distressed were numerous and that they must be grateful for finally having gained some attention, not to mention being lifted out of the slough they had been sinking deeper and deeper into for years. If they could be organized and got to vote, there was a potential mass that overweighed any other interest in the whole country. But who would organize them?

The answer to this was making itself clear. Hopkins was preparing the way with his national rescue team of social workers working closely with local politicians—an unlikely alliance that nevertheless was proving marvelously effective. Hopkins' people could easily make it seem that local bosses had access to the relief rolls or public work—most of the funds were gifts to local governments anyway, taking the place of expenditures for maintenance they ought to have made but had been unable to do for years. Streets were cleaned, garbage collected, parks improved, and many other neglected services performed by the relief workers.

The bosses, then, would get the recipients to the polls and see that they voted the Democratic ticket. Why, they must have wondered, had they supported Roosevelt's rivals for the nomination—almost lost it for him, in fact—in 1932? Anyway, they were now the most effective corps of supporters any politician could want. In 1936, even in 1934, there would be millions of new adherents.

Another remarkable force in the making was the newly energized industrial workers. Once collective bargaining was firmly legalized, union membership began to expand and to become more militant. This was already apparent in 1933. Labor's leaders were as visible in Washington as those of the farmers; they could not yet match the lobbyists for industry, but it could be seen that they soon would. They had an advantage that any politician must recognize: they represented a vast number. Compared with their old opponents, the employers, they were a far more numerous constituency.

Roosevelt was certainly the first popular hero the poorest Americans had had in a long time. The populists of the middle states had never had a sympathetic president; neither had the 1912 or 1924 progressives; neither, for that matter, had any recognizable group except business. Hoover, Coolidge, and Harding had been answerable to the combination of special interests dominant in politics because businesses furnished campaign funds. They still had that in their favor; but a vitalized labor movement might well gather the resources to rival them.

As this realignment went on, it did not matter much, politically, that financiers were being persecuted, or that NRA was likely to fail. What was important was that people's immediate needs were being satisfied.

It will be recalled that NRA, in its inception, had been favorably thought of by many influential industrialists; had, in fact, been pushed by them. Henry I. Harriman, president of the U.S. Chamber of Commerce, had helped to put it together. So had Gerard Swope of General Electric and Fred I. Kent, the New York banker. They had caught the notion, each in his own way, that industry could not go on in anarchic fashion and that it must regulate itself if the system was to be saved. Their ideas had seemed to catch on, but when the codes were being made the temptation to take advantage of the loose organizing processes had been too strong. The countervailing principle, each industry opposing the tendency in others to exploit it, had somehow been lost to sight. Some, the most powerful, had written advantages for themselves into their codes, and found Roosevelt compliant. Besides, the necessary public oversight had been omitted, and this was fatal.

These mistakes meant nothing immediately to the sufferers from depression. If they were still unemployed, they had relief or there was public work. Their homes were no longer likely to be taken away. Many even of the neglected rural workers were being reached now by Hopkins' social workers.

If there was reason to be disappointed about AAA and NRA, about consumer protection, and, indeed, about much else, there was still Roosevelt's commitment to the general welfare. The mistakes might not be beyond correction and Roosevelt might still make the attempt. He had experimented; he had moved too fast. He could learn and he could slow down and make corrections. He was saying that he would.

If I did not allow my disappointment to overcome my faith that ways would be found to improve matters, there was also the fascination of watching Roosevelt at work. I had no administrative position of importance; but I was something of a favorite with Ickes, with whom

I shared a clearly emotional feeling for the nation's estate, and I was respected by Wallace, who knew that the policies I advocated were right. Neither Wallace nor Ickes, the ablest of the cabinet members, was intimate with Roosevelt. I had the advantage of those past evenings in Albany when the exploration of future policy had been taking place.

The Brains Trust had not prevailed then; the campaign had not revealed any of the conclusions we thought Roosevelt had reached, nor were they uppermost here in Washington—at least not yet, although some things were turning that way. I had, however, learned a lesson. This was that no plans are important if they cannot be realized; and that the means for realization is political leadership. I must assume that Roosevelt was doing what he thought he must. I could at least watch from close by and have some things explained. Altogether, the opportunity to have a part in public operations went far to overcome the disappointments of that first year.

Most of all it was fascinating to watch the spreading confidence in Roosevelt among those who had cause to be grateful. They had put him in office with a kind of despairing hope. It could be seen that they would keep him there because he was doing his best to fulfill that hope.

CHAPTER 7

Persistence

SOME GOINGS-ON in New Deal Washington were of a sort to repel political purists. I was no longer one of these, having been hardened by experience; but anyone still capable of indignation had much to be indignant about. I had seen the open rapacity displayed by the professionals, both in and out of government. I no longer expected anything else. I had been perfectly placed to feel the weight of the processors' lobbies as the agricultural legislation took shape and as the AAA began its operations. The organization was, in fact, now controlled by them. Davis' ears were open to the pleas of millers, meat packers, and textile manufacturers. There seemed to be none who could be said to have the slightest interest in the larger problems of recovery and stability.

Wallace, who was concerned enough, had in fact lost control of the agricultural complex he nominally presided over. He was by now engaged in public persuasion, writing pamphlets, making speeches, and meeting with all sorts of people. His effort centered in reducing the isolationism he felt the nation was falling into and in persuading his public that the nation faced a crucial decision. What that decision was, I must confess, I was never entirely clear myself; but it had to do with international arrangements. It involved freer trade with other nations—something American farmers had never favored; but he was pleading for tolerance and cooperation. The mystic in him was always latent, and this caused him to evade hard decisions and outright taking of sides. This, at a future time, would lead to associations and affiliations with esoteric movements of embarrassing kinds and be very damaging. The politicians then, as later, were not willing to regard him as salable to their constituents.

Wallace, I now knew, would sometimes look the other way while things went on that should have caused him to erupt in indignation. This is not fair, quite; it is more accurate to say that he accepted them as conditions necessary to the situation he thought it important for us to occupy. He was intelligent. He was not really looking the other way; he was ignoring what he felt he could do nothing about if he was to carry out what seemed to him his mission. This was not to be administrator of the Agriculture Department or of AAA; it was to be a political leader, to be a presidential associate and possibly a successor.

Staying on in the Washington of 1932-33 required a certain tolerance of the number and presumption of fixers and power brokers who descended on the capital along with the new officials. It would not be believed, I often thought, that there could be so many with claims on Democratic politicians after so many years of Republican incumbency. After three administrations they might have been expected to have disappeared. But many had survived somehow. Others had suddenly become Democrats and were claiming privileges for their clients. They were incredibly unabashed and matter-of-fact in their demands. It was not jobs the early birds were after. The patronage crush had been delayed until the special session had closed and Farley was freed to begin satisfying congressmen's demands. The early fixers wanted arrangements made to ease up on regulations, to lower fees for services, to place projects, to favor contractors—all that sort of thing. Some were notoriously successful, and these set up headquarters in the Mayflower, the Willard, or the Shoreham, where there was a constant swirl of activity and where hospitality was lavish.

When the hunt for jobs began, there was a good deal of jostling. Each of the emergency measures, especially those appropriating funds for public works and relief, carefully specified that employees were to be engaged without regard to Civil Service requirements; but the impact of this on the departmental and other agencies was not anticipated by those of us who were newcomers. It was true, as Wallace had remarked, that there appeared to be an amazing number of Mormon secretaries and clerks, placed there by the longtime Senator Smoot; and it would hardly be contended that replacing them with Democrats would be detrimental to our work. The politicians argued that there must be Democrats with credentials as adequate as those of Republicans who happened to be Mormons; and, of course, they were right. But the changeover was disruptive.

We were much relieved when Farley placed one of his party men in our building and allowed him to control the process of substitution. He conceded that they must be qualified and that they should be below a certain level, mostly stenographers and clerks. Pressure for jobs was thus deflected. If only those not requiring special skills were to be filled in this way, we had no serious complaint to make. Julian Friant was assigned to be our protector. He proved to be a useful go-between. He conscientiously observed his instructions and managed to keep rapacious congressmen from making direct demands on us. They tried at first, thinking that if they were members of committees we had to deal with they could get favored treatment; but we were able, after we had Friant, to hide behind him. It was a matter of party loyalty, we said. They were naturally suspicious of Wallace, who had all his life been a Republican until he had defected to Roosevelt, and of me, who had only peculiar academic credentials, not expected to be found in an assistant secretary. The politicians remained unreconciled to both of us, but Friant gave us the protection we needed.

The substitutions were numerous; and there were many new jobs. AAA's staff of thousands was to be appointed without formalities; but this was true throughout the emergency agencies. During the first year there was a rising flood of incoming Democrats to operate the new programs. Many Republicans who had no protection from sponsors departed; but it was mostly expansion that offered the enlarged opportunities.

I was curious about the actual usefulness of this system to the congressmen who made so many demands. They were frank. They were not only rewarding their supporters; they were strengthening their future support. How could this be when clerks, stenographers, and others were being moved to Washington? I was told that they had relatives back home, and that, moreover, a congressman who was able to hold out a credible possibility of rewards was much more likely to have a base he could depend on. Since representatives had to run for reelection every two years, they were involved in an almost continuous campaign. Senators, having six-year terms, were somewhat freer, but not much. There was always a governor or an ambitious congressman ready to take advantage of any weakness. Occasionally there were others. Sometimes it was convenient for congressmen to have potential rivals, or supporters of rivals, in Washington rather than back home, and to have their indebtedness clearly centered in the officeholder with a claim on the administration.

To have an organization made up in large proportion of workers who owed their jobs and their security to a politician who had no interest in their work was a poor way to begin operations; and the emergency agencies were in fact deplorably inefficient. Much of this was excused as the inevitable result of rapid expansion, and there was no general indignation. There was, in fact, not much criticism of the system. The only serious attacks for obvious slackness were made on the relief workers. They were unmercifully lampooned in the midst of a bad winter when their distresses were most humiliating.

The filling of new government jobs by patronage could be called corruption of a sort; but the more flagrant corruptions were of other kinds. There were, we discovered—although we were not innocent enough to have been ignorant that such arrangements were common— many businesses and many individuals whose incomes depended on close relations with public officials. They were not necessarily contractors who gave less than they should for what they were paid. They were in some way regulated, perhaps, and could profit from the easing of requirements; or they carried on subsidiary operations that depended on the location and size of government projects. There were others who used public facilities such as the range and timber lands controlled by the Forest Service. Their interest was in minimum fees and permissive regulations. They had the western legislators, almost to a man, on their side. Arguments concerning overgrazing or overcutting, and the resulting effect on soils and streams, fell on deaf congressional ears.

It must be supposed that in any but a socialist government with all property owned by the state, those who had private claim to it or partial control over it would try to maximize their profits by influencing those who could arrange for the private use of public property or who could affect the income they could expect. There were continual contests over such matters as privileges, fees, and regulations. A forester could have life made miserable for him if he made difficulties for cattle men or lumber men. The Service heard, in explicit terms, from congressmen who could affect its budget.

Sometimes these controversies boiled up and got beyond our capacity to handle; but Wallace was in somewhat the same position as Roosevelt. He had to think of other issues whose outcome might be jeopardized by a taking of sides objected to by important legislators. Roosevelt sometimes explained, as he did in the instance I am about to describe; but he assumed that he did not really need to. It was his responsibility to determine what causes he would support and what he must choose to neglect for fear of being hampered in the solution of a problem he considered more important.

The cause I suffered much from losing and one that seemed to have the worst of all excuses—money to be used in politics—appeared when prohibition ended. The formal adoption of the Twenty-first Amendment, reversing the Eighteenth, was on December 5. Preceding this, beer, low in alcoholic content, had been legalized in March. The amendment had been on its way to ratification by the states for some time and had been the object of interest by all those who recognized the failure of prohibition but who would have liked to see such controls imposed on spirits as would take private profit out of the trade.

One of Roosevelt's rather ambiguous promises during his approach to the presidency had been that since prohibition was a failure, it was time to think of ending Hoover's "experiment, noble in purpose." There were still convinced prohibitionists in many parts of the country, but they were no longer able to influence legislation. When it was proposed to make repeal an issue in the Democratic platform at Chicago, there had been some opposition by delegates from dry regions; but it had been overborne. Roosevelt had hardly mentioned the subject during the campaign. The old saloons had occupied so many corners and had been the hangouts for such a breed of dissolute loafers that the Women's Christian Temperance Union, after years of earnest endeavor, had forced a congressional surrender; and state legislators had been equally compliant. The remnant of these reformers was still something to be treated with respect by a candidate.

Dissolute drinkers had not disappeared when the saloons had gone out of business. The had found ways to get illegal liquor, and consorted in a new kind of institution—the speakeasy. The bootleggers had grown wealthy and lived in arrogant splendor. They had corrupted the police and enforced their own laws. All this became intolerable. But when Al Smith, the Democratic candidate in 1928, had openly campaigned for repeal he had alienated a large segment of voters. Four years later, however, the situation had become so much worse that Roosevelt had cautiously let it be known that he would support repeal. Now that he was president and the necessary amendment was progressing through the state legislatures, there was the immediate problem of what to do when three-fourths of the states had ratified. When, in December,

Utah had become the thirty-sixth state to accept the amendment no policy had been formulated.

In anticipation, however, there had been a tussle going on. The speculators, interested in the golden prospect of spirits flooding into the markets, naturally thought the occasion one for making a killing. They had millions of gallons waiting in storage. They wanted as little restraint as possible, and they wanted it lodged where they could best influence it. That seemed to be the Treasury, where it had been before prohibition. Some of us felt, however, that the opportunity for a rigorous control should not be missed. When the liquor industry had been relatively free it had made itself thoroughly disreputable. A return to the old conditions could easily be avoided, and we thought it should be.

There were no visible vested interests. There was, in fact, no liquor industry—at least none that was lawful. We conceived the idea of public dispensaries placed between distillers and retailers. Those who saw the scheme as a bar to the easy money they had anticipated used every device they could invent to discredit the notion. It was, of course, more "communism." Besides, it might encroach on the states' rights to set up their own systems.

For some time I thought Roosevelt was persuaded. He recalled well enough all the old abuses. We prepared several memoranda and drafted a law we thought adequate. We had several talks about it, and he seemed to approve. Then he changed. He told me privately that there were those who were so influential that they could almost certainly defeat the necessary legislation. He outlined the arguments they would use. Anyway, he said, the legislative leaders had warned him not to try it. In their warning was an implied threat to much else he was asking for; so temporary codes for the industry were set up instead, and a federal agency was organized on the old plan.[1]

One of the proposals we had made was to separate beer and wine from spirits, making the beverages easily available in retail stores just about as any other commodity would be. Spirits, we thought, should be sold in franchised stores. It would have been simple to have had a

[1] In 1935, after NRA was declared unconstitutional, and the codes were no longer operative, an act was passed by the Congress and the Federal Alcohol Administration was assigned to the Treasury. In the *Public Papers* (II, 511-14) a note outlines what happened. There is, however, no suggestion of the controversy and the disappointments involved.

subsidiary corporation in each state where it was wanted—there were still some with majorities against any traffic in liquor at all.

Our effort was wasted. The government did impose taxes on spirits, but the distillers, most of whom were soon consolidated into a few groups, were soon selling what they pleased at the prices they themselves set. Immense fortunes resulted for those who had been forehanded about acquiring distillery securities or stocks of liquor. It could be called a minor disappointment, but at the same time it could be taken as another lesson in realistic politics. A certain percentage of the profits was given in gratitude to cooperating party managers.

The experience with the liquor interests, those with the cattle and sheep men, others with the processors of farm products, and still others with the beet-sugar growers who meant, if they could, to exclude the Philippines and Puerto Rico from the American market, all coming so close together, induced in some of us not exactly despair but certainly a conviction that drastic change was necessary.

Roosevelt, in the White House, fended off such corrupters of public policy as he could; or perhaps he turned them to other uses—as when a percentage of the profits from the trade in spirits was siphoned off to party funds, or when representatives of the cattle and sheep men were induced to vote for public works funds they detested. What return he exacted for abandonment of consumers' interests was not always visible; but he continually made deals with legislators to get what he wanted in return for approving what they wanted. The deals were often extremely complicated and were seldom explicit on either side. They were, of course, carried out faithfully enough in the professional mode. The prevailing rule seemed to rest on the recognition that the system depended on the exchange of favors. It was what they lived by and what allowed them to continue in the trade. They could seldom afford a doublecross. So the unwritten rules were almost never broken.

The weighing of losses and gains was something done only in the minds of those involved. It was clear enough that Roosevelt understood the system thoroughly, operated his part of it smoothly, and was satisfied that he was making progress toward the accomplishments he held to be most important. What these intentions were, I thought I had begun to see. They went a good way beyond what had yet appeared as specific proposals. The rest would not appear until the proper time arrived—his judgment of the time; and that in turn would depend on how well the present understandings turned out.

Fascination with what I was watching and was learning about, I am sure, accounts for my willingness to ease up on the efforts I made to right old wrongs. Mine was not an independent position, and choices were not mine to make. I had come to believe that Roosevelt would do immensely good things for the nation. He had only to be given time; his actions would result in the necessary support.

What were those good things? I had been allowed glimpses, sometimes had even been given previews; and I had been rather patiently treated when I had been excited by some immediate possibility—as I saw it, but as he did not. I believed he meant at some stage to bring about such changes in government as would excise many of those corruptions we now had to suffer. With that done he could go on. What he meant to go on to was a better life for all Americans. There must be less fear of poverty, fewer humiliations for the aged, and an end to blighted lives for children. This would involve a lot of reforming and a lot of rebuilding. In private he saw no reason for not being explicit about some of this. In his foreseen future there were expanded public preserves, forests tended and parks improved. There were protected waters. The public estate would be enlarged and made available. There was a good deal more in his general intention. There was, for instance, a system of national security to be devised, and this was a preemptive concern.

Very few Americans were worrying just then about what was going on abroad; but their president had to concern himself with looming troubles in many places, especially Germany and Italy. Even this early he was thinking of ways to frustrate the plans of Hitler and Mussolini to subdue the democratic world to their visions of a purified racial elite with lesser peoples reduced to slavery. He worried also about Japan's rapacity. Experience with attempts to encourage New Deals in France, Britain, and elsewhere had ended in their attempt to secure an American stabilization of the currency they could profit from by not stabilizing their own. There was no hope in them for what he had conceived as a system of democratic peoples. He must maneuver carefully, accumulating support at home and using such powers as he possessed to put off until it could be met the confrontation he believed was coming.

So I learned the lessons of those months with the best of all tutors, sitting occasionally beside his desk with the flags and the wide views across the lawns for background, or in the room upstairs he used for work in the evening. Sometimes he explained; sometimes he hinted; more often he left much to inference. He was never very solemn about it. There were always expedients, experiments, elaborate bargains under way. He had the assurance by now that I was what he once called "a good soldier." He used that phrase once in a meeting of the Executive Council when I might have felt humiliated by refusing to authorize something I felt ought to be done. That was not perhaps a great reward, but no one ever got more from him.

I made suggestions, when I became notorious, and, as I was afraid, a liability, that I should withdraw; but this was not the way he saw it. He was, in fact, as he said, able to use such "thunder on the left" as could be called up. It scared some conservatives into compromise. When I cited my obligation to Columbia, he wrote a letter to President Butler, something he would have to repeat at a later time.

I heard, moveover, but not from him, that he was preparing a promotion. An undersecretary for agriculture was to be created, and I was to be the nominee. How, I wondered, could he possibly profit from the agitated attacks this would precipitate when it went to the Senate for confirmation? Anyway, it seemed, this was not immediate; and I stayed on, pursuing such activities as were within my province.

When a Columbia colleague who wanted me back asked me what I judged I had accomplished in Washington during this year, the best answer I could think of was that I had annoyed a good many people who ought to have been annoyed. It seemed a feeble accomplishment for the expenditure of so much energy. There was one other thing, I said; I had learned a lot. Whether what I had learned would ever be useful, I could not say.

ADDENDUM

A *Chronology, March 1933–March 1934*

4 Inauguration, with the banking crisis demanding immediate action, was nevertheless in traditional style. The Democrats were taking over after an exile of 12 years.

5 Wallace and I introduced ourselves to the Department of Agriculture.

6 The president proclaimed a national banking holiday.

9 Recommendation was made for legislation to control the resumption of banking, and the Emergency Banking Act was passed, confirming measures taken by executive order in preceding days. The act loosened Federal Reserve loans to member banks and authorized the purchase of $2 billion in gold or foreign exchange—a first step toward devaluation.

10 An act passed enlarging the Reconstruction Finance Corporation, and Jesse Jones was appointed chairman. The president held a press conference, the first of more than 100 during his first year.

12 There was a fireside chat, the first of four such radio addresses during the year.

13 An act was signed legalizing the sale of beer defined as non-intoxicating, generally recognized as a prelude to the end of prohibition.

15 Conferences began (Moley, Feis, Bullitt, Warburg, and myself) concerning the international negotiations about to take place. We would be pressed about the debts; and there would be talks about monetary agreements, tariffs, and other issues.

16 A message was sent to the Congress recommending the Agricultural Adjustment Act.

20 A law was signed "to maintain the credit of the U.S. government," giving the president power to abolish and reorganize agencies, generally spoken of as the Economy Act. It allowed the president to reduce the pay of officials by 15 percent. (Request for this legislation had been made on March 12.)

21 A message was sent to the Congress on "three essentials for unemployment relief": Civilian Conservation Corps, Federal Emergency Relief Administration, and Public Works Administration. (The resulting act was signed on May 12.)

22 An executive order consolidated Federal Farm Credit agencies. (Morgenthau was appointed to be governor of a Farm Credit Administration on May 27.)

24 Legislation was recommended for the protection of investors. (The resulting Securities Act was signed on May 27.)

APRIL   5 The Civilian Conservation Corps was established by executive order after weeks of intensive, sometimes acrimonious, discussions.

6 Prime Minister MacDonald arrived to discuss the world economic situation (April 22 and on following days statements of accord were issued). We learned that Roosevelt had agreed to the June 12 opening of the World Economic Conference. The prime minister, representing a coalition cabinet, was accompanied by Sir Frederick Leith-Ross and Sir Robert Vansittart.

10 A message was sent to the Congress recommending a Tennessee Valley Authority. The act was signed on May 18.

27 The president made a joint statement with Premier Bennett of Canada, followed on subsequent days by others with Herriot of France, Jung of Italy, Schacht of Germany, Soong of China, and others. Statements were uniformly optimistic, avoiding difficulties.

MAY   4 My book *The Industrial Discipline and the Governmental Arts* was published. It was followed by editorial comment and publication of excerpts.

12 The Agricultural Adjustment Act was signed; it had been preceded by intensive discussions and was followed by controversies concerning its organization and policies to be followed. It included the so-called Thomas amendment authorizing the issuance of $3 billion in unsecured currency.

17 A recommendation was made to the Congress for a national recovery act; this too was preceded by intensive preliminary discussions and controversies over drafting.

31 The delegation to the World Economic Conference, headed by Hull, left for London.

JUNE 6 A food and drug bill was introduced (by Senator Copeland).

10 An executive order abolished some agencies and consolidated certain functions, but nothing very important.

13 The Home Owners Loan Act was signed.

16 The National Industrial Recovery Act was signed; an executive order appointed Johnson to be administrator of NRA; another established the Public Works Administration, under authority of the NRA Act, and appointed Ickes to be administrator.

I at once began to act as a member of the Special Board for Public Works, representing the secretary of agriculture. Similarly I began to act as a member of the National Recovery Board.

The so-called "Hundred Days" ended. They were actually 95 days.

17 Roosevelt left Washington to begin a cruise on the *Amberjack*, starting at Mattapoisett, going up the coasts of Massachusetts, New Hampshire, and Maine to Campobello. This was his first visit there in twelve years, since his attack of polio.

19 Moley left for London, carrying instructions from Roosevelt.

24 I addressed the Bar Association of Western New York: "Design for Government."

JULY 1 After a day at Campobello, Roosevelt left on the destroyer *Ellis* to board the cruiser *Indianapolis*, proceeding to the lower Potomac, where he would transfer again to a destroyer and land at the Washington Navy Yard.

Roosevelt sent a message to opposing factions in Cuba: this was the beginning of the Good Neighbor policy.

3 Roosevelt sent a wireless (the "bombshell") message to the London economic conference insisting on larger recovery objectives than mere currency stabilization.

4 Roosevelt returned to the White House.

8 Roosevelt left for a weekend cruise on the *Sequoia*.

9 The first NRA code was signed: that for cotton textiles.

11 The Executive Council was established by executive order.

14 Roosevelt left Quantico for weekend cruise on the *Sequoia*, accompanied by Mr. and Mrs. Wallace and myself. This was the first for them and me.

21 An executive order was issued delegating to the secre-

tary of the interior powers necessary to organize subsistence homesteads.

27 The Central Statistical Board was established by executive order.

The president's Reemployment Agreement was announced.

28 Roosevelt left for a stay at Hyde Park.

AUGUST   4 I gave my first radio speech on the land problem.

5 I began my syndicated newspaper articles (ended January 28, 1934).

A National Labor Board was appointed: Senator Robert F. Wagner, Chairman; Wm. Green, Leo Wolman, John L. Lewis, Walter C. Teagle, Gerard Swope, Louis E. Kirstein. This was authorized by Title 7A of the National Recovery Act.

11 Roosevelt left Hyde Park for Harrisonburg, Va.; and visit to CCC Camp No. 1, accompanied by those who had helped in its organization, including myself; the first of several such visits during the summer.

15 I began my first visit to western states to assess departmental activities.

19 Roosevelt left Washington for Hyde Park.

27 Moley resigned (effective September 7) after the harassment following his return from the London economic conference; he announced that he was to be editor of a news magazine, *Today*, backed by Astor, Harriman, and others.

SEPTEMBER 5 Roosevelt returned to Washington.

21 A program to furnish the unemployed with surplus foodstuffs was announced. This was followed on October 1 by organization of the Federal Surplus Relief Corporation. This was Frank's invention to escape the dilemma of crop reduction while need for food and clothing persisted.

OCTOBER 8 The *New York Times* began intensive reporting of opposition to the Food and Drug Act.

16 The Commodity Credit Corporation was authorized to be organized as a Delaware corporation by executive order.

17 Letters were exchanged wih Mikhail Kalinin opening the door to recognition of Russia. This was followed by exchanges with Litvinoff and the establishment of normal diplomatic relations.

29 I addressed Chicago Adult Education Forum on "Sound Money"; amazement in Britain reported by the *Times*.

NOVEMBER   8 An executive order was issued creating the Civil Works Administration; Hopkins was made administrator, with $400 million "to remove from relief rolls all employable persons."

10 I was invited by Moley to write for *Today*.

11 I was appointed to Yale University as research associate in law.

An Executive Committee on Commercial Policy was created.

14 I spoke in Grace Church Parish House, Brooklyn, on administration policy.

15 F. A. Silcox was appointed to be chief of the Forest Service at my recommendation.

17 An executive order was issued establishing the National Emergency Council.

Roosevelt left for Warm Springs, Georgia.

26 I spoke at Swarthmore College on "New Strength for the Soil."

29 An executive order was issued establishing the Public Works Emergency Housing Corporation.

DECEMBER   4 The Federal Alcohol Administration was established by executive order.

5 A proclamation was issued completing the repeal of prohibition by the Twenty-first Amendment to the Constitution. It had been submitted to the state legislatures by the Congress, February 20.

6 A statement was issued that agreements under negotiation by the AAA would be turned over to NRA. Exception was to be made for manufacturers engaged in "first processing of agricultural products and handlers previous to first processing."

Frank C. Walker was appointed executive director of the Emergency Council.

9 Senate committee hearings on food and drug bill ended.

11 Peek's resignation was announced.

16 The *New York Times* carried a story that "Senator Copeland would redraft the Food and Drug Bill." This ended hope of quick passage.

19 An executive order was issued adding members of Special Industrial Recovery Board to the National Emergency Council, thus abolishing the board. This followed a show-

down with Johnson, precipitated by me, on codes I believed ought not to be approved.

29 I addressed the American Economic Association on "The Place of Government in a National Land Program."

1934

JANUARY

1 Woodin resigned as secretary of the treasury.

2 Davis announced the reorganization of AAA; three assistants were appointed: V. A. Christgau, H. R. Tolley, and A. D. Stedman.

3 The annual message was sent to the Congress; also the budget message.

4 Copeland introduced a revised food and drug bill.

9 The *New York Times* reported that I was to be made undersecretary.

15 Roosevelt requested "legislation to organize a sound and adequate currency system." This was the end of the gold-buying experiment for the control of prices.

25 I spoke at Union College on "The Progressive Tradition," published February in *Atlantic Monthly*.

26 I spoke at the University of Cincinnati on "Taking Stock."

28 The *Times* reported organized opposition to the Tugwell bill by the U.S. Chamber of Commerce.

30 A federal judge in Florida held the AAA unconstitutional in a citrus-fruit case.

31 A proclamation was issued fixing the weight of gold in the dollar, ending the Warren experiment in "reflation."

FEBRUARY

8 A request was made for legislation to help the sugar industry. I was assigned to oversee these developments.

9 A recommendation was made for legislation establishing a Securities and Exchange Commission. (The act would be signed June 6, 1934.)

13 I addressed the Columbia Alumni Federation on "A New Deal for Consumers."

15 An act was signed authorizing funds for the extension of relief and civil works.

26 A recommendation was made for the creation of a Federal Communications Commission. (The act would be signed June 19, 1934).

28 Roosevelt made a statement concerning relief. New appropriation by the Congress ($950 million) to be used for: (1) distressed families in rural areas, (2)

stranded populations, and (3) unemployed in large cities. FERA to be demobilized.

MARCH   3 I left for Puerto Rico and the Virgin Islands.

5 Roosevelt addressed code authorities of 600 industries: a survey of purposes, accomplishments, and failings. (On May 9 a policy board was established and on September 27 the National Industrial Recovery Board would be appointed to replace Johnson.)

23 An executive order was issued establishing the Office of Special Adviser to the President on Foreign Trade (to accommodate Peek). (The office would be abolished on June 16, 1935.)

Index

Index